PRAISE FOR *GIGMENTIA*

"GIGMENTIA is a heart-felt view of life from behind the drum kit and the writer's desk, a winning story of art, music, and, especially, life. ."
—Jess Walter, #1 New York Times Bestselling Author of
Beautiful Ruins and The Cold Millions

"I love this book! [*GIGMENTIA*] needs to be required reading for anyone who is willing to take on the life of a drummer."
—*Liberty DeVitto, Drummer, Billy Joel*

"As an accomplished musician, poet, and novelist, Michael B. Koep is a modern day renaissance man, whose writing echoes his musical vocation: he writes with lyrical intensity in the pulsing rhythm of a drumbeat. In his new memoir, *GIGMENTIA,* this literary gift flourishes. *GIGMENTIA* takes the reader on a riveting journey through band and musician life, fathering and marriage, caring for a mother who has acute dementia, and ultimately saying goodbye. I highly recommend this book."
—*Michael Gurian, New York Times Bestselling Author of*
The Wonder of Children *and* The Wonder of Aging

"This is a thoroughly original and deeply engaging exploration of the sometimes bizarre, often touching, but always fascinating public and private experience of working musicians -- and a moving depiction of friendship, parenthood, biological and created families, and the losses and gains that constitute life lived intentionally and well."
—*Michael B. Herzog, Author of* This Passing World *and*
Pilgrimage

"Koep captivates with spellbinding, lyrical prose. *GIGMENTIA* is a moving exploration of artistic process, of friendship and family, of memory, of grief and loss— joyful, nuanced, and heartbreaking."
—*Nspire Magazine*

By turns wistful, instructive, funny, and unabashedly candid...always revealing... *GIGMENTIA* is a call to understanding the creative life, and ought to serve as an inspiration to anyone seeking to live fully and mindfully.
—*Stefan Rudnicki, Grammy Award winning audiobook narrator*

"This author has a gift."
—*Books! Books! Books!*

ALSO BY MICHAEL B. KOEP

The Newirth Mythology:

The Invasion of Heaven

Leaves of Fire

The Shape of Rain

GIGMENTIA

A DRUMMER'S LOVE SONG TO ROCKSHOWS, FATHERHOOD, WRITING, AND THE PASSING OF A BELOVED MOM.

MICHAEL B.
KOEP

For information contact:
Will Dreamly Arts
info@WillDreamlyArts.com
www.WillDreamlyArts.com
www.MichaelBKoep.com

For information about special discounts for bulk purchases,
please contact Will Dreamly Arts Publishing at (208) 930-0114

Will Dreamly Arts can bring authors to your live event.
For information on how to book an event contact Will Dreamly Arts Publishing
at (208) 930-0114.

For more on The RUB and KITE:
www.RubTheRub.com
www.KiteTheBand.com

FIRST EDITION

Designed by Will Dreamly Arts
Cover art and illustrations by Michael B. Koep
Back cover portrait by Mark Rakes

Hardcover ISBN: 987-17341383-7-5
Trade Paperback ISBN: 979-8-9885326-9-9
Ebook ISBN: 978-1-7341383-8-2

1 3 5 7 9 10 8 6 4 2

Library of Congress Cataloging-in-Publication Data has been applied for.

For my brother, Bob,
because you said drums were cool.

Long ago it must be
I have a photograph
Preserve your memories
They're all that's left you

—Paul Simon

Suddenly, you were gone
From all the lives you left your mark upon.
I remember. . .

—Neil Peart

PROLOGUE

THE GIG BAG

There it sits on the other end of the ironing board. It looks a lot like a rucksack, but it is a third of the size. There are three outer pockets and a center hole with a drawstring at the top. Army green canvas. Padded shoulder straps. Inside is everything I need or might need to do my job.

I hit things with sticks. I'm a time keeper.

Ordinary items in there—in the gig bag. Water bottle. Beanie with built in headlamp. Work gloves. Small tool kit which consists of a Leatherman multi tool, drum key, allen wrenches and a mini LED flashlight. A toiletries bag with ibuprofen, a First Aid kit, toothpaste, and brush. Three pens. Chop sticks. A bamboo spork my cousin Jane gave to me. A tin box of curiously strong mints. Two small vials of glitter—one gold, one silver. An eye liner pencil. A banana. A set of Promark, hickory 747 drumsticks and practice pad for pre-show warm up. And finally, a Pilot Precise V5 black ink pen and a green cover Moleskine journal.

All because I hit things with sticks. I keep time.

After thirty years of banging out a living behind the drum kit, I've learned that I will use every one of those items in their turn. When, on a cold night during load out, a head lamp will light my way from the stage, through the snow, to the vehicles, and back again. When my guitar player wants to *glam it up a bit, get some sparkle on,* I'll lend him my glitter. When I split my knuckle from bashing it across a cymbal edge, I have the medical tape to keep the blood from splattering all over me, the drum kit, and the audience—oh, and of course, the ibuprofen to ease the pain. And while moments pass, I'll attempt to grab hold of as many moments as I can with a few scratches in my journal. Ordinary things, yes, and integral for the job. As it would seem, few people would care what's in there.

But I do.

I lift my pressed white shirt from the ironing board and carefully fold it. I choose a tie, lay it and the shirt down carefully into the center hole of the bag. 4:30PM. I have a little over two hours to get to the venue to meet my band mates, Cristopher and Cary, for load in—then sound check before the 9:00PM show time.

The front door opens. My partner, Sheree, bursts in like a sunbeam. "Hi!" She grins as she sets her bag on the table. Her blonde hair shines. "Are you getting ready to go?"

"I am," I say, moving in for a hug.

"I'll be there by the second set," she says.

"So will I," I say.

We laugh.

On the stove, linguini boils. Steam fogs the kitchen window. A pot of marinara sauce with mushrooms and onions heats beside. Coffee is brewing. I check the pasta by tossing a noodle at the wall. It sticks and hangs there.

Then a kind of pre-show food-dance begins. Dropping a piece of bread in the toaster, I strain the noodles, tong them onto a plate, and ladle the red sauce, the mushrooms, and onions over the top. I pour a cup of coffee. I pour a glass of water. Toast pops up. I butter. I sit. I sigh.

Drummer fuel. A humble meal of essentially carbohydrates, water and caffeine. I will need all three ingredients for the gig tonight because from set-up to tear-down, from the first song through the three 90 minute sets, to the last bombastic train-wreck finale, my body will have worked and smashed the drum kit the equivalent of running ten miles or more. I think, *I should have taken a nap.*

A battered three-ring binder is open on the table beside my plate. It is the third draft of my third, soon-to-be published book, *The Shape of Rain.* I scan a few paragraphs and make notes in the margin with a red pen while I slowly twirl a fork in the linguine.

I eat.

I scribble.

I fret over the seemingly endless stream of corrections that need to be made in the manuscript. Dumb mistakes. Typos. Things I missed while I was hurrying to make a point. Worry tugs at my focus as I reconcile just how late I am in delivering the book. Lifting the coffee to my lips, I wonder about my publisher, Andreas, and what he is going to say when I tell him I need a few more weeks (when I truly feel that I need a few more months—maybe years). My head shakes at the thought. The thing is already late. We've agreed that I must now deliver it by May 12th in order for the thing to publish on October 1st, 2018. I'm overwhelmed. I try not to panic. Then I shift to a practiced dictum: *stay in the now. Stay in the now.*

I re-craft a sentence while I chew. Outside, dusk looms. It is spring. Walter, the sugar maple tree beside the house, is birthing tiny bright green buds out of the tips of his branches.

After dinner and dishes I brush my teeth. The mirror shows me how grey my beard has become. My eyes are red and tired from all that reading. My long hair is silvering. Thinning, too. This year, in November, I turn fifty. Five decades—and over the last three decades, I have been a professional drummer—a hitter of things with sticks—nearly my entire adult life. Somehow, against the staggering odds of being a working drummer from North Idaho, I have managed to earn a relatively decent wage, tour the world, and help to form a band that has somehow become somewhat sought after—or fully booked—or doing quite well—or more accurately, still doing what we set out to do: make people dance and smile. Better still, in our tenth year, we still love playing together. And, it seems, there is no slowing down now.

Our band was manifested right out of a dream I had. Cliche', I know. Waking that long-ago morning and wiping the sleep out of my eyes, I had all the pieces: the members of the band (myself, Cristopher Lucas and Cary Beare), the name of the band, The RUB (the name stemming from a Hamlet monologue, and the delicious powdered spices one works into fish, beef or chicken—oh, and of course the word "rub" is a sort of sexy word without being a sexy word), the way the band dressed (back then I had a fascination with the glittery androgynous fashion of 1970's glam rock—high platform boots, eye shadow, ruby red lips—think T Rex—think Ziggy Stardust—think The New York Dolls), and along with all of that, a sneering, kick-your-ass, hard rock edge—aggressive, melodic and not-to-be-trifled-with disposition—pieces that define power trio.

A day later, I phoned Cristopher and Cary and shared with them what we must do. Our first gig followed soon after. I wore glitter. Cristopher wore a mechanic's jumpsuit. Cary wore fake white fur. We failed miserably at the androgynous thing, but the music and the connection seemed to work. Audiences grew.

That was ten years ago.

And now, strangely, unexpectedly, for the first time since I've begun to play the drums, only now, in this season, I feel a sort of fulfillment. Maybe even a kind of success. Maybe because I have come to recognize the items in my gig bag as the primary characters of the story I've been living—the story I've been maybe missing and trying so hard to collect. Maybe because people keep coming to see us. Maybe because we've made it ten years together without killing each other.

There were other bands, too. Way back there in the early years. Mostly original bands. I still play with a band called KITE from time to time, though we've been on a long hiatus—call it an extended vacation. Mark and Scott are my bandmates in that group. There are stories to tell of those adventures, as well.

This is not the story you've heard on a rock radio station, on NPR, or read about in Rolling Stone. This not a memoir from a world famous rock icon or Pulitzer winning author. There is not a Grammy to boast, or a platinum album, or even a gold record. No weighty name drops or tales of chance meetings with established rock and roll royalty. Nothing of triumphant, sold-out shows at Wembley Stadium or Radio City Music Hall. None of that wonderful stuff, at least, not yet (one should always dream). No debaucherous tales of trashing hotels (alas).

Of course, it is well known that for every discerning music lover, there are bountiful stories available about such extraordinary, fantastical, and heart-stopping accomplishments—a plentitude of iconic rock biographies. Full remote-controlled, side-scrolling rows of Netflix original rock docs. There are countless biopics and historical documentaries of musicians and craft outlining the effect of an artist's influence upon culture, and the challenges they faced as they rose to fame and fortune. Cautionary tales of excess. The big money. The drugs. The sex. And of course, the rock and roll. The brief histories of meteoric stardom. The thermonuclear fusion of hydrogen, helium and Stratocaster guitar solos echoing song and radiating starlight into our hearts. How rockstars are made. The crushing impact of right time and right place—and ultimately, thankfully, how the sounds of such collisions become the soundtracks to our memories.

Those are the stories that have fascinated me since my first vinyl record (The Beatles, *Let It Be*). They still do. On the occasional Sunday afternoon, my older brother Bob and I gather to watch the latest rock documentaries on artists like Queen or Heart or Peter Gabriel, Dave Grohl, or Jeff Buckley. In Bob's living room, the sound system volume is always louder than it should be; his cooking is delicious, the drinks are strong, and I always take away some new anecdote, some new tidbit of amazement about how one of my chosen art forms comes into being. We have questions we didn't know we had answered about favorite artists or our favorite or songs. For example, just how did John Bonham get that incredible drum sound and slap delay on Led Zeppelin's *When The Levee Breaks*. Or, what was it like for Paul McCartney and his wife Linda to start over again in the early 70s and build a new career with Wings? Just how many cars did The Who's Keith Moon drive into swimming pools? How much weed does Willy Nelson smoke? Is it possible that the KISS demon, Gene Simmons, has never taken a single drug—and not that it is polite to ask, much less to even consider bringing up, but did he really have sex with nearly 5000 women? What craziness.

There are books, interviews, YouTube videos, movies and more that will tell all you desire to know about these larger-than-life artists and their lives riding upon lightning. Are these tales really tales of rare magic with a hint of divine intervention? Are there legends and giants walking the earth?

It makes me wonder if the characters that inhabit such stories have gig bags. And if they do, are they filled with ordinary things? Ordinary memories? Quite likely. But doubtless, our appetite for the sensational might be fed by much about, say, the ordinary comb in Elvis' back pocket, or the contents of his gig bag compared to something juicier. (Save, of course, if his gig bag contained the Colt Python fire arm he loved to brandish within his gold curtained Las Vegas suite.) Comb or handgun? His comb or the story concerning Elvis' drug-addled belief that President Nixon was seriously considering him as a potential FBI agent. Have you heard that story? Good shit. When The King, it seems, has finally gone mad—and how we love to go mad with him.

How we love to watch the stars burn in the atmosphere.

As I pass into the living room, clicking lights off as I go, I see my gig bag waiting for me on the dining room table. It looks heavy. I consider the coming summer season and the sort of delicious tequila-driven moments ahead, the long nights, long drives, countless smiling faces, and sore hands.

We call it festival season. The busiest year yet for The RUB's tenth year. Between the months of May and September in 2018, The RUB is scheduled to play some fifty or so dates. Each show completely different than the next. As opposed to the arena superstars whose performances are virtually repeats of themselves throughout a long tour, The RUB will perform outside and inside. In small clubs. In huge bars. In theaters. On outdoor festival stages. In barns. In the woods. In backyards. At tiny restaurants. At concert venues. Audiences will range from ten people to three thousand.

Tonight is the first show of this oncoming season—the whirlwind storm of summer shows ahead.

And very few people will see us load the gear across the wet lawn to a make-shift plywood stage, or note the tangled spider web of black cables networking us to them, or the depleted roll of gaff tape being used as a drink holder at Cristopher's feet. Of course, those things aren't what we came to show. We came to sing to them. To make them smile. To inspire. That's the mission. That's the reason.

From time to time on social media I, will come across a meme that attempts to build an empathetic case for musicians and artists and shed light upon their seemingly woeful plight. You've seen them, I'm sure. Here's one that popped up recently:

THINGS YOU'LL NEVER UNDERSTAND ABOUT A MUSICIAN.

1. We aren't in music to get laid.
2. Not being famous is actually okay for us.
3. We are artists. Artists are weird.
4. Music isn't a dream, it's a way of life.
5. Just because you haven't heard of us doesn't mean we aren't successful.
6. There are many more levels of musician than starving artist and chart topping superstar.
7. Keeping time means something very different to us.

Now, I don't necessarily appreciate the author's solipsisms, nor the *neener neener, you'll never understand us, so you're out of the club* attitude. But my career has taught me that there is a kind of ubiquitous notion that musicians and artists are indeed misunderstood, different, or just plain weird. And while I would probably debate each of the meme's points and question the author's intention in penning the thing, it does give a nod to the fact that few people outside of the arts really know what happens behind the curtain. I think it might be safe to say, few people care. And besides, that's not why we came to play.

I walk out to my CRV Honda that my son and I have named, Finn (Finn because when you squint your eyes the car looks like a Star Wars stormtrooper's helmet—and our favorite stormtrooper is, of course, FN 21-87, or later dubbed Finn by Poe in *The Force Awakens*). Opening Finn's back hatch, I double check my gear. Packed in like a well played Tetris game is my green sparkle DDrum Kit with hardware, cymbals and monitor speakers. Also tucked in there are two light trees, Par Cans and our colors—our flag, if you will—the large, wood RUB sign with a green glittered logo that pronounces our dominance by flying over every stage we play. I run a mental check list to ensure that I've got all I need (the luggage compartment is another kind of gig bag). I start the engine and go back inside to make a last check.

What is it like to play the song, *Sweet Home Alabama,* 403,975 times, and why won't I play it 403,976 times? What is it like after playing a version of *Hotel California* to have an African American soldier, 7'1" 350 pounds, cradling a loaded M-60 machine gun, hug, hold and thank you in tears for playing his favorite song? How many drumsticks can I throw up into the air during a performance and catch again without missing a beat? What happens when you miss one? What is it like to have your bass player launch his body into your drum set as if he were diving into deep clear water, and you, because you can't help it, dive in after him as splashes of beer, tequila and shouts of pure frenzy explode from the audience?

This book tells these kinds of tales, too.

For most of my life, I've tried to remember moments and put them on paper. Too often, I fall short—so many details—so much to take in—not enough time. By accident, a few years ago, Cary coined a word for the condition. At an airport in Oakland, he was confronted by a fan of the band and he couldn't recall the person's name. Slightly embarrassed, he kindly offered, "Sorry, I have *gigmentia.*" When he shared the story and the term with me, I could immediately relate. The invented word fascinated me.

Here's a shot at a definition.

Gig, a slang word coined in the 1920s by jazz musicians, short for *engagement* or live musical performance, combined with the suffix *-mentia,* meaning, condition of the mind, *gigmentia* might be defined as the confusing state of too many shows, too many late nights, too many repetitions to remember accurately—or at all.

That will serve as a start, anyway.

This story is an attempt at capturing the *life* of a festival season of rock shows; the road between the signposts. It is an essay to render the everyday working musician/author/artist/dad/son/partner from a small town in the Idaho panhandle. While what follows might not shine out the kind of worldly successes and sensationalism mentioned above, the forthcoming reflections focus on the space between the beats, to use a drumming metaphor—the music that happens in silence and the spikes of crazy that happen along the way. Simply, a drummer keeping the time.

I see my gig bag on the dining room table. I open it and pull out my journal and a pen. I make a quick entry:

May 5, 2018
First show of the season tonight.
The sky is endless blue. The coffee maker beeps four times, counting down to sleep. Bright sunlight glows auburn from the wood floors. But who cares about these things?
I do, damn it!

I close the cover over the words and tuck them back into the gig bag where I keep all of the other ordinary things.

CHAPTER 1

BOYS OF EARLY SUMMER

It is difficult to talk about climate change in Idaho. Not only is the subject a challenge due to my state's citizenry leaning predominantly conservative, but mostly because North Idaho weather is consistently inconsistent, and with such freakish and dynamic conditions being the norm, it makes the discussion of change a moving target. One of the many Idahoan dictums goes something like this: "Don't like the weather? Wait five minutes." With our region's wide shifts in temperature during the transitional seasons of spring and fall, North Idaho can experience heatwaves in April and snowstorms in September, and vice versa. "It's always been that way," most Idaho elders claim. "Mild one winter, and the next, snow up to your elbows. Never know what to expect, but you can always expect weird."

Science tells a different tale, alas. According to the Environmental Protection Agency and the Intergovernmental Panel on Climate Change, Idaho temperatures have risen a degree or two over the last fifty years. As is true for neighboring Canada, Washington, and Montana, our mountain snow packs are melting earlier every year, runoff water is declining, and widespread forest fires browning out our summer crystal-blue skies have all become normalized. Despite Idaho's lowest-carbon-emission-ranking in the US, mostly due to our low population, the decrease in field burning in the late summer, and some of the environmentally conscious strides the state has taken to at least give a nod to climate change, Idaho weather will remain freakish even if its an average Thursday in February with snow, sunshine, and rumors of a small tornado funneling across the Palouse, or even if the earth's climate shifts to cataclysmic, apocalyptic weirdness. Either way, an Idahoan would likely not acknowledge or mention it.

Now, I would never call a crystal blue sky weird, necessarily, yet this May 5 sky, with its endlessly clear, pristine and perfect blue is both an impenetrable wall of color and a wide open view into forever. So, a bit weird for early May. And it is hot. Mid 70s. (Well, Idaho has a different idea of *hot*.) A slight spring chill still hangs in the shady areas, but in the open, the unfiltered sunlight seems strangely dangerous. As I open the door to my car, I pause a moment to feel the weight of the heat on my face. I wonder briefly if I have sunblock in my gig bag. I should make a note of that.

Twirling a drumstick in my right hand, I merge onto I-90 toward Spokane, Washington, and I notice a huge billboard advertisement. A giant, golden beer bottle, glistening with beads of moisture, towers beside two freshly cut bright-green limes. In the background, a perfect beach of fine sand borders idyllic blue sea and heavenly blue sky. The tagline reads: "Grab summer by the limes." I am suddenly reminded, noting the Corona logo across the bottle, that today is May 5th—Cinco de Mayo. I shake my head and hear myself say, "Oh dear, oh dear."

Then I think of tacos. Then I think of tequila. Then I think of margaritas. Then Mom pops into my head. She loves margaritas. I grab my phone and call.

"Borracho," I tell my mother.

Her voice is distracted but genuinely interested, "Where? Now, where is that?"

"It's in Spokane," I say as I adjust my headphone ear piece. "Right downtown."

"That's a strange name, *Borracho*. Do they serve margaritas? I love margaritas."

"Of course they do, Mom. In fact, they're known for them."

"Will you take me sometime to have a margarita?"

I stare at the oncoming road for a moment. "Of course I will."

Tonight's venue is a beloved Mexican restaurant and bar on the corner of Main and Division in downtown Spokane, and it has become known for its great food, its fine mescal and tequila menu and its outdoor patio for live music. While the venue is a popular hot spot year round, Borracho on Cinco de Mayo is without a doubt the place to be. And the name—the apt name is not to be trifled with. It means what it says. Borracho: drunk.

Cinco de Mayo is the observed date that commemorates a victorious battle for the Mexican Army over the French Empire in the year 1862. While most people somehow mistake the holiday as Mexico's Independence day, which is September 16th, neither the real reason for the celebration nor the mistake seem to matter. Over the last forty or so years, the date and its meaning have transformed into a Mexican-American cultural fiesta hosted by huge beer and wine companies. It is reported that Cinco de Mayo beer sales match Super Bowl revenues. At the grocery stores, straw sombreros and fake black mustaches show up beside registers, tortilla chip and salsa shelves empty out, and up the street, seemingly every bar has dollar shots of tequila, every Mexican restaurant has partitioned off its parking lot to make way for taco tables, margarita stations, and, thankfully, for music lovers, live music.

I share a few of these things with Mom as I maneuver through I-90 traffic. She listens and asks several questions. I answer as best I can. Moments later she asks some of the same questions. I respond with the same answers. I imagine her sitting in her chair beside Dad—part of her is smiling because she is driving with her son to Spokane to watch him play drums; part of her is confused and frightened because she can't remember where I am going. And sometimes, she can't remember where she is.

"Do they have margaritas?"

"Yes, come to think of it," I say, "they do."

"Are you going to play Elvis?" she asks.

I grin. How she loves The King. "Of course I'll play an Elvis song for you tonight, Mom."

The RUB has played Borracho several times over the years. A few of those shows have been on the 5th of May and each one has been memorable, well played (despite some blurring due to their famous jalapeño margaritas), and accompanied by a fair share of weirdness.

I feel a smile form as I recall, a few years earlier, Cristopher, Cary and me, standing outside the venue a short time after soundcheck, when a Latin-American man wearing a poncho, a spectacular purple-velvet sombrero, and criss-crossed bandoliers fitted with mini tequila bottles, sauntered up leading an adorable grey pony with thick fur and soft brown eyes. Soon thereafter, we and the burro were getting our picture taken together. The Latin-American man then placed hats and mustaches on our heads and faces, and the camera kept clicking. He pulled out three tequila bullets, we shot them, and he was on his way down the street.

Sometime later a photo from that chance meeting showed up on Facebook. Of the many comments (most of which concerned the burro and its cuddly demeanor), one in particular noted the band's hats and fake facial hair and called us out for blatant cultural appropriation. "You should be ashamed of yourselves— and you should know better," the commenter commented. "I'm so disappointed. RUB: FAIL."

It took a moment to get my head around the comment because the last thing on my mind was making fun of Latin-Americans, much less appropriating their amazing culture and rich heritage. While I could defend our carelessness, I won't. The commenter was right about one thing—we should have known better.

It is quite possible that at that time (maybe four years ago), I might have ignorantly thought that Cinco de Mayo was Mexico's Independence Day. Certainly, I was unaware that the donning of hats and mustaches had developed into a cultural insult comparable apparently to the blackface or a green top hat on St. Patrick's Day. Or am I mistaken? Where is the line? Is there a line? What is the right thing to say here? Notwithstanding, no matter how seemingly harmless, the hats and mustaches are troubling to some—and to others, a downright insult.

Arguably, there is some oversensitivity on such issues just as there is not enough empathy for how such caricatures continue to hold their power and harmful characteristics. But it is not this writer's place to sway anyone. What feels right, of course, is that if something truly hurts somebody, it is best to stop it and offer an apology. That's what my mom would say. Then she'd ask for a margarita.

Cristopher did not take kindly to the Facebook post, recognizing the author as a well-known Spokane Facebook troll. It seems the troll had an extraordinarily long nose and loved to narrow his eyes down it every time there was a faint hint of social injustice. His reputation was rude, unfair and his language did more to anger and divide people than to educate. So, instead of firing back on a public post, Cristopher went about trying to get the troll banned from the social network altogether. Whether Cristopher was successful, I don't know. But for us, the comment disappeared and the name of the troll was forgotten. Old weirdness.

I applauded Cristopher's actions, yet I am still torn between someone's valid grievance to educate others versus the negativity of shaming. I recall saying to Cary, "I wish trolls had more tact." Cary shrugged and replied, "Trolls. . . Trolls will be trolls." While the hats and furry lips may have been taken to a point way beyond, we were just wanting to hang out with the snuggly burro. And the burro didn't seem to have an issue with anything. Not even the mustaches.

Circling around the venue, I maneuver through the alley where I am stopped by a drunk couple (the girl wears a sombrero) staggering across my path. The guy holds his arm out to me, palm flat like a traffic cop. His eyes are red slits and his smile is lazy. I tilt my head and tap the wheel while he and his lady laugh and ooze their way from one bar to the neighboring bar.

Around the corner, I park on the sidewalk beside the back patio entrance marked by a dented green dumpster. Opening the car door and stepping out onto the pavement, I can hear three Latin American songs blasting from different directions, the rush of heavy street traffic, and the obvious sound of laughter mixed with tequila. A sour fume wafts from the dumpster. The heat from the sky is both vexing and thrilling. I reach into my gig bag and produce my work gloves.

I can see Cristopher over the sidewalk fence. He has already moved the sub speakers, the cable cases, and monitors to the stage. Our eyes meet and we nod while I pull my gloves on.

"It's hot!" he yells.

"Weird, right?" I call back. He ducks down behind the wood slatted fence.

Opening Finn's back hatch, I breathe a sigh of relief and joy. The first item out is my newly-acquired, black cage, high velocity air fan. I feel a grin spreading on my face. I lift this new friend up and out and raise it above my head.

"Cristopher!" I shout. "Behold! I have a fan!"

He raises his head and nods. "It's about time," he replies.

At that moment, Cary's red pickup pulls up next to Finn. I turn toward him and hug the fan to my chest. He grins. "It's about time!" he says through the open window.

You see, rock drumming is physical work. Not for all drummers, of course, but we'll get to that. The way I play, for better or worse, it is. I hit hard—and I sweat. For years now both Cristopher and Cary have suggested that I should purchase a box fan to lower the temperature in my stage area by a degree or two. I resisted the climate change, not believing it would make a difference (after all, I'm from Idaho). But, year after grueling year, the idea has grown on me. Then one day, I recognized that I indeed had the the power and control to alter my environment—I chose to pursue the technology (imagine that). With another glance at the hot blue above and the fully exposed stage area, I kiss the face of the fan.

Another addition making its gear debut at this show is a new piece to my monitoring system: a QSC KSub powered subwoofer. *You should know if you don't,* monitors are stage speakers that face the musicians so they can hear or monitor their performance. Very often these days, you might notice a band with little ear buds in their ears instead of the clunky, stage hogging speakers at their feet. It is true that the newer technology of in-ear-monitors has its benefits, but this hitter of drums has his roots firmly embedded in being able to hear the room itself. Call me old-school. Perhaps one day when I'm consistently playing a chamber or arena too big to hear, I'll transition to closing off all else and going *in-ear*. But until then, I'll stick with speakers teetering on the edge of feedback.

The aforementioned KSub works in tandem with my smaller vocal monitor, but its real use is to add very needed low end or bass frequency to the stage sound—in other words, more kick drum. Kick drum or bass drum is the heartbeat of most popular music, and none-more-so than in rock music. It is the exhilarating thump in the chest sensation that you feel when hearing a good-sounding rock band. Unfortunately for most drummers, too often, that thump disappears behind the larger PA speakers and the stage sound can sometimes sound flat and uninspiring. Cristopher, our primary sound engineer since the band began, has often struggled with my incessant requests for more kick drum on stage. From show to show he must try to sate me while trying to keep a happy balance between his taste, Cary's taste, and the overall front-of-house sound. Not an enviable position—the sound-guy. More on that later.

The long and short of having this new monolithic cube of low end thump means that Cristopher will be able to thread a thick kick drum sound into the stage mix which will, in turn, keep the audience and me inspired.

With the fan in one hand and my snare drum case in the other, I move to the back gate fence. I wrestle a moment with the door latch. I hold my breath to keep the sour stench of the dumpster from entering my head. Throwing the door open, I wedge a chair in as a doorstop.

There are maybe twenty tables with red umbrellas, a few without. The raised stage is a single step up onto a wooden deck. Near the restaurant entrance is a long rectangular fire place bar where patrons sit on high stools. I set my gear down in front of the stage, out of the way of Cristopher and Cary, and turn back to begin the back and forth dance—the gear haul—the load-in. There is an old musician bit that goes like this: We play for free, we get paid to set up and tear down. Very often that feels all too accurate.

Another set-up bit we play at is taking on roadie names and personas. We'll often interact with patrons during set up and claim that we are not actually the band but instead we are the band's roadies.

I return to Finn and thread out the RUB stage-sign from the back hatch. It is made of wood—the size of a small kitchen table —its perimeter is wired with old-school Christmas lights, the RUB logo painted glittery-green. It is our badge, our banner, our colors and our primary stage prop. It is both epic and kitchy. As I enter into the patio area, I raise it up and in my best English accent, I proclaim, "All hail, The RUB hath come to sing!"

A few people grin, most don't notice, and those that have come to see us before either applaud or chorus, "All hail!"

As I hang our sigil high at the back of the stage and turn, I notice a table with four guys in the center of the venue, turned toward me. They wear baseball caps. They look as if they are in their late twenties, early thirties. They look pissed off. I pause a moment to take note. One of them mutters something. I don't catch the words, but the vibe is strangely threatening. Another laughs. His buddy takes a shot of tequila. One of them looks me up and down as if choosing just how to take me out.

Damn, I think, *not a good start for the day.*

As I pass them on my way out to get more gear, I offer a friendly greeting, "What's up, fellas?"

"Shit. . ." one of them says.

Another mock repeats my greeting, "What's up fellas?"

I stop and level my eyes at the *shit* guy. His face appears as if it is capable only of sneering. He wears the ratty-rebel-urban-civilian fashion that is alpha-male: toxic-black, grey and baggy. A chain dangles from his hip and rounds back up to his pant pocket. Some wildly indiscernible tattoo swirls like a bad acid trip up his forearm to his thick shoulder. His hair is short, and I assume it to be painstakingly clear-cut beneath his ball-cap. Obvious fastidious vanity had gone into the shape of his sideburns.

Before I can ask if there's a problem, being careful to not culturally appropriate, I hear my name. "Michael!" I look up to see Jade, our main host/waiter at Borracho walking toward me with a huge grin.

"Hi Jade," I say. We slap our hands together in a handshake and embrace (like guys do at a tequileria).

"How you been, man?" he asks.

"I've been well. You?"

"All good, bro. All good. I got one for Cristopher already, you ready? You ready?"

I know what he is suggesting without him naming it: their mind-mangling jalapeño margaritas.

I smile. "I'm always ready, though—I should get my gear to the stage first."

"You let me know," he says. He then looks at the four asshats, "How you fellas doing? More drinks?"

Two of them nod.

I am slightly relieved that Jade's sincere hospitality diffused what seemed like a kind of stand-off. As Jade turns back to the bar, Cristopher steps forward, his chest a little thicker than usual, his expression laced with mild sarcasm and mocking enthusiasm.

"Hey Jade," he almost laughs, "bring us six shots. Put 'em on my tab." He stands at my side uncoiling a mic cable. "Happy Cinco de Mayo, fellas. Let's get this done right."

A chill drags down my spine at his tone. He is using all the right words, but his tone just said, without any question: *Try me, you fucking dough-heads.* With a quick glance to me he turns back to the stage and says over his shoulder, "We'll do one with you."

A sense of pity fills my abdomen as I continue lugging the drums, hardware cases, monitor speakers and light trees inside. Instead of seeing four tough dudes, which is what they evidently wanted everyone to see, I see four scared kids. Angry faces, closed minds and looking for any reason to show rage.

Not the first time I have encountered such men (boys), and I quickly activate the first protocol for dealing with them: kindness and caution.

A few trips from Finn to the stage later, I am ready to begin my construction of the drum kit. Jade appears with a tray of six shots of tequila. Cristopher steps up beside me and we join the four troublemakers for what I hope will be an unspoken peace offering. "Happy Cinco de Mayo," Cristopher says. A flash of flame in his eyes says, *we are not to be trifled with*. The ball-capped men raise their glasses, nod and drink. One offers a thank you to us, the others remain unmoved.

Our stage set up unfolds and is ready for soundcheck in less than two hours. I crouch down behind my kit and adjust the air speeds on my new fan. An unfortunate electrical pop crackles out of the monitor speakers when I make adjustments. Cristopher's head jerks to me, "What was that?" I gesture to the fan and shrug. "Try plugging it into another power strip," he growls. I agree and move to another outlet. Still, the switch emits an amplified pop. I shrug at Cristopher again. He shrugs back.

I climb onto the drum throne (note *throne*—always have loved that the seat for the drummer is called a throne), and Cristopher and I start into the drum soundcheck ritual.

This part of soundcheck begins with me playing the kick (bass) drum by itself while Cristopher makes adjustments to the drum's tonal character over the PA system. After twisting knobs to create a thick, meaty, hit-in-the-chest kick sound, he gestures for me to start on the snare drum. I then hit the snare over and over while he crafts and listens. When he is satisfied, I move onto the first tom-tom—and so on, around the drum kit.

If you've ever heard a drum soundcheck before, it can be a bit irritating. The boom-boom-boom, crack-crack-crack while you're sipping your early evening drink isn't the ideal background for relaxation. Some bands don't care one way or another how bar patrons feel or react to the disruptive pounding. Many times I've experienced a drummer and his sound tech work a drum sound for forty-five minutes or longer. It is true that the process must be done, but for The RUB, we have always tried to make our soundcheck easy to listen to, brief and, if possible, somewhat entertaining. Despite my attempts at courtesy, being the drummer (the one that must do the hitting and center of the irritation) can often be awkward. After all, who wants to be the guy interrupting conversations? Not me.

And this is one of those times I would rather not call attention to the stage, as our asshat ball-capped dudes are still here looking drunker, and becoming more and more irrational. As the drums bang out through the PA, they turn to the stage—their faces unmistakably pissed-off.

Fortunately for me, the shot of tequila has settled my nerves a bit. I hold their eyes and begin hitting the snare with carefully directed weight and accuracy. CRACK! CRACK! CRACK! They stare back at me. I try to send a kind of telepathic message to them that might read like this: *Boys, despite all of your toughness and alpha-posturing, don't provoke a man that makes his living by striking two sticks of wood against various targets around him, for hours at a time, without missing, with some degree of speed and force—while seated on a throne—please consider Cristopher's warning: "We are not to be trifled with."*

As I make my way around from drum to drum, Cristopher asks that I play the whole kit. He moves out beside the boys' table and I lay into a rather aggressive, mid-tempo groove. I lean forward into the beat, channeling a Terry Bozzio eagerness, yearning for each and every touch of stick to drum—stick to cymbal.

After a few bars, Cristopher raises his hand and makes a hand gesture—as if his fingers are the mouth of a puppet speaking. A signal that says: *test your vocal mic.*

I keep up the weighty beat and begin to sing an antithetical melody, The Beatles' *If I Fell.*

If I fell in love with you / Would you promise to be true / And help me to understand. . .

Tequila, I think, as I sing the beautiful refrain at the table of angry boys.

If I give my heart to you / I must be sure from the very start. . .

I see Cristopher let shine a little smile at my veiled aggression. He signals for me to stop. I stop. My sound check is done. I set my sticks down on my floor tom and stand, taking one last glance around the kit for anything I may have missed.

The ball-capped boys say something I can't quite hear. Cristopher says something back to them that I can't quite hear. A moment later, he walks back to the stage and continues to make adjustments on the mixer. He is smiling when his eyes tick to me.

We both know the outcome, for this isn't our first rodeo, as the saying goes. We've seen and have had to deal with our share of asshats. Before the show is through, we'll see just how tough they are. When the songs do the things songs do, we'll see a changed, enlightened crew.

It is also quite possible that the situation could go the other way—a sudden memory of Cristopher in an after-show wrestling match with four Marines at a military club at Mount Fuji in Japan smashes through my memory. I can still taste the cheap beer and see him standing on the bar about to pounce. If I remember correctly the exchange was all in good fun. Or was it? Another memory flashes of a guy wearing a cowboy hat rushing the stage and smashing his fist against Cary's jaw during a performance— all because he thought Cary was making fun of him when in truth, Cary was playing the country song he requested.

I lift my gig bag, cross the patio to the restrooms to change into my stage clothes while Cary begins his guitar check—loud riffs—soaring high pitched notes. Passing the bar, I order four carne asada tacos. I shake my head at how good the guitar sounds tearing through the air. I scan the room for cowboy hats.

At a table in the back of the shadowed restaurant, I sip my jalapeño margarita and munch a taco. I gulp water. My eyes stray to the quickly-filling patio and bar. The energy is bright from the sunshine, the flowing booze, and the spirit of holiday celebration.

Finishing my meal, I pull out my drumsticks and begin to warm up my arms and hands by tapping out various rudiments on my thigh. Cary joins me with his bean burrito (his vegan choice). We chat about the day, the heat, my new K sub speaker, and we nod to the not-so-nice baseball-hatted men and the potential problems they may pose.

"What weirdness awaits?" Cary asks.

It's the right question.

An hour later, we are on stage, and Cary's guitar drones, cello like. One long, lulling note, warm and inviting. The smoke machine emits a low, ghostly cloud that coils around the band. We are patient. We let the sound linger for at least three, maybe five minutes. Slowly, the audience begins to wake to it. One by one, faces turn to us. Some as if in question. Some knowing. Some simply wasted and wondering, *what the fuck is that sound?*

Meditation. Relax. Listen. That thing Cary does with his guitar—that mind-fuzzing, ultra-relaxing pad of tone gets me every time—and I use it like a drug. It is the herald of the show to come. I slow my breathing. I let the soothing vibration push the stress of the day away—the traffic, the tedium of set-up, the weirdness of angry boys with something to prove, the sun's heat, the day-to-day worry that is sometimes inescapable. There is only that sound. There is only the green-sparkle drum-kit arrayed before me and Cristopher to my right, Cary to my left. The fume of the fog rises and its scent becomes the incense to the temple that is the stage. . .

(Oh, good grief.)

Sure, a little heavy, but that's how it feels. Truly.

And so it begins.

At the end of the second set, some two or so hours later, the boys are no longer wearing their ball-caps. One is slumped at his table. Two are standing at the front of the crowd directly in front of Cristopher. Each of them has one arm raised into the air while their other hands slosh their drinks onto the patio pavement.

Along with the shoulder to shoulder crowd, they are howling, laughing, and yelling for more.

"More coming! Be right back!" Cristopher shouts into his mic. He is nearly drowned out by the jubilation. "Shots! Time for shots!"

The two dudes open their palms wide, seemingly desperate for a high five. Cristopher slaps their hands. They lean toward him, blathering on and on—I can only catch phrases: "Fuck yeah, bro," and, "dude, fuck yeah," and, "you fucking guys kill it, bro," and, "you guys rule, fuck." I feel my lips smile. Cristopher glances at me. We both knew this would happen. The ball-capped boys have been disarmed in the best way known—perhaps the oldest way—we sang them a song.

Sweat stings my eyes. I retreat from the drum throne, spin, kneel, and lower my face into my new whirring fan. It feels like heaven. I worship. The heat is lessened and I can feel my skin cool. Goose pimples rise along my upper arms. I take a long pull of water from a straw. My body feels good. My hands are strong. Two sets to go. I make a mental note that I've tossed five sticks into the air in that showman sort of way and I've caught four. Not bad for the start of the season.

"Shots!" Cristopher beckons. I turn as he unslings his bass from his shoulder. "C'mon, bitch."

"One second," I say gravitating back to the fan. "How did I go so long without you?" I ask its rushing air. "How I love you," I whisper to it.

During our breaks, I typically rush off stage to find a quiet, out-of-the-way place where I won't be disturbed to catch my breath and dry off. Most of the time, I'll find Sheree for a quick kiss before I disappear. In fact, she's right over there. Just a second. . .

Unlike my colleagues, I have a job that demands an exponentially different set of physical challenges. While what they do is important, singing and moving their fingers with the occasional leggy, wide-spread rock-stance, the athletic reality that it takes to play drums is seldom acknowledged. Certainly there are those kit players whose approach is akin to a marathon runner: calm, focused—reserving the high energy and emotive expressions for just the right crescendo, the right climax. Good on them. Well met. Oddly enough, I was once such a player. In those days, I leaned more into a technical, memorized and rehearsed style, which, as its upshot, provided a worthy and stable control. An incredibly important developmental stage for me. It taught me discipline, forethought, and, perhaps a not-so-awesome, implicit, *need* to control. Thankfully I feel I've retained the best lessons from those days—but somehow a kind of reckless abandon has *paradiddled* its way into my playing since The RUB played its first gig. And if I were to name it, I'd call it, *Moonishness* maybe (see Google: Keith Moon); it has forced my limited facility to take the kind of chances behind the drums that my former self would never attempt: improvisational fills, grooves—and songs—throwing myself into songs I have never played, much less, ever heard. Not to mention this new risk-taking behavior of tossing drumsticks high into the air and catching them just to see if I can get away with it. From our very first conversations about The RUB, we always said that every note should count. And I took that seriously. So seriously that I threw seriousness out the window and realized that the word *count* should only ignite in one body: the audience. What counts is *their* experience. And reservation, calm methodical playing won't do. Even technical drum fireworks won't do. If I'm on fire every moment, maybe. . . just maybe. Therefore, drumming now is an essay in reflecting the joy that music brings—all of the euphoric potential, the giggles, the high-dive wonder, and each boyhood dream of playing a great show (like Jack Black says in *School of Rock*—"Playing a great show can change the world!"). To change the world, a drummer must keep the time. We are the pulse to the audience and we must not fail.

Of course, the responsibility to my bandmates is also paramount. The great Buddy Rich once said, "An average band with a great drummer sounds great, a great band with an average drummer sounds average." Therefore, I strive to lay that solid foundation so they can shine. Drumming is always a challenge of endurance, focus, and serious business—minus most of the seriousness.

"Yo!" Cristopher calls me out of the cool fan air. "Shots!"

Here's a fun fact—speaking of Buddy Rich—Cristopher's dad, David, was Buddy Rich's drum tech for a number of years. Growing up, Cristopher referred to Buddy as *Uncle Buddy*. If that isn't something to keep me on my toes. . .

"Shots, yes. Coming," I say.

Our friend Perry, in his sixties, bald, warm smile, eyes like Marlon Brando, has poured from his jacket flask a cluster of shots for us. The RUBBISH (the RUB's official tongue in cheek fan club: Sara, Rodd, Doug, Dennis and Maggie—and Perry, too), Amidy, Cristopher's girlfriend, and Sheree, gather around the table closest to stage left. A tequila aficionado, Perry tells us that he has brought this particular bottle back from his recent trip to Mexico and has waited a long while for us to sample it. As he prepares to serve, the tray of plastic shot cups tips and spills. We all groan. Perry stares at the travesty. His face shows injury— pain. Rodd, lays a hand on his shoulder and comforts him. We all offer Perry our condolences. He doesn't seem to hear us but, instead, continues to puzzle and play out just how and why fate has spilled and killed this special moment he had planned. The tequila drips over the table edge.

"Thanks anyway, Perry," I offer, needing to retreat to some place quiet and cool. A bead of sweat finds its way into my right eye. It stings. "I'll have Jade send us all a shot to start the next set."

"No, no," comes Perry's distant reply. Still fixated on the spill, he says, "I'll get us something nice."

From a far corner in the back of the restaurant, not completely private but at least out of the noise and chaos, at a tiny booth, I can see a line of people at the door extending down Division

Street and around the corner. I feel a slight chill at the thought of The RUB drawing this many people for a show. Or maybe it's just Cinco De Mayo. Maybe both. Nevertheless, it is still exciting.

My hands throb. My arms feel warm and fluid. An ever-so-slight buzz settles in my shoulders. The sweat is now drying and my skin has cooled off a bit. The brain is quick (or at least, I think it's quick). These are sensations I've grown to love and appreciate over my career. I suppose athletes call it being *in the zone.* That feeling of confidence, focus, and commitment to the task at hand. When the body fuses with intention. Or maybe it is the tequila. Maybe both.

I lift my journal out of my bag and scribble a few notes:

Is it true that peak athletic performance begins its decline somewhere around 26 years of age? Did I read that somewhere?

I frown. I tick to the backward-baseball-capped antagonists—now, seemingly, Cristopher's best pals. He stands beside them near their table. They laugh together. He has tamed them. The boys all look to be in their mid-twenties, early thirties. Quite likely at their peak athletically. Probably peak fighters. Yikes.

I flash again to that night at the base of Japan's Mount Fuji, and Cristopher, arm in arm with a host of beer-soaked Marines, as they together slurred and crooned the Eagles' *Take It Easy.*

I smile.

I make another quick note:

Stick throws tonight so far: 4 for 5. Not bad. (Four catches for five throws.)

Jade appears before me.

"Great show, man! Can I get you something?" he asks.

"Is it true that peak athletic ability starts to fade at age 26?" I ask him half-jokingly.

"Something like that," he smiles. "Why?"

I look down at the note scribbled on the page, then back to him. "I'll have a Patron on the rocks, please." He nods, smiling. I answer his question, "I must be seeking my twenty-six-year-old self."

"Me, too," he says as he turns away.

When I get back to the stage, the inevitable has begun. The asshats have started a fight with another table of asshats (careful not to place baseball hats into any kind of cultural appropriation). Two men begin a shoving match. Three intervene. Five gather closer. It is a familiar chain-reaction and always an unwelcome sight. In moments, the venue's bouncers are pulling the men apart. The back gate opens and our ball-capped pals are ejected. Cary and I watch from the edge of the stage as they staggeringly resist the expertise of the house security. Their anger shifts to shock and then to incredulity. I think I hear one of them say something like, "It wasn't me, man!"

Weird.

The patio audience watches as the exchange escalates into more shoving and cussing against the bouncers' cool demeanor. Then, in an unexpected and freakish move, two of the ball-capped asshats break out of the fray, dash to their vehicle parked just beside the patio, pile in and start the engine. Their escape prompted by likely noting that well down the block, but not yet arrived, are approaching police cars.

I take an anxious breath as their vehicle throttles into the busy intersection—several oncoming cars screech—some to a halt, some to maneuver. There is the nauseating crunch of fenders and glass. My eyes widen at the way the scene plays out like the kind of car chase one sees only in movies. The hat-boys' tires scream and weave through two tight fissures in the crowded four-lane— they rip through a red light—they swerve uncontrollably right, taking out a road-sign as their right fender is lopped off and clatters onto the sidewalk. As they disappear around the corner of the building, there is another crunch of metal as they tellingly smash into some unseen obstacle.

Police cars swarm in from all directions, surround and close the corner off. Their blue and red lights flash in the dusk. We watch for a few minutes. I close my eyes and hope no one was injured.

The evening is cooling, but I think I scent the oncoming summer on the air. And at that moment, I hear Cary's guitar begin to sigh the opening tones to our version of Don Henley's *Boys of Summer.* The heady sound compliments the mood, as if the venue's collective experience was indeed a scene of a surreal and bizarre movie. I circle behind the drum set, sit and quickly stretch my hands and fingers to prepare my entry into the song with Cristopher. I let the lulling guitar draw me in and we start, entranced.

We play the piece in half-time, and instead of using sticks, I play the snare and toms with my hands and fingers, much like a conga or djembe—the pattern and idea inspired by Graham Broad and his work with Roger Waters (and likely some John Bonham influence, too). As Cristopher sings the first verse: *Nobody on the road / nobody on the beach / I feel it in the air / The summer's out of reach,* I watch the blue and red lights strobe across the pavement, reflect in the building windows around us, and glitter and dance in the sheen of my cymbals. When the audience raise their voices in the chorus, I feel an electric chill:

> *But I can see you*
> *Your brown skin shining in the sun*
> *You got your hair combed back and your*
> *Sunglasses on baby*
> *I can tell you my love for you will still be strong*
> *After the boys of summer, have gone[1]*

And so the climate changes within the patio area. Cristopher's song choice is the perfect weather shift for what we have all just

---

[1] From Don Henley's, *The Boys of Summer*, lyrics: Don Henley, ©1984. From the album, *Building the Perfect Beast,* Geffen Records.

witnessed. The boys wearing the ball-caps are forgotten, the anxious incident is replaced by a beloved tune, and both old and new memories ride upon its melody. And just like that, the weather shifts from a storm to a sun-shower. I smile at Cary and think, *Nothing weird about this. Nothing weird at all.*

CHAPTER 2

CRISTOPHER LUCAS

As we begin another show, I'm listening to Cristopher vamping a heady bass guitar riff. Yesterday was the drunken, testosterone-driven chaos of Cinco De Mayo—today an audience of forty or so people—families and kids. Some are seated in the grass, some gathered around potluck-laden picnic tables, others stand and listen. Today's show is a private birthday party, in a small park called Higgin's Point, atop a high hill crowned with budding deciduous and evergreen trees. Early spring flowers fleck the path that leads down the hill to the lake. Today our "stage" is a slightly uneven patch of dewy grass beside a small picnic area. The day is gloriously mild with the previous day's sky of ever-blue.

I sit beside Cristopher, leaning my elbows on my snare drum, waiting. I think I can see the slight hangover tugging at his patience—or maybe he is seeking some relief in the sound of his bass. Either way, he's struggling a little. I know because, well, I know this fellow.

Or maybe because I'm struggling a little, too.

And I know the song, I think. It has a familiar vibe. I can almost hear the melody. Cristopher plays on. He won't look at me, as it might telegraph the song too early—and he's in a playful mood—and if he gives the song's identity away, the little guessing game he likes to play with Cary and me would be over too soon.

An introduction to Cristopher. Here's an article I penned for the regional lifestyle magazine, NSpire, a few years ago, about my friend, bandmate, and partner.

THE SING BACK SCHOOL

Those of us lucky enough to be lake-people know the gift of this kind of day: from the boat's bow, the blue sky is dimensions deep, July heat, windless and little chop, the water is cool, and the sun rides long on the horizon. Certainly there are a few spirits in plastic cups, frequent stops for refreshing dips and, most paramount to this writer, at least, great songs blasting from the stereo—all those songs we know—earmarked memories. We gather for moments like these.

And it was on such a day in 1998 when I met singer/songwriter, Cristopher Lucas.

After introductions, our reveling lake-company clustered around Cristopher on a friend's dock near Beauty Bay. Cristopher, sitting on the edge of a moored boat with his feet flat on the boards, pulled a guitar from its case. Conversations fell away to a deep pocket guitar rhythm. Before he opened his mouth to sing, I felt that I knew the melody to come—as if I'd heard it before, though I was mistaken. The tune was familiar, but wholly unique and original. It resonated with everything I adore about music. A hypnotic pulse, a transforming melody hinging on the right turn of phrase. Organic and current. Before his first song was over, I was compelled to sing the final refrain. I was singing back to him. And so was everyone else.

I recall thinking, How did he do that? He wrote these songs he's singing? Who are you, really?

Cristopher comes from a clan infused in song. His parents, Deanna Sylte from Rathdrum, Idaho (of the famed a cappella group, The Sylte Sisters) and David Lucas, from Buffalo, New York (renowned producer and advertising jingle composer—his hooks you'll likely recall: ATT's *Reach Out and Touch Someone* and G.E.'s *We Bring Good things To Life,* among a great many others), met on a European concert tour in the late 60's. Born in New York, Cristopher grew up in recording studios, became accustomed to family dinners with some of the hippest and most talented musicians in the world, and was baptized in the sounds and the moods of the city—the slick, pop sensibility, the razor-sharp harmonies and the hooks that make hits. The alchemy that brings people together—the very elements of our fast-paced life score.

When his parents split up, Cristopher's big-city experience and New York savvy sauntered onto the family cattle ranch in Rathdrum, Idaho. What might have been culture shock for someone else, Cristopher's feet found a second home among his relations. The meteor showers, the summer pine, and the slower days of the Pacific North West charmed him, and the music of his new surroundings would eventually define a writing style all his own. His family sings. Many play instruments. He became steeped in traditional folk, gospel, and country, and, soaring over it all, were voices raised up in harmonies.

The roots of a musician's life of practice. Years of honing his skills as a guitarist and singer. Recording his original songs onto cassettes and giving them away as gifts to family and friends. Cristopher released his first major CD, *Southbound Patriot James* in 2000, followed by the acclaimed *Cruxlife Volume One, 2005.* Then countless gigs, from tiny smoke-hazed Idaho dives to inner city clubs in New York, all across the country and overseas. And his unique and eclectic sound always gathered people together, drawn by that familiar hook that somehow defines them—and they sing along.

"When you're blessed with friends who love you and support you—and you can give them songs they want to sing, and there's a little of everyone in the tune—that's the joy of music. That's the sing back school." —*Cristopher Lucas.* [2]

•••

The tune he is thumbing is moody and sublime. It matches the day, the surrounding green forest and the breathtaking view of

---

[2] *The Sing Back School,* by Michael B. Koep. @2016 NSpire Magazine. Reprinted by permission from NSpire Magazine.

Coeur d'Alene Lake down the hill. Sunlight glitters and vibrates on its surface. Off to the north is a smear of purple storm clouds. The light breeze carries the scent of rain.

Through the trees and straight across the lake, I can see the very boat dock on which Cristopher and I met for the first time. I stare at it and try to wrestle with the math. *Was that 1995? 1996? Have we really been playing music together on and off for over twenty-five years? Thousands of shows.*

Oh, the gigmentia.

I'm suddenly reminded of our first gig together.

Not long after our initial meeting, Cristopher was invited to a sort of semi-official audition for the band I was playing with at the time, Manito, named after a beautiful park in Spokane. Manito was in need of a new bass player and, given the magical nature and magnetism of Cristopher, we asked if he would come and play a few songs with us. On that same night, my older brother, Bob, also a bass player, asked if he might join us to play a tune or two.

The evening's venue was a little bar on Coeur d'Alene Lake called One Shot Charlies, in Harrison, Idaho. Named after its owner and operator, Charlie Jenicek in 1949, it is said that due to Charlie developing Parkinson's disease over the course of his bar-owning days, he had a tendency to over-pour booze, or provide a heavy *one-shot.* I am here to testify: the shots remain large.

My brother, Bob, played a partial set of some relatively complex songs and performed quite well. He and I had played in our first, early bands together, so for two brothers to be laying down bass and drums was comfortable, tight, and as plumb as any group would want.

When Cristopher came to the stage, however, something more came with him. At first I felt his accuracy on the bass to be somewhat rudimentary if not slightly lazy. While he managed to hit some of the right notes some of the time, he would often drop out leaving the drums, guitar and vocals to form the structure. Then, at just the right moments, he would enter back into the mix, injecting the song with a dose of excitement—a fresh and inventive take on an arrangement. After a few songs, Cristopher and I interlocked. Instead of attempting to lead his stylings, I joined them—and I felt by the ease of the grooves and our individual nuances that he was meeting me where I wanted to go. It was the true give-and-take that well-meaning musicians long to experience with other players.

But there was more.

Cristopher sings. His voice took full verses of songs he'd never attempted. He joined into three and four part harmony parts finding places that we didn't realize were empty until they were filled. All of these vocal stylings and subtleties were the product of a genuine grasp of the music's essence and obvious, practiced musicianship.

I was stunned.

But there was more.

By the last set, we had achieved the audience's attention, their adulation, and perhaps even a higher sort of recognition: the flashing of bare breasts by four slightly older, not-so-steady-on-their-feet women (bless their hearts, after all). While recorded history tells us that the flashing of breasts during raucous celebrations goes all the way back to ancient Rome, then reimagined for our more recent Mardi Gras, Fat Tuesday parties (all for Christians to get a little naughty before the coming of Lent), and even more recently, the practice finding a new bearing (fully intentioned pun) during the glam rock days of the 70's and 80's. As a group, for the lack of a better way of putting it, we were appreciative. The gesture is rare and, only occasionally, would a woman or a group of women feel compelled by a song or show element to share that somewhat intimate, exhilarating, and sometimes comedic gesture. Alcohol might play a role, too. Perhaps more than one shot at Charlie's. All of this bounced (again, intended) across my thoughts as I continued to hit the drums. It is, in the end, a confusing thing, exhibitionism, especially at a little dive bar in Idaho, in early summer, in the 90's. And the breasts, while not altogether spectacular, made me giggle—as did the sheer madness and weirdness of why such an occurrence should occur. Boobs. Well then, alright. Very good.

In contrast to my rather introspective take on the history of such a gesture, Cristopher's response was perhaps more apropos.

When the ladies donned again, Cristopher, in an amazing feat of coordination and speed, dropped his shorts to his ankles, stooped just enough to cover his pelvis with his guitar and screamed out the refrain of some rock song I don't seem to recall at this time. There, just beyond my hi-hat and rack tom—his bare ass, white thighs, and sun browned calves, with his bass slung just low enough, was the bass player who would become my other half—my counterpart—the one with whom I would inhabit my career's most enduring and enlightening rhythm section: Cristopher Lucas.

Certainly not a spectacular sight, his ass, yet Cristopher's mirroring sort of gesture to these well-meaning women seemed to complete whatever unspoken audition criteria or expectation I had concerning the incoming bass player to our band. Not only was he a thoughtful musician and singer, he was also an entertainer, a comedian, a borderline provocateur with the best of intentions, and what I would learn and come to depend upon later, a dear and loyal friend.

And now, whenever I am asked how long Cristopher and I have played together, or what our first show was like, if I don't have the time to tell the whole story, I usually say something like: *The first show we ever played together, Cristopher played his pants off.* I knew then that whatever lay ahead for our relationship would not be boring.

A breeze crosses through my kit as Cristopher continues to play. Finally, I recognize the song: Radiohead's, *Creep*. The three of us fall in together and find our places in the song. A few songs later, Cristopher places a microphone in the hand of a little girl who is eleven or twelve and broadcasts to Cary and me a tempo and a cluster of chords. Another curveball. The song registers as *Zombie* by the Cranberries. The young girl roots her feet into the grass, holds the mic to her lips, and out comes the sound of Dolores. A sudden jolt shoots through us. Cristopher and Cary are grinning at the girl's focused effort. I shake my head at the sound. It was just months ago (January) that the tortured Cranberries singer, Dolores O'Riordan, was discovered drowned in her hotel room—a combination of what doctors called a "therapeutic" amount of sedatives and alcohol. It appeared that she fell asleep in the bath. Tragic. I'm uncertain as to why I can recall this piece of rock history, for I've never been a Cranberries fan, particularly. Dolores's voice, however, I've always thought to be stunning. And today, atop a hill in North Idaho, her voice is renewed. When the young girl finishes, she rushes off to hide behind her parents. We can do nothing but applaud.

As we launch into the final few songs, I can feel my back begin to ache. Looking down, I take note of just how uneven the ground is, and I shift my weight on the throne to compensate. It is terribly difficult for this drummer to play drums on uneven ground. In an effort to find some comfort, my eyes find a sail boat out on the lake, and I imagine that we're performing on its deck—the rolling waves forcing each of us to keep our balance.

Rain dots my clothing as we start loading gear from our grassy stage to the parking area, some fifty yards away. Those distant indigo clouds arrived just as the last of our audience was making their way down the hill. Piece by piece, the machine is disassembled and lugged across the lawn and puzzled into the vehicles. I hang The RUB sign from a branch in a nearby tree, and Cary and I shoot a comical little phone video—I ask him, "Hey, Cary, what kind of tree is this?" and he replies with muted incredulity, "This? It's a RUB Tree. Don't you know? It's self-explanatory."

I close Finn's back door. The three of us hug. A few minutes later, on the drive home, I'm playing a counter-rhythm on my steering wheel to the sloshing windshield wipers.

CHAPTER 3

CARY BEARE

Cary is huddled over the mixing desk in his recording studio. I sit in the high-backed, green chair tucked in the corner, with an open notebook in my lap. At the top of a blank page, I've written, *Starlight and Sky.* Now I bite the end of my pen and stare into the white, hoping for words to appear. Hoping that the right lyric will come as we move along in the process. In the air is the sound of starlight—or Cary's guitar interpretation of what starlight might sound like. There is a glittery, gleaming quality to his playing. Underneath is a lightly punctuated drum track accenting the etheric drone of bass. Kind of like Pink Floyd.

As Cary twists knobs at the desk, changes EQ settings, and considers the next production steps, I raise my eyes to a framed photo on the wall next to my chair. I see the photo, recognize the people in it, then look back down at my blank page and continue to wait for a visitation of words. A moment later, I am looking at the photo again—only this time looking a little harder—pausing to really see it.

I know the story. Cary has mentioned it before. A rare, thankfully captured moment, to be sure.

In the photo is Cary Beare. He wears a brown corduroy jacket. His hair is long (as usual), he has a beard (not terribly usual, but great), and his eyes are kind and confident (as usual). Also in the photo is Jason Thomas Gordon, his songwriting partner, drummer, and vocalist from one of Cary's other groups called KINGSIZE. In the center is the King of Pop, Michael Jackson, and beside him is his wife, Lisa Marie Presley. At first glance, my mind simply registered, *There's Cary with Michael Jackson— seems appropriate, and quite normal.* What now strikes me is that it is *not* normal, necessarily, to see a friend of mine standing next to Michael Jackson—and yet, what interests me, is why it does—as if it's just another day in the life of Cary.

I met Cary in 1987 after my Mom arranged an introduction while he was on a break between sets at the Coeur d'Alene Resort's, Shore Lounge. Mom was lead concierge for the newly built five-star hotel, and when she became acquainted with Cary, she told him about her son, me, and gushed that I was a drummer, a poet, a guitar player, and quite likely issued forth a thousand more motherly dotes. In spite of all that, Cary, thankfully, agreed to say hello. I remember thinking one word upon meeting him: *otherworldly*. His soft spoken manner, and his genuine caring and empathy for me and my story made it easy to simply converse, even in a loud and busy bar. He has that effect on almost everyone he meets. (I was too young to be in the bar, by the way, but I managed to sneak in just to meet Cary.)

On the phone, a few days later, we agreed to meet at his home in Rathdrum, Idaho to, in his words, "See if we can write something. How does 6 AM sound to you?"

"Early," I said, "and I'll be there."

When he answered the door that morning, he was wearing only a T-shirt and boxers. (Apparently my band mates don't like pants.) In his hand was a half eaten bowl of chocolate Malt-O-Meal. Long dark hair draped, like a towel, around his shoulders. Eyes genuinely happy to welcome me. After he got dressed, we talked about our favorite bands, our goals as musicians, and finally sat down to play some songs. Leaving, later that morning, I felt a new and powerful friendship had been forged.

Cary's life chasing sound began osmotically. For the last four months of his mother's pregnancy, his father played guitar everyday, mostly Buddy Holly tunes, to the not yet born Cary. At three-years-old, Cary heard his mom's piano, walked to it and clunked around on the thing, and soon thereafter played his first show at church. *Kumbaya*, of course. His grandmother showed him his first guitar chords and a musical vocabulary began to form.

When his cousin dropped the needle on Boston's *Rock and Roll Band,* and later Rush's *2112*, combined with Cary seeing his first rock concert, a band called Lytz (*Lights,* clever) at a high school dance, for him, like so many before him, like me, his future unfolded before his eyes. Cary would chase sound. He would find success as a musician. He would be a rockstar. It was on.

In a short span of years, Cary went from starting his first band at thirteen (Crossroads), to becoming the bass player for the band Lytz, to a number of other groups until finally landing a position in the Inland Northwest's biggest group at the time, a glam rock outfit called LION (*LYON* would have been clever). The up-and-coming ensemble had management, a record, a tour, and even a bit of fame. The only lacking element: a worthwhile paycheck.

This forced Cary into playing covers in bars to survive. Ultimately, his talent, along with the eclectic group of musicians aligning with him, created a surprising, lucrative career. Before long, Cary and his partners, Dave Dupree and Bob Burdette, were packing out the Shore Lounge as the house band, playing six and seven nights a week; and for Cary, proving that for the first time it was indeed possible to make a living (a rather decent one) singing songs for people. Better still, according to Cary, what he did made people happy. And for me, his taking time to give a leg up to a kid that couldn't even get into the bars yet, was my first lesson in generosity from a musician. His gesture was secured in my memory and his example of paying it forward is something I practice to this day.

Cary makes an adjustment to the mix, swivels in his chair, and says, "I think we should put a guitar here." He turns up the volume slightly, nods in the air to the place, and I listen. There's certainly an empty space.

"Yes," I say. "Can't wait to hear what you do."

He snickers, "Ah, making it up as I go. . . that's what I do."

He reaches for his guitar. I look back down at the still empty lyric page. The title still hovers there: *Starlight and Sky.* My thoughts linger back to the framed picture. Michael Jackson is in all black, with a brimmed black hat. His expression is the same as it is in all of the pictures you've seen of him—thoughtful, sure of himself, immeasurably deep. Ticking to Cary's face, I can't help but see the same qualities—the same artistry.

Cary's band in the late 80s was called *Gotham*. So money hungry was Gotham, they felt it unnecessary to employ a drummer. Instead, they ran a drum machine with a foot switch. For me, and most drummers in that era, such a move was blatantly disrespectful and downright cheesy. But as I stood outside and watched through the window, the careless crowd danced and drank, carelessly listening, carelessly not giving a shit whether there was a drummer or not, and loving the carefree trio singing like birds, I couldn't help but understand the meaning of the phrase *bitter-sweet.* Bitter *or* sweet, they were making money.

But Cary was soon disillusioned. He had set out to chase sound, not cash—well, not cash only, so, in late 80s, he left Gotham to pursue his star-lit dreams in Los Angeles.

There is no direct line to success in the music business. There is not a college course with a job waiting after graduation. There is no railway nonstop journey from Obscurity Station to the coveted City of Rock Gods in the county of Fame and Cash.

To make the trip, one must have hope. One must have focus—an unwavering work ethic. Must sacrifice. If there's anything akin to a straight line to achievement in the art of rock and roll, it's determination. But even then, success may not look like the success you had in mind. Success, if there is real success, is found as you go along, made up as you go.

In 1989, Cary plunged into the Los Angeles rock scene and found himself stapling eight and a half by eleven paper flyers to telephone poles, living in one-bedroom apartments with six other people, surviving on ramen, rice, and burritos, and performing whenever and wherever—each time, with the explosive fusion of starlight and unrelenting resolve. Cary's tenacity moved him from his first LA group, Slam & Groove, to a position in a fledgling, making-it-happen, hard rock blues band called The

Riverdogs. He was now suddenly connected to the machine. A first success—a tour, some recording, a bit of short-lived financial relief. Then, back into the breach.

From those days to these, Cary's journey is marked by such high points, but there were heartbreaks, too. His character and reputation landed him auditions with acts like Aldo Nova, Alice Cooper, Tommy Shaw—for all of which, he got the gig—for all of which, he was scheduled to either tour, record or both—all of which, only fate knows why, fell through a day or a week later. Try, if you can, to imagine the preparation, the practice, the phone calls, the luck of getting the number to the agent or manager, the call with a scheduled shot, the week before, the call to your mom to tell her about the chance, the feeling on the morning of the audition, the nervous energy playing *School's Out* with Alice writhing like a snake to your right, trying to be cool, slam dunking the part, slapping hands with the band members, driving back to your apartment to eat a bowl of ramen, going over in your head every note, expression, sound, dynamic of each and every moment, getting the call the next day, holding your breath as the manager tells you, "You killed it kid. Come on down next week and we'll go over the tour and we'll get you an advance for a few thousand." You tell everyone. You consider maybe moving to your own apartment. You call your mom. You buy organic (more expensive) vegetables. Then, two days later you get the call and find out Alice has canceled his tour because he wants to do a cameo for *Wayne's World 2*, and his old bass player is available for that. You're out.

Rock and roll.

Fuck.

It is the desert. It is desperate thirst. It is the green palms and blue pool of water just over the next dune. As you collapse, just yards from it, it dissolves into dust.

But you don't die. You don't wither under the sun. You keep making it up as you go.

Some time later, country music's Deanna Carter picked up Cary and kept him on as her guitar player, songwriting partner, and engineer for over fifteen years. During a break, Cary auditioned for the Seattle based band, Heart, got the gig, and performed a short stint of shows as their bass player.

He's had several TV and feature film music placements, two of which were prime time's *Less Than Perfect* on ABC and *Gary Unmarried* on CBS. He's even done a cameo appearance on Tim Allen's *Last Man Standing.* He's toured, and toured, and toured. He's written and produced with John Ondrasik of *Five For Fighting* and Annabella Lwin of *Bow Wow Wow,* and countless others. He toured with Willie Nelson. He's written over 1000 songs. He's written and recorded several of his own records, including his solo masterpiece, HERMIT, *Behind the Veil* in 1997. Over the years Cary has built a relationship with the great Bill Ward of Black Sabbath, as his mentee, his friend, and recording partner. To this day, Cary still harnesses and demonstrates a phrase Mr. Ward made certain to impart: *"Make every note count."* Cary has always done just that. And more.

Of course there's a lot left out. But I would be remiss not to include my fateful phone call to Cary about a dream I had involving a band named The RUB, and Cristopher in a mechanic's jumpsuit, and me with gold glitter eyeshadow, and Cary with ripped bellbottom jeans, black Converse, and a snarling guitar ripping through a stack of Marshalls.

In the photo on the wall, Cary Beare is as I've always seen him, genuine and quite simply, doing his life's work. To be in a photo with Michael Jackson seems to be right and proper. He could be in a photo with Cristopher and me, and he would still carry that same grace, and wizard-like glint in his eye. He is one of my oldest, dearest, and most trusted friends—and he is also a teacher, an unshakable stage pro, and makes the best cup of tea I have ever had.

He turns again from the recording desk. With a knob twist the volume rises. "What do you think?" he asks.

"I love it," I say. The music feels like the only words I've scribbled down on the sheet. Starlight. Sky.

"Time for you to sing," he says as he sets up a vocal mic on a stand.

I turn the almost blank page toward him so he can see it, "I don't have much," I admit.

He smiles, Gandalf sparkle in his eye. "*Starlight and sky? Sounds like you've got it all. Make up the rest as you go.*"

CHAPTER 4

SHIT-KICKER'S BALL

Finding the route to the stage in the Spokane fairgrounds' maze of roads has always been slightly complicated for me. Each time we've played here, there are strangely placed detour signs, roads are blocked off, or gates to some parts of the park are closed and locked. Annoying. Especially when you need to use the restroom.

I spy the building where we are to perform and hurry into a parking place. I can see that Cristopher has already unloaded his gear and Cary is sitting in his truck, thumbing his phone. I jump out and rush to the nearest restroom.

Every year, The RUB tries to play at least four benefits for charities. Given our relative success in the region, we have always felt it important to offer our time and performance to support various local causes. The S.K. Ball is a recurrent gig we've played a handful of times. S.K. for *Shitkicker*—a cowboy, western-themed event—barbecue feast, auction, Gunsmoke costume party, and rock-and-roll booty-kick-ball for the Inland Northwest's generous business folk and those fairly well-to-do. Billed as a barn dance, it's a chance for a thousand or more cowboys and girls to enjoy cocktails, line dancing, corn-hole tournaments, a mechanical bull, accompanied by a hell of a lot of whooping and hollering as they donate to the worthy efforts of Spokane's Ronald McDonald House. The evening concludes with us RUB wranglers driving them on to more hollering and whooping.

Held at the Spokane Fairgrounds, the event is spread throughout a massive steel building with a lofty ceiling, cross-hatched with brown steel girders over grey concrete floors, and a high perimeter of large windows. Lots of flat surfaces. The room seemingly made to echo. Loud. But it has a whole lot of cowboy about it and feels barn-like. One can almost scent the cow pies— hear the horses' clip-clops.

Washing my hands in the rest room, I learn, from talking to one of the building's greying custodians, that the first Spokane County Interstate fair in this location took place in 1952—and the first Fair in the Inland Northwest was held in 1886 at a place called Corbin Park a few miles north of downtown Spokane. "40,000 people attended the fair here in 1952," he tells me. His eyes smile through black square rimmed glasses. "And last year, almost 180,000. That's a whole lot a folks."

I agree. "A whole lot a folks."

He tells me he's been pushing a broom on the property for almost twenty-five years and has seen a "good deal." I note his uniform: blue button-up shirt and black suspenders. Looking me up and down, he points and says, "Musician?" I nod. "Thought so."

"The long hair?" I ask.

He laughs. "No. The vibe. Lots of people have long hair. Musicians are different. Something about 'em."

I dry my hands with a paper towel.

"Must be my hand-wash technique."

He smiles, "Or your long hair." He eyes me for a second. "Guitar?"

I shake my head, "Drums."

He smiles. "Yeah, drums. The most important instrument."

I like this guy. "Yes. Don't tell my bandmates that."

He then rattles off a number of shows he has worked during previous fairs, like 2011's Weird Al Yankovic, and Joan Jett and the Blackhearts. "I will always love Joan," he says. His tone almost longing. "Then there was Huey Lewis and the News, and Styx in 2012, and Cheap Trick in 2015. . .Glen Campbell. The Beach Boys," and on he reminisces. I nod, smiling. "There's a lot of shows I can't remember."

"I know the feeling," I agree. "We call it gigmentia."

He smiles and considers the word for a moment. "Gigmentia?"

I nod. "It's a word we use for the condition of not being able to remember shows and their details. So many shows, too little room in the brain."

"That must mean I have gigmentia."

"Me, too," I say.

"Well, shows are one thing," he shifts, "for me, the fair is about the *food*. American, no-excuses, fried goodness. Never mind the high-minded healthy movement," he grins licking his lips. "Donut hamburgers. Elephant ears (fried dough with sugar, if you didn't know, or might be worried), funnel cakes, ice creams, huckleberry chocolates, Philly sandwiches. . ." and on he goes.

After a few more descriptions of deliciousness, he tells me he is looking forward to hearing the band tonight. I thank him for the short history lesson and for making me hungry.

"Oh, don't you worry," he comforts, "I've seen the barbecue spread that'll be rolling out soon. There's a whole lot a good stuff to eat." He then tilts his head. "Tell me you don't play *country* music."

"Goodness, no," I say, my arms outstretched, feigning terror— then lowering them, "but we do play a couple-three *good* country songs."

"Thank the Lord Almighty," he sighs. "I can handle *real* country music, but that's it. The shit they're calling country these days is, well, shit. Music for idiots."

I laugh.

As I move to the door he says, "You're here for a good reason. Good on you boys for playing for these Ronald McDonald folks. They do this event every year, and there's folk that need 'em. You're doin' a whole lot a good hitting those drums. . ."

"It's a privilege," I tell him. "They've helped me out before. I'll always try to lend a hand back."

Returning to Finn, I begin the load-in ritual and pull the first cases out and roll them to the stage door. Cristopher's somewhat descriptive itinerary notes tell me that this show is *plug and play*, short hand for any show that does not require us to supply our own PA system and light rig. We need only arrive at the venue and set up our instruments. A sound and lighting company hired by our client handles the rest. They cover the front of house sound, the PA set up and tear down, along with the staging and lights. Plug and play shows are alright by me. Less time setting up, less energy, and less fatigue before I run ten miles behind the kit.

We are also setting up nearly four hours before show time. Some shows require that we set up and soundcheck earlier in the afternoon when a dinner is to be served before our performance. It makes for a long day and night.

As I roll the first cases backstage, I'm delighted to see line array loudspeakers flown above both sides of the stage, six massive bass-sub speakers aligned below, and four stage monitors complete with monitor desk. Out in the center of the huge, airy room is mission control, the front-of-house mix-desk and light boards. Everything is already placed, wired, lit up, and making sound and light.

Again, plug and play shows are alright by me. *By a whole lot a. . .*

I turn and a friendly fellow with short-dark hair, wiry glasses, black T-shirt, and an ever-so slightly distracted demeanor extends his hand, "You're Michael?"

"I am." I shake his hand.

"I'm Justin," he says. "I'm your front-of-house engineer tonight."

"Nice meeting you. The system looks great. I can't wait to hear it."

"The RUB will sound killer," he says, his eyes narrowing as if he were aiming a weapon. "Love you dudes."

He introduces me to a couple of other crew guys, both of them very nice, professional and smartly dressed in black. While I head back to Finn for more gear, I think, as I so often have since I first began playing shows, *I need a roadie.*

I'm impressed by Justin and his sound company, *Amp'd*. It isn't often that a sound crew is so polite and deftly focused; to this drummer, it means the world. With that kind of stuff and attitude, *they are in the band.* Or we're in theirs. When there is a rapport with anyone assisting us doing our job, the job becomes that much more fun, and so much more powerful.

An hour or so later, Cristopher, Cary and I are on the stage making our final adjustments to our personal gear. Justin asks if I'm ready to drum check.

I go from hitting kick drum, to snare, to toms, to cymbals to my vocal. The concussions reverberate and echo through the empty metal hall.

Floating up in the ceiling girders are a number of black and white balloons, spotted like holstein cowhide. I'm reminded that in the back of Finn, I brought a cowboy hat to adorn my stage clothes, and that very soon the room will be full of costumed ranchers, desperados, and outlaws. I then notice, at the back of the hall, the elderly custodian, leaning on his broom, watching the soundcheck.

Suddenly, a song comes to mind, and I can't help but sing it to check my vocal.

> *Where, where, are you tonight?*
> *Why did you leave me here all alone?*
> *I searched the world over,*
> *And thought I found true love.*
> *You met another and*
> *Phht! you were gone.*[3]

Cristopher and Cary are standing out behind the front-of-house desk. I can hear them raise their voices up in harmony and sing

---

[3] *Phfft! You Were Gone*, Bob Newman/Lee Roberts ©1952. King Records

along. It's too much fun. I round the chorus again, adding a half time, weighty Bonham groove on the kick and snare.

The custodian shakes his head at me and smiles. "That's one of the good ones," I say to him over the P.A. He waves. "A whole lot a good."

Wikipedia has a great definition for *greenroom*:

In show business, the greenroom is the space in a theatre or similar venue that functions as a waiting room and lounge for performers before, during, and after a performance or show when they are not engaged on stage. Greenrooms typically have seating for the performers, such as upholstered chairs and sofas.

It is quite rare for The RUB to have a greenroom. Sure, one show might be in an old theater in downtown Seattle—greenroom at the ready, with a bathroom, cooler full of ice-cold bottles of water, retro purple velvet furniture and maybe even a complimentary snack tray. But the next show will invariably be on top of a forested hill beside a lake where the electricity is cabled in from two hundred feet away, or just outside a barn on a twenty-acre ranch and the stage just nailed together by two guys that had been drinking beer all day, or in a smoky bar in North Spokane, or in some parking lot. Because the stages we play are varied and expectedly unusual, it can be a challenge for us to find a quiet place to prepare to perform. To tell true, not having a greenroom is a trifle annoying.

Each of us has our own pre show ritual. In an ideal situation, after set up and soundcheck, I prefer to have at least forty minutes in the greenroom to change into my stage clothes, eat, and warm up with sticks and a practice pad. It is also preferable to be gathered with Cristopher and Cary so we might connect on the day's job, anything newsworthy in our personal lives, or just a laugh before we get down to business. We covet this time together and try to keep the occupancy of the greenroom to us only. If at all possible, I will eat pasta with a red sauce or tossed in olive oil and lemon, and a piece of bread, followed by hot coffee—sometimes a tequila on the rocks is part of the menu, but not always. Both Cary and Cristopher have their own distinct tastes when it comes to pre show faire. Cary is a vegan and it can be tricky sometimes to find just the right food for him—but he usually brings along something he can eat in a pinch. Cristopher has his favorite foods and is eclectic in his tastes. He loves to try specialties of a given venue or restaurant. If pasta is not available for me before a show, Cristopher and I often end up ordering the same thing. After a few years we noticed how often we would order the exact same dish from a menu. It became a running joke. At one point Cary claimed that who ever ordered first would simply be matched by the other. Both Cristopher and I protested, and went about proving the contrary. The next time we were at a restaurant before a show, we all scanned the menu and I whispered into Cary's ear my choice. When Cristopher ordered, I grinned at Cary. "Judgement?" I called. He laughed, for Cristopher had indeed made the same choice. That fun little anomaly recurs to this day.

Well, for this show there is no greenroom, and conditions are far from ideal. Backstage, I fashion a small cubicle out of several rolling cases. It's private enough to change into my stage clothes, so I rifle through my gig bag, lift my shirt and tie out. Feels a little awkward, but there is nothing terribly unusual about it—changing in a corner of a backstage area. I shake my head and think, *How many times have I done this?* I've dressed in parking lots beside Finn, behind trees, in public bathrooms, behind a pool table, in board rooms, in closets, in busy restaurant kitchens. I've even changed into my stage clothes in the dark behind my drum set with a huge crowd waiting for the band to start. My word, I've even changed on stage behind a rolling case when the stage was fully lit.

I pack my RUB T-shirt back into my gig bag, take out my sticks, sling the bag on my shoulder and flip my cowboy hat onto my head. On stage, I leave the gig bag beside my floor-tom, and I can see that the room is starting to populate with people with their own cowboy hats. I see Cristopher sitting at a table at the far end of the room.

An incoming text tells me that Sheree has arrived and she would like me to meet her at the main entrance. I drop my sticks off at the table and make my way to her.

She's wearing a brown top with bare shoulders, a faded cowboy hat and dark jeans. I consider her for a moment and resolve that she looks nothing like a cowgirl; rather, like an elvish maiden trying to dress like a cowgirl. Her blue eyes are bright and she is vibrating. First thing she says through a grin is, "I can't wait to dance." We thread our way through the growing audience, pass the mechanical bull to the bar where we buy a couple of tequilas.

The event begins. The auctioneer begins her rapid breakneck chant—that, "*20 dollar bid, now 30, now 30, will ya' give me 30? 30 dollar bid, now 40, now 40, will ya' give me 50? Y'abletabid?*" It's hypnotic, rhythmic like a good drum beat, and makes the room feel electric, like money is changing hands and things are selling quickly. Later, when I asked the auctioneer the purpose of the chant, she told me that it does indeed provide the perception she is selling items in a rapid manner, and the music of it invites people to spend.

Auction paddles go up. The auctioneer's pitch rises until she lands a solid "Sold!" like the cymbal at the end of a drum fill. And money changes hands. Thousands of virtual dollars are tossed through the air. I'm delighted to be a part of it. All of this support for the area's Ronald McDonald House—assisting families with sick children, financially, logistically and emotionally.

We eat spicy barbecue ribs, sip tequila, and watch the auction. Half way through dinner, the M.C. plays a video that outlines and demonstrates the need and the charity's mission—the reason we're gathered. Children afflicted with illness and hardship are interviewed, along with their families. They speak of how the Ronald McDonald House has been the only light during the darkest of hours. I tear up. Both Cristopher and Cary stare at the screen, their expressions sad and thoughtful. Sheree's eyes glisten. My eyes tick to my drum kit on the stage and I'm reminded of the importance of what we do.

I know all too well the fears that these families speak of. My son Michael Scott was born with a rare condition called Klippel Feil Syndrome, which affects the development of the bones in the spine. People with KFS are born with abnormal fusion of at least two spinal bones (vertebrae) in the neck. All of the bones in Michael's cervical spine are fused save two. When his mother and I were given the diagnosis, we were in complete shock. Somehow we knew that nothing would ever be the same, and there would always be a shadow of fear when it came to Michael's health.

During those days of nauseating uncertainty, our finances were tight—and the travel to and lodging costs for Seattle Children's Hospital were burdensome, to say the least. The Ronald McDonald House was a soft landing place, and I will never forget their kindness, their support, and their solemn mission.

By the time we play the first song, the audience is ready. They cluster up to the front of the stage, dance and sing, and whoop and holler. Justin manages to wrangle the massive chamber's echo into a focused sound. The stage monitors are thick and crisp. Cristopher and I pocket into tight grooves. Cary is his wizard-self. Through the entire show, I picture the faces of the kids in the short documentary. I'm warmed by the nearly two-hundred-thousand dollars raised. The audience is having a wonderful time. We play almost three hours, with two short breaks. I'm reminded yet again of The RUB's mission—to elevate, to bring joy—to bring light.

As we play an encore, I again pick out the custodian at the back of the hall, watching us. He's smiling. *There are reasons for doing what we do*, I think. A whole lot a reasons.

CHAPTER 5

THE NEWIRTH MYTHOLOGY

1:20 AM, two days later, I am sipping hot coffee on my porch. The massive sugar maple we've named Walter stands beside the house with his branches splayed against the sky. Stars burn between his naked limbs. The air is strangely warm for May. Stepping back inside, I can smell the toast and the steam from Sheree's shower.

Lined up on the floor beside the door are our bags, packed and ready for a long-planned journey. Our flight leaves at 5:15AM. We're going on a vacation—a real vacation—something I don't think I've ever had. It is strange to think that with all of the travel I've done, I've not had a *real* vacation.

Last year, while planning the final chapters of the third book in my trilogy, *The Newirth Mythology,* I began plotting a well deserved respite with Sheree. A holiday. A ten-day relationship with ocean and beach, relaxing and enjoying uninterrupted time together. Hawaii. And well timed, I think, because just yesterday I delivered the final draft of book three, *The Shape of Rain*, to my publisher, Andreas. Delivered with a resounding sigh.

The book was challenging to write. Not only because of the pressure to tie up the story, but my life had taken a dark turn during its composition: a divorce, a disillusionment, fear and loathing, loss of balance and belief in all things. During the worst of it, I often laughed at myself between the tears. I've always thought myself clumsy in relationships, act, and deed—maybe a condition of my artistic sensibility, but during those nightmarish days, clumsy transformed to near complete malfunction. And working on tying up the complexity of the book and the mythological tales I'd begun in the mid-nineties (or arguably when I was thirteen, in 1981), playing a weekly set of three to four RUB shows, parenting, moving, falling, and climbing back up, let me just say the entire process was, well, tricky.

I'm sure I'm not the only one.

I had a lot of support for which I am eternally grateful, both personally and professionally. Close friends gathered around me —as did family. My publishers and partners, Mark and Andreas, my editors, and my band allowed me to feel my way, bump and fall, and knock things over, as I navigated the darkness and found my way back to life.

Standing beside the packed bags, feeling the excitement of the vacation ahead, my eyes scan the room, lingering on pictures, trinkets, and the amber light in the air. Much has happened in the last couple of years. How this household has changed. How I've changed.

On the dining room table is the final ARC (advanced reader's copy) of *The Shape of Rain*. I flip it open to the afterword, a summation of the last year, of restarting my life, of finalizing the book, of coming back to life.

(as printed in *The Shape of Rain*)

LATE WINTER
Tying Things Up

Boy, there are a lot of things to tie up.

In a corner of this empty living room I have peeled back the carpet to reveal another layer of carpet. Getting my fingers beneath it, I pull and discover yet another layer—a spectacular circa-1973 olive green and orange over white crotchet pattern. I can feel my eyes widen. I like the look of it. I don't know why Farah Fawcett, The Fonz, and my mom's date bars come to mind (likely Sunday evenings when I was a kid, lying on the basement floor, watching TV with my brother). The memories are dashed, for as I pull now on this bottom layer, I quickly learn that it has been glued down. Taking a firm grip of the triangle of carpet layers, I pull and my legs push. Staples snap, the backing rips and the wall trim splinters. A thick tar-like residue remains adhered to the floor like a black, foamy sticker. And cat. Oh yes, cat—you know the stench. The house hears my first string of heated profanity—something about wanting to meet the bastard that thought gluing was a good idea—I suggested plagues upon him —upon his own house—et cetera. A few minutes later, I am scraping the tar. I find the floor. Douglas fir, aged wood floors. Scarred, stained—perfect. But this is going to take time.

The carpet's stains, the cat piss, the furniture crop circles read like a diary of the house. How many memories, footsteps, wine spills, nervous, hundred-turn paces happened on this floor? How many pitter-patter sprints to the Christmas tree? How many wrestling matches?

I lie back, stare at the ceiling, and whimper, "Boy, there are a lot of things to tie up."

It is another story altogether to explain why I am lying here on three layers of carpet in a house that was built in 1910. A house my son and I have just purchased. Another story entirely to explore the shocking and unexpected turns of matrimony and how it breaks. Another tale for another time to discuss the better part of the dark four years that have knocked me down on this overly cushioned, mattress-like floor. And, I think, if I stay down here, where it's dark, I'll stay here—so I sit up, I climb to my feet, I put my hands on my hips, and I say to the house, "All right, my darling, be that way. I'll have your coverings. There are new memories to make. Out with the old—in with the new. Let's get on with it. Boy, there are a lot of things to tie up."

Why do I keep saying that? *Boy, there are a lot of things to tie up*. Probably because during all the monumental shifts in my world over the last few years, I've been in the process of writing the third and final book of a rather involved trilogy. The story was seeded sometime around 1996 and has since crowded my daily thoughts, my journals, countless conversations and, I'm thrilled to include now, it has inserted itself into a relatively notable number of readers. And it has been remarked by many that the Newirth Mythology is, thankfully, not spoon-fed fiction, but rather, "Thoughtfully complex and meticulous with plenty of unexpected pathos." (I didn't write that, someone else did.) Aside from the story's penchant for a cliffhanger or two—or three— there's the occasional unresolved philosophical meandering (for instance, the heavyweight "why am I here" puzzlers), and never mind the time jumps from a witch's pyre in the 14th century, to an evening with Led Zeppelin's Jimmy Page, to a psychologist's journey across an ocean of death to what some may name the place where artistic inspiration is birthed and others, the Afterlife. Bearing all of this in mind, my publisher, Andreas, Dad, my friend Scott, my editor, Allison, the very nice gal at Safeway, nearly every fan I've met at signings, almost every person who knows I'm working on the last book of a trilogy has, in one way or another, expressed, in no uncertain terms, a kind of proclamation or unchallengeable edict from deep within the collective knowledge of spun yarns, for don't we all know a story or two ourselves—and by God, we all know that stories should end a certain way. They have all said regarding my not-yet-released third and final installment: "No pressure. But boy, there are a lot of things to tie up."

Other reader comments include—this one is my personal favorite—"How does it end?" That's a toughie to answer. Second place is, "Do you know how it will end?" I typically shake my head gesturing *no* while I say, "Yes, of course." And coming in third, but not necessarily last, "What's it like putting a book together? Because, hell, there must be a lot of things to tie up." Sometimes I think I just might have the right energy and vocabulary to effectively answer. Certainly I've been doing this long enough to at least offer my particular method and process when it comes to creating a long piece of fiction. For example, I might talk about how most of the story develops out of simply doing the work, staying at the desk and writing it. I might discuss themes and plot and character development, et cetera. But in the end, endings and knowing how to put together a book have mostly to do with, well, you've likely guessed: tying a lot of things up. Into a neat little package—with a bow, no less.

Meanwhile, I make lists for the house: paint (hobbit colors: burnt umber, yellow ochre, autumn leaf crimson), brushes and scrapers, electrical tape, masking tape, work gloves. Call on new furnace. Call a flooring company. Make a dump run. Fix the ceiling fan, the back door hinge, the leak in the kitchen, the broken railing, the rotted porch steps. Create a room to sleep in. A room for Michael, my son, to sleep in. Make a home.

I crimp my eyes shut after a few hours of demoing a water-damaged bathroom floor and keep reminding myself: the house is scarred, stained, and perfect. I take a break from hacking out the bathroom floor and survey the rest of the house to determine the right position for a temporary writing desk. It isn't long before I fully understand that I can only do one thing at a time. One foot and then the next.

Daylight slips into evening. I pour a scotch. Dusty and tired, I sit on the porch and watch a violet sky fade into purple.

In the morning, I wrestle a desk into a corner, open my laptop to the where-I-left-off-place, and turn to the kitchen to brew coffee. The wreckage of my life crowds around me—boxes and boxes of books, LPs, a turntable, two drum kits in cases, and art supplies. A bag of tools sits beside a massive pile of old, stinking carpet.

I think of the trilogy's main character, psychologist and writer, Loche Newirth, and his horrible plight. How the stories he has written—his works of fiction—have become real, and they are destroying not just the lives of those surrounding him, but worse, eliminating the promise or chance of life after death. I recall thinking early on about worst case scenarios for my story, and how I wanted to do something I'd never seen done before. Typically, the worst-case scenario for one's characters is, well, death. Imagine it: the gun is held to the captive's head, the bad guy says, "Don't take another step or else" So, now we've got some tension, right? Death and its permanence—and we all agree to define that as bad. Well, for *The Newirth Mythology*, I wanted death to be a scenario, but certainly not the worst case. Instead, I put into harm's way the hope of an Afterlife. The destruction of what some might call Heaven. It took some doing. First, you need to provide some plausibility that an Afterlife truly exists outside of mythology, outside of the hearsay, "I saw the light" stories and the old, "There's an afterlife because, well, it would be stupid if there weren't." Then you need to surround the Afterlife with potential killers, put a gun to Heaven's head, and say, "Take one more step and the Afterlife gets it," and so on. Needless to say, Loche is in a bad way. And so is everyone else. You too, I expect, if you happen to be hoping there is a place waiting for you beyond this life

SPRING
Supernatural Trickery

Let me make this perfectly, abundantly (add more adverbs here), clear—I do not believe in the supernatural.

I do not believe in ghosts, hauntings, or what the Immortals in my story would call Bridging Spirits or Bridgers, or *Godrethion*.

I do not believe in gods, prophets, or messiahs.

I do not believe in planet-position-personality-predictions, augury lifted from palm wrinkles, nor foretelling from flipping a few cards.

Neither do I hold faith in McKenna mystic psychonauts, meditation, shamanism, yoga, crystals, essential oils, new age manifestation, Hicks existential high vibrational gonna-get-it-done-now-to-find-fucking-meaning spiritualism."

I share these personal laws aloud one late, rainy afternoon in May as I witness my new bedroom door close entirely by itself, accompanied by a Stokerian hinge creak—a groaning, longing, spine-scraping, torture chamber creak—the kind the vampires of Transylvania pay high dollar (or lay) to have installed. I stare at the door, mid-stride with a bucket of paint hanging from one hand, and in the other, a raised hammer. I wait for the gooseflesh to smooth out—my breathing to slow—my eyes to find the reasonable answer.

I tick through logic. Wind? No, there's no wind inside. The heat is off. I bumped it when I passed? No, I am on the other side of the house—and have not been to the bedroom in hours. My heavy footfalls perhaps? I say aloud, "It must be. . ." and I drop off. I try again—my inflection rising questioningly, "The explanation is easy Scoob—the door opened because—the weight—of the—tri-layered—carpet—being gone—has allowed the foundation—to settle—a little ——bit."

I open the door, press it to the wall and place a doorstop at its base.

After this, I begin talking to the house in earnest.

I place a book or two upon a shelf. I say, "Hello, House. I'm placing a book up here." The last piles of cruddy carpet I heft into a dump pile outside. I say, "House, I'm cleaning up your floor. Making room for new memories." All the baseboard trim has been removed for the painters coming tomorrow. "House," I smile, "new clothes tomorrow." I startle at another sound. Hail clatters on the porch and the metal roof. I listen carefully to make sure it is not a chain being dragged from room to room upstairs. After some time with my head tilted ceiling-ward, I'm still unsure.

Later, at my desk, I try cleaning up a few paragraphs from the day before. I stack words into new sentences. Tools and dust and bent nails and sandpaper clutter the corners of the room around me. Ignoring the chaos, I secretly wish the bedroom door, there on the other side of the dark living room would yawn and creak closed again. Loche Newirth would love for that to happen. But then, I think, with all he's been through now, Loche might likely use a scary groaning door as a sleep aid.

Part Three, The Shape of Rain has its share of supernatural bumps in the night, or to be more accurate, bumps in the mind. If *Part One, The Invasion of Heaven* dealt with the power of stories and the transforming influence of myth upon beliefs and behaviors, *Part Two* tells of the repercussions of said beliefs— murder, assassinations, the descent into the maelstrom of madness. These stories tell of supernatural lovers. Betrayals. Of trespassing gods upon the Earth and an Order of guardian Immortals sworn to send them back across the threshold of death —and all of this, created and penned by the main character, a conservative psychologist and non-theist, Loche Newirth, whose writing has altered the course of history, and whose catalogue of created characters are all now living and plotting to interfere with our mythical beliefs of afterlife, our notions of gods, and the hope that our lives, in some way, matter—*Part Three, The Shape of Rain* wrestles with it all. Each day I have errands within the narrative. Lines to follow. Plans to see through. Each day there is seemingly something new. I move my characters through the paranormal while they struggle to see through their new lenses of reality.

SUMMER
The Burrow

My son and I have given the house a name. We call it *The Burrow* after JK Rowling's description of Ron Weasley's house in the Harry Potter series. A house, she wrote, "that looked like it was held up by magic." In the center of our Burrow is a staircase that coils its way up to four small, almost hobbit-sized bedrooms, each meeting at the stair landing. It feels like a fort, as Michael describes it, "Like Ron Weasley's fort. . ." Thus, we call it the Burrow.

But long before the name *The Burrow* caught on, I wanted the interior of the house to match what I imagined Bilbo Baggins's home, Bag End, would look like. Now the walls are painted a parchment yellow. The old-world wood trim around the doors I have stained to a rich mahogany. And the floors? Did I mention the floors? After cleaning, sanding, a few repairs, and swathing an oil color stain somewhere between burnt sienna and chocolate, the hardwood patina turned out better than I could have imagined. These are Bilbo's floors. This is the floor of an Irish pub (only slightly cleaner). And now when I rise in the mornings, the entire house glows amber and gold. There's handmade crockery in the kitchen, and swords in the hall, and medieval maps on the walls, and candles. Quill and ink on the desk, and old books on the shelves. And tucked away in a room near the back is a desk lit with a single lamp. Four coffee cups, two empty, two half-full, stand guard around an open laptop.

It seems that the more I find the proper places for things, the more I find places that need filling. A lonely corner of the living room is without a lamp. The empty walls up the staircase need framed pictures of Sheree, auntie Jo, auntie Mel, uncle Stan, Shakespeare, Buttercup and the Man in Black, Jeff Spicoli, a picture of my bandmates Cristopher and Cary, Scott and Mark.

Then, at the same time, I feel as if I have too many things, (or better stated, too much shit). The pack-rat genetic trait has been firmly lodged in my DNA. My father's voice, "You never know when you'll need—" insert peculiar metal rod that's been leaning in the corner for twenty years, or bag of old coat hangers or the weird tool that does that thing that you found with the stuff that you got from that guy that time when you needed that thing. . . you know, that thing. Why do I continue to haul around this Barry Manilow record? Why do I keep T-shirts that are over thirty years old—when I don't wear them? And while these questions deserve consideration, all I can think of is, where in the hell do I place the T-shirts, the Barry Manilow record, the coat hangers and that thing I got from the guy with the stuff that time. For some reason, all of it needs to stay.

Head scratcher. . . head scratcher, indeed.

Michael has left a wooden sword leaning just beside my desk. It is in my best interest to pick it up when I rise to refill my coffee cup, lest I be defenseless against an imminent attack. Outside, the backyard is shaded beneath the canopy of a walnut tree. Moving patterns of electric-blue sky wink between the leaves. It is hot. Michael and I should be at the beach, but there's a book that needs to get written. There is so much to do. So much to tie up.

The messy baggage of the roommates of my mind. . . these characters of mine. I have shared the very small place that is my head with Loche, and Basil, and William Greenhame, and Albion, and Julia, and Helen for over twenty years now. Their stuff is scattered everywhere. I have Loche's earliest thoughts, Basil's first paintings, William's history drawn from countless sources. There are so many pieces and parts that I have decided to include several appendices at the end of this final installment, *The Shape of Rain.* Call it excessive. Call it Tolkienesque. Call it what you want. All I know is—these things need a place. They need to stay.

In order to begin telling Loche's story, it was necessary for me to complete the history of the *Wyn Avuquain* Immortal race, their belief systems, and their heritage. At the same time it enabled me to offer the Pacific Inland Northwest of the United States a mythology of its own. Included in the appendices are maps, character lists, historical timelines, treatises on Immortal culture, charts outlining the *Itonalya* influence upon astrology as we know it, rules for the game of *Shtan*, and various definitions and footnotes.

Also, I've made room for a few of the earliest *Itonalya* folk tales—for example the Lay of *Melithion* and *Endale,* which tells of the love story between the Earth and her guardian, the Moon.

The final section of the appendices is dedicated to the *Itonalya* language, *Elliqui.* Included are usage rules, grammar, pronunciation tables, letter and tone charts, along with both English to *Elliqui* and *Elliqui* to English dictionaries. The effort is a culmination of work that I began, I think I can safely say, when I was in middle school. Since then, the language has grown considerably in both its depth and sophistication. But in the last decade the lexicon has taken on a life of its own. Words have begun to link larger meanings—metaphorical if not etymological.

FALL
Scarred, Stained, and Perfect

The sun's light slants and adds a little extra shadow to everything. Trees along the street explode into reds and golds. Mornings are brisk. Frost on my windshield.

Days roll together as I face the final few chapters not yet written. I rise before Michael to make his lunch. I brew coffee. I wake the boy and we wrestle into clothes, brush hair and teeth, and on the way to school, discuss the finer points of swordplay, dragon culture, why leaves turn colors. When I return, I notice how the house looks more like a home. I've managed to pull together some furniture. There's art on the walls. There are coats hung on pegs, clothes in the closets, and things placed where things should be placed. At least for now.

Truth is, I don't have any idea how to do this whole house/ home thing. I don't really understand how my furnace works, or how to fix a sink, or if the sofa is really in the right place. And this thought occurs to me: there will always be loose ends. Each year, the leaves will pile up and they will need to be raked. The washer and dryer will break down. We'll change the paintings on the walls and swap out the pictures on the shelves. There's no end to what we'll do here. Things will always be a little scarred, stained—and perfect.

I settle in behind my desk, scan emails, put fires out, then I fill the screens with the book. I read, edit, work a few sentences. I stand; I pace. The coffee is bitter. I try a thread, pull it through the fabric of the story. It tangles an hour later—I pull it out—cut it—try another. Sometimes I move the story forward: Astrid Finnley to Venice—Loche through the gates of *Wyn Avuqua* in the year 1010 AD. Fausto's shop. Hours pass.

Truth is, I don't have any idea how this book will end—not until I arrive there. Rain taps at the roof. In the back of the house, I think I hear the bedroom door creak ever so slightly. The thought occurs to me that I've been listening to that recording of voices saying "Boy, there's a lot of things to tie up," over and over since I began *Part Three*, and now I suddenly question if this vein of logic is true. Do all stories have to end neat and tidy, wrapped with a bow? How tidy is a life after all? And how beautiful is the ragged hem that is our story? A rage and defiance rises up within me. Embrace the unexpected, and what is natural. Don't over-think. Let go and accept the chaos—take the non-novel path—as in life, so too it is in fiction. "Yes!" I tell the Burrow. "Yes!" I shout at the lines of text on the screen. Maybe it is not about tying it all together, but rather, unraveling it—to find what is inside. Pull back layers. Find the floor.

When Michael bounds up to my desk with sword in hand, asking, "Are you done yet, Dad? How does it end?" now, for the first time since I began, I truly believe I have an answer for him. "Dad, how does it end?"

I tell him, "It ends scarred, stained, and perfect."

—mbk, 2017

Sheree touches my shoulder and I lift my eyes from the book. She is in a towel. Her hair is still wet. She smells of citrus soap and patchouly.

"Can you believe you've finished it?" She asks.

I close the cover. "That's funny. I don't think I finished—I just had to give up."

She rests her palm down on the book and says, "Let's go to Hawaii." She kisses my cheek and walks into the bedroom.

I take stock of all that's shifted. My son, Michael, is happy and healthy. His mother is well and we have since found forgiveness, compassion, and forged a new respect and kindness for each other. And Sheree has come, bringing a family of her own to Michael and me—and to my family and friends—and a love and connection I've never felt before. There is so much ahead for us. There is so much to look forward to. How blind I was. How very blind.

A few minutes later I am loading our packs into the back of Finn. A drumstick rolls out from underneath the seat. I pick it up, twirl it in the air, and catch it as I turn back to the Burrow. Sugar Maple Walter cradles tiny stars. Luminous green blooms tip his long fingers.

CHAPTER 6

NEW YORK & CHICKEN

Sunshine, pineapple, electric blue ocean, body surfing, watercolor sunsets. . .

After returning from our much needed and near-perfect Hawaiian vacation, and spending four days at the Burrow with my son, Sheree and I, along with Andreas and his wife, MJ, have flown to New York to herald the coming of my third book, *The Shape of Rain,* to a rather indifferent host of book people in Manhattan at BookExpo America (BEA). BEA is an annual book trade fair in the United States held over four days in late May and/or early June. Nearly all significant book publishers along with many small presses and publishing houses in the United States, and many from abroad, have booths and exhibits at BEA, and use the fair as an opportunity to showcase upcoming titles, sell current books, socialize with colleagues from other publishing houses, and sell and buy subsidiary rights and international rights. Authors, librarians, and buyers for book retailers also attend the event.[4]

I watch the New York skyline glitter as we cross the Queensboro Bridge. The sun is setting. The sky is a bright pink. I think of one of Mom's favorite sayings: *Pink at night, sailor's delight. Pink in the morning, sailor's take warning.* I shake my head at the strange memory.

I squeeze Sheree's hand. Her eyes are wide, staring at the oncoming city. Every time I visit New York, I am overwhelmed by its size, its vibrant energy, its stories—it is *New York*, after all. How many movies, books, pictures, cultural icons, and historical events have sprung from these streets? Glancing down at my journal, I am aware of my inefficacy at constructing a sentence to capture the sight. I raise my eyes to the window—the Empire

---

[4] As of the time of writing this, BEA has been retired indefinitely due to the Covid 19 pandemic and an organizer's rethink to "explore new ways to meet the community's needs through a fusion of in-person and virtual events." —Wikipedia.

State Building, its crown like a retro sci fi rocket. I squint. I think of King Kong. I think of bi planes swarming its height. Machine gun clatter. Through Queensboro's blurring cantilever truss I can see the Freedom Tower down south like a spike of silver. Tires hum on the pavement. This is the 59th Street Bridge in Simon and Garfunkel's *Feelin' Groovy*. In the movie *Almost Famous*, the band, Stillwater, crosses it in a limo—Zeppelin's *Misty Mountain Hop* fills out the mood. This is the bridge where Sollozzo's driver loses a possible Corleone tail in *The Godfather*. So many stories—and that's just this bridge.

I give up on words. I close my journal. Maybe Mom can help me forget my sad ineptitude.

I press the phone to my ear.

"I thought you two were in Hawaii," Mom says.

"We were in Hawaii. Remember, I told you yesterday when I saw you that I had to go to New York for the new book," I say, knowing she won't remember. I shake my head.

"Oh," Her tone is confused. "Maybe I remember that. Yes. When are you coming home? You've been gone a long time."

"I *was* just home. But we won't be long. The book-show is only three days. We're going to stay one extra night to sightsee and then we'll be back."

She doesn't answer.

"Mom? Are you there?"

"I'm here. I'm just a little confused, that's all."

I can feel the muscles in my face wrestling with a frown. With each passing day she seems more forgetful. More confused.

"Did that beautiful girl go with you?" I sense a sudden flash of light—I imagine her smiling.

"Sheree is right beside me, yes. We're in a cab on our way into the city right now."

"How exciting!" she says.

"Yes. The buildings are lit up against the sky. The sky is pink, you know."

She doesn't miss a beat, *"Pink at night, sailor's delight."*

I laugh, "Yes, that's right."

Her tone shifts suddenly as she asks my dad, "Ken, we've been to New York, haven't we?" I hear him mutter something. She then asks, concerned, "Don't you have shows to play?"

"I've a busy summer of shows coming up, yes. But the band has known about me needing this time off for a long time."

She asks, "Why are you there?"

"We're here so I can sign some books and meet some people and introduce my new book."

Across from me, Andreas says, "We've a trilogy to introduce to the world!"

I smile.

Mom asks, "Your new book? You wrote a new book?"

I can't tell if what I suddenly feel is humor or a hammer-like sadness. "Yes, Mom, I finished the third book."

My travel companions turn to me. Sheree squeezes my hand. After a few more questions and answers, an *I love you,* and a quick update from Dad, I hang up and stuff the phone into my gig bag. I sit back, still pushing against that frown.

Andreas says, "Ugh." He taps my knee and adds, "Scotch soon." His wife MJ, a hospice nurse for many years—has seen dementia and much worse—offers concerned, empathetic eyes.

I sigh. "Likely not going to get better for her. Scotch will be nice."

The taxi drops down into Manhattan. The buildings seem to lean in and stare down at us as we enter.

It is a delight to have Sheree and MJ along with us on this trip. A rare thing. Andreas and I have had a long standing policy to use our business travel as a way to concentrate and focus without the distractions of home—to reconnect both personally and professionally. But on this trip, we thought we'd make an exception. With a very clear agenda for BEA this year, we felt it was time to bring our other partners along, so they might get a different perspective on the size of the book world and the challenges we face as we try to lodge our work into the marketplace.

After checking into our hotel and freshening up, we all meet in the lounge for a cocktail, then walk a few blocks up 7th avenue to Times Square where we marvel at the massive movie screens, the frenzied lights and sounds.

For the next three days Andreas and I will attend Book Expo. I will do two book signings and meet hundreds of book lovers and fans. I will get the opportunity to talk to other authors and agents. I will appear for an online video interview for the Independent Book Publishers Association (IPBA). Andreas will connect with our distribution company, and affiliate publishing houses and set up meetings for the coming year with major book outlets and booksellers. We will network. In the evenings we will take our ladies out for dinner and drinks in Manhattan. We will walk everywhere we can. We will take the subway. We will eat as many pizza slices as our bodies can digest. We will drink all of the scotch. I will text Cristopher a note or send a picture several times while we're here, to remind him of his old stomping grounds. A photo of a subway sign, of a dollar pizza slice, of a grey and cobalt apartment building with a black fire escape.

We will eat heartbreakingly divine Italian food.

On our second night in the city, Andreas and I take Sheree and MJ to one of our favorite restaurants, called Mimi's. It is just a short cab ride from our hotel over to Midtown East. En route I tell the ladies the story about how we found it. Or, I try.

"On our first BEA trip a few years back, we were starving— out on a walk," I start.

Andreas cuts in, "Italian food."

"Right," I nod, "We were searching for Italian food—but just out walking."

Andreas: "Walking aimlessly. We could have stopped several times but we just kept on walking."

"Kept on walking," I echo.

"And just before we were going to give up and look up a restaurant on our phones. . ."

"I saw," I say.

"He saw—"

"I saw that we were walking up 52nd Street. I say to Andreas, 'Hey, we're on 52nd Street. How cool. Have you heard that Billy Joel record, *52nd Street?*' He said he hadn't. I tell him it's the one with *My Life* on it, and *Big Shot*. I stopped and took a quick photo of a 52nd Street sign and texted it off to my brother, Bob. Then I said, 'Liberty Devitto.' He asked, 'Liberty, what?' I said, 'Liberty Devitto—Billy Joel's drummer—one of my all time favorites.'"

"And then we saw it," Andreas says.

"Yes, that's when I saw—"

"He saw—"

I hold my hands up and draw squares in the air, "The red and white checkered table cloths—"

Andreas grins. He breathes the words, "Red and white checkered table cloths," sounding as if he had just spied an aquamarine oasis after a month long trek through a dry and barren desert.

The ladies listen. They wait for some kind of punchline.

Silence inside the car for a few moments.

Andreas says, "Then. . . then there was Chicken."

"Yes," I agree, "Chicken. And nothing was the same."

They stare.

I say, "Maybe you had to be there."

Andreas: "Be here."

The cab comes to a stop.

I hand the driver some folded bills. We step out onto the sidewalk. Andreas points at the restaurant window. "Red and white checkered table cloths, see?"

Entering, I am again charmed by the hanging plants, the stained glass, and the well-worn piano bar.

"Hello, Mama," I hear Andreas say.

A short woman in her middle sixties, with arms specifically designed to hug grandchildren—an expression that simultaneously scolds and sweetly dotes, golding-white short hair and thoughtful mascara—looks Andreas up and down a moment.

Andreas says, "You probably don't remember, I'm Andreas." He points at me, "And that's Michael, remember Michael—he's an author."

I smile, a little embarrassed.

Her eyes tick to me, tock back to Andreas, and for a split second I see some flicker of a memory appear in her eyes—as if she remembers, but can't quite place us. As if the three times we visited Mimi's in the thirty-or-more years she's hosted, wined and dined multitudes of tourists, musicians, actors, authors, poets, business tycoons, and regular New Yorkers, night after night, *as if* we made some lasting impression.

It is certain that Mimi's made its impression on us. Without doubt.

"Ah, yes," Mama says after a beat. Her smile is a mother's smile. Like my mom's smile. "Michael," she says—a faint Italian accent. She grabs my hand and says, "Yes, I remember your glasses. You like scotch, yeah. Scotch. And you, Andreas, you, too."

We both say, "Yes."

Could she really remember, or is this the magic of nearly every New York restaurant? They bring you in like you're home, and Mama is there.

"And who are the pretty ladies?" She lets go of my hand and takes a hand of Sheree and MJ. We make introductions. Mama ooo's and ah's at our significant others, then picks up menus and leads us to our table. There is a white tulip in a glass vase. A flickering candle. Red checkered table cloth. Sheree is glowing.

Not two minutes pass and drinks are delivered. We sip. We listen to the piano player. A grey-haired woman with thick, pop-bottle-lensed glasses and a leopard print dress, microphone in hand, warbles a Sinatra tune. Outside, endless traffic streams. Headlights sparkle in the windows, in our glasses, across the bar.

We order hot and cold antipasto and nibble on shrimp, eggplant, and mushrooms sautéed in garlic—salami and olives that taste like the sea. The bread crust crackles as I break it. I dip it into olive oil—I sip scotch—the piano player drops into Billy

Holiday's *You Can't Take That Away From Me*. Andreas raises his glass. His blue eyes flash. He says, "Here's to being here. Being here together. May we have many more. . . Here's to *The Shape of Rain*." Our glasses ring as they touch.

After my linguini and clams, and an espresso, I hear Andreas say, "*Chicken*." His eyes are raised slightly over my shoulder. I turn and see a sickly pale, bald-headed man in his early seventies, somewhere between portly and gaunt, somewhere between a bright light and a hidden illness. He wears head-to-toe black. Around his neck and wrists are coils of brightly colored beads. A pressed fabric cross hangs on his chest along with a bright yellow sun pendant. In each ear lobe is a gold-wire earring.

I'm excited to see him. I'm about to wave and say, "Hello, Chicken. We've missed you. How have you been?" But I stop myself. After all, we've only met and listened to Chicken play and sing three times—and he sort of remembered us last year—so I hold back and wait, not wanting to create an awkward moment.

I wonder, like Mama, how many nights and drunken requests has Chicken managed and juggled over the years? From behind his keyboard, how many faces must have blurred together. I know from my own experiences playing show after show that faces, names, and connections can smear and wash away like memories of performances themselves can fade away completely. *Gigmentia*.

So many thousands of shows. So many faces, conversations, songs and words, meetings and greetings—not enough space in the mind to remember it all.

Gigmentia.

I think suddenly of my mom.

As Chicken makes his way to take over the piano for the main event, *The Chicken Delicious Show*, Andreas says, "Hello, Chicken."

He stops. His pale blue eyes scan Andreas's brow, cheeks and chin. A slow, thin-lipped smile stretches as he says, "Hello, Andreas." He looks at me, "Hello, Michael."

It must be noted that Chicken's voice, accent, and tone is so unusual, unique, and haunting that it will take a sentence or three to capture it. Upon hearing him for the first time, you hear a trace of Southern drawl. Slow. Slippery. There is an effeminate quality, too. Not a lisp, nor overwrought gay male speech, but certainly the stretching of *s* sounds and a female's ease from word to word. He lingers a little long on vowels, yet there's a weird droning music to it—a familiar tone you want to immediately repeat back. As if you know that later you will be working on your own Chicken Delicious impression.

"Hello Michael, it is so nice to see you again."

He asks about my books and if things are going well. We tell him in brief that we've come to BEA again and we wouldn't miss the chance of spending an evening listening to him play and sing. He seems pleased, but troubled. I introduce Sheree and MJ. As he shakes their hands, he studies them. "Such pretty girls, boys," he says the way he does.

When he starts the show, his fingers tap out some familiar but unplaceable melody. He says, "Good evening, everyone. My name is Chicken Delicious. I come from Mississippi and I live on the kindness of strangers." He nods to his tip jar. "I play almost everything but tonight I'd like to play Andreas." He grins across the piano bar. We all laugh. He gives Andreas an alluring wink and a chuckle.

The room begins to fill. We eventually make our way to the stools at the piano bar just in front of Chicken and we sing along, make requests and become the fodder for his/our entertainment. Two older women adorned in gold jewelry and thick glasses hog the microphone. They beg Chicken to play number after number. He plays their songs with ease and manages to move the mic to other hands until eventually it lands in Sheree's lap.

Sheree grins with delight. She is quite a good singer, and her blood to alcohol ratio is near perfect for a New York piano bar crooning. She kneels down beside Chicken and they lean into deciding upon a song. Mama brings more drinks. I hear Andreas laughing. After a couple of key checks, Chicken begins playing

Elton John's *Goodbye Yellow Brick Road* a little slower than expected, his eyes checking in with Sheree as if asking if what he's playing is correct. I will learn later that she was trying for Sara Bareilles' cover of the track—a haunting, minimized version that Chicken has never heard. Nevertheless, the two deliver the song in a memorable way without too many memorable bad notes. All in all, a delightful duet.

When the applause dies, Chicken tells us that he will take a break. Sheree again kneels down and the two huddle into a conversation. I smile watching them. I lift my camera and take a couple of photos. I am reminded of the first time Chicken engaged me, kneeling beside his piano four years ago.

Born Lewis Hunter Stowers III in Jacksonville, Mississippi, in 1943, he was a shy introvert, a painter, a traveler, a motorcyclist, an eccentric storytelling musician. In the late sixties, he met known occultist and psychic, Joseph Lukach, and through to the middle 1990's, Hunter would be his apprentice, his manager, and his accursed slave. During this period, Hunter would witness healings, miracles, and black magic. He would study a blend of Afro-Caribbean religions like Yoruba, Santería and Voodoo as well as converse with the dead, practice witchcraft and numerology. He would open a botanical store and sell herbs and potions. "Witchcraft in the early seventies wasn't really unusual," he told me, "it was just one of the arts. Jimmy Page, The Stones, Dylan—they were searching like all of us." Hunter crossed paths with many of these characters, including John Lennon and Yoko Ono. I'll never forget him eyeing my round glasses that first night and saying, "Michael, you look like John, you know. I've played his piano at the Dakota a few times." At that, I marveled. I recall thinking, *I can't wait to tell my brother Bob this story.*

While much of this might ring sinister or frightening, I felt no fear during that short conversation. I felt light, kindness, genuine interest, and most of all, awe. He framed his past as a journey that challenged and broke him, and he returned enlightened. His "slavery" ended when Mr. Luckach died and Hunter discovered that the outside world had seemingly shifted from the old magic to a new technological deity. Friends that he thought were close proved to be false. A new chapter was about to open. That was when his muse lured him back to the piano for the rest of his life. And it was this muse that told him to change his name. He told me that the spirit said, "People won't think of you as an old man, but an old Chicken—that made me smile." Thus, Chicken Delicious was born.

At our first meeting, he asked me my birth date and I shared it. He considered the numbers with closed lids and divined: "You're tenacious, and you've worked hard," he paused, peeped one eye open and squinted at me, "you don't ever give up. You sometimes work *too* hard. Makes some of your friends and family uncomfortable. You've paid your dues, as they say. You've quite a ways to go yet, but you will reach a success beyond your wildest dreams." He closed his eyes, "I see Andreas there, too. And someone you've not yet met." He smiles. "You wish your work came easier to you, but you're not afraid to fail. That's good. Some life changes are around the corner. Tough ones. You'll be okay but they'll be painful. You're worried about the health of someone." He thinks a moment. "Your mother? Your son? Maybe both." Feeling just the right scotch buzz, I stared at him, dumbfounded. We chatted for a minute or two more and he shared with me that he hasn't been feeling very well. I tried to inquire further, but he changed the subject.

I returned to my seat at the bar in a kind of trance. Andreas and I stayed to listen to a few more songs while we finished our scotch. My mind rolled his words over and over.

Now, as I watch Sheree kneeling beside Chicken, I feel a chill. From a very young age, Sheree has had a keen interest in all things spiritual. A born healer, she has also done her share of study in essential oils as well as becoming a Reiki master. What is more, she claims that she's seen mysterious, unexplainable occurrences, can feel otherworldly energies, and has paranormal sensitivities beyond that of most people. While I don't generally hold with such claims, I try to remain open—because after all, there are more things in Heaven and Earth, *Michael*, than are dreamt of in your philosophy. Most certainly, Chicken will sense Sheree's eagerness, her energy, and her willingness for augury. I have the feeling that their meeting will live long in her memory.

Chicken crosses the room to take a break. Sheree sits down with us again. She says, "He's amazing—a true light."

"What did he tell you?" MJ asks.

Excitedly, Sheree begins sharing Chicken's visions. "That I would never look or act my age—that all will be well with my son. . ." and so on. I listen. I feel my head shaking with wonder at his pinpointed detail.

Chicken returns to his piano wearing a Billy Joel paper mask. He sings *Piano Man* and *Scenes From an Italian Restaurant*. He changes it up and there, behind the keys, is Elvis, then Queen Elizabeth, Marlyn Monroe, Elton John, Frida Kahlo, and others. It is hilarious, bizarre, and disturbingly entertaining.

At his next break, I'm able to get a private word with him. I crouch down beside his piano stool and notice the dark circles under his eyes. He looks tired, drawn, distracted.

"How have you been?" I ask him.

"Not well, Michael. The doctor tells me I need to slow down. But I have too much to do. I have so much more to share, just like you do, Michael." He tells of health and financial challenges. A couple at the bar interrupt us with a song request. Chicken places his pale hand on my wrist and says, "Don't worry about me, Michael. We're here now—and we have angels all around us."

There are more songs and more jokes. I catch myself glancing toward the street. Cars pass in streaks of light. We need to be getting some rest for BEA tomorrow. I wonder what my son, Michael, is dreaming in his bed back in Idaho. I wonder if my Mom knows where I am. I think of Cary and Cristopher and wish that The RUB had a gig here in New York. I consider the angels around us.

A tug of worry pulls at my heart when I consider the work ahead—the strangers I will meet tomorrow—the book executives that may not care a fig that we've come. The dues I've yet to pay. The words I've yet to write.

Andreas reaches for his jacket. He says, "Getting about that time—let's get some sleep. Tomorrow we've a trilogy to introduce to the world."

As we rise and move to the door, we all wave to Chicken. He grins, finishes singing his refrain, and drawls over the mic, "Good luck at your book show tomorrow. What you've got is good for this world."

That was the last time I saw Chicken Delicious.[5]

[5] Hunter passed away from heart surgery complications in July, 2019. Here is his obituary: It is with a heavy heart that we are sharing with you that he has gone on to his next fabulous journey. Hunter has left an indelible imprint on the hearts of so many by sharing his wisdom and exquisite piano playing talent. A gifted teacher, fine artist and virtuoso musician, Hunter was a true original, unmatched in his quick-witted humor and outrageousness. His radiant spirit will leave huge voids in the hearts of many, that he would want us to fill with joy, thank you's and the good memories we have of him that we all treasure.

CHAPTER 7

THE DUES

At 7:45AM, Andreas and I stand on the corner of 37th and 7th, sipping coffee from cardboard cups. We are shouldering our document bags, laughing and reminiscing about last night. Morning sunlight warms the wet pavement; steam plumes from a round grate in the shiny grey street. The air is thick with spring humidity. Given the amount of scotch I imbibed last night, I'm shocked at how awake I am. How clear. *Must be the city*, I think. I can't be sure, but I feel as if my feet are vibrating.

We take a cab from the street corner in the Fashion District west to the gargantuan Javits Center, just off the Hudson River. This convention space of nearly 800,000 square feet is a sight to behold—a sprawling exhibition center constructed of primarily steel girders and massive panes of glass. Reading the pamphlet on the way, I learn that the building's footprint matches the size of the man for whom it is named: Jacob Koeppel Javits. Mr. Javits served as New York State Attorney General, a U.S. Congressman, and U.S. Senator in the mid 20th century. A liberal Republican, he was deeply committed to social issues: civil rights, labor unions and education. Best of all, at least to me, Mr. Javits had a big hand in creating the National Endowment for the Arts.

I mention a couple of these facts to Andreas.

"Busy guy," he says. "I wonder if he ever wrote a book and went to BEA—now *there's* a challenging prospect."

This is my fourth BEA at the Javits Center, and each time I have had to catch my breath at the event's enormous scope. Hanging from the arena-high ceilings are hundreds of insidiously huge, billboard-sized book covers that herald the coming year's most anticipated titles. New Harry Potter editions, new Dan Brown, new Stephen King, new Grisham—everywhere, full color graphics and power fonts—author's names in bold, booth numbers, signing posters, publishing house logos, distribution company logos—it is as if we've walked into a teenaged giant's bedroom and she has plastered her walls with the posters of her heroes. Just as I did the first time I saw this, I say to Andreas, "Can we get one of our books up there?"

Andreas puts his hands on his hips, cranes his neck, taking in the massive Dan Brown *Origins* banner and says, "Of course. It's just a matter of time."

I look back up. The larger than life book covers are intimidating. Almost oppressive. They seem to say that there's a powerful group of people that want everyone to pay attention to the words in this story from this author. *Look here*, they all seem to call out. *Look here!*

"Yes," I reply, a little deflated, "just a matter of time."

He must have noticed my mood shift. He says, "Remember our first time here? We had nothing but a book. Now we've got three books, a distribution company, an audio book deal, BEA book signings, interviews and we're being featured by IBPA.[6]" He raises his chin and stares at the massive covers hovering above our heads. He admits, "Though, it would be bitchin' to have the Trilogy flying up there next year. More dues to pay. It'll happen."

"It's a good thing we love the process, paying those dues." I smile.

"There'd be no reason to go on if we didn't," he says.

We both nod. We both study the upper architecture of glass, steel, sky, and new books.

Beyond the lobby is the food court and the subdivisions of exhibit space where the book industry has set up its own city scape. We wander through the streets of bookmakers, book writers, book designers, booksellers, book printers, book stores, book borrowers, book lenders, book mailers, book promoters, book movers, book shakers, and, most importantly, book lovers. Sally Field is signing books at the Hachet booth—the line of fans

---

[6] Independent Book Publisher's Association

curves around the block and out to the food court. A tall, dark-haired man with kind eyes and a yellow tie is scribbling his signature into his books at the Harper Collins booth. There is another line of fans. A woman in an apricot pantsuit and blue tinted glasses speaks to an audience of maybe fifty people about intellectual property rights. I see a sign advertising that the Daily Show's Trevor Noah will be speaking at the BookExpo Breakfast about his new book, *Born A Crime.*

I love Trevor Noah, I think.

It is a county fair, an inner-city farmer's market, a carnival, a theme park. It has everything you want to know about the printed word and more.

We part ways. Andreas heads to his first meeting of the day. My video interview isn't until after lunch, so I decide to walk the Midway and attempt to see what's what.

Ahead, I can see the Walt Disney booth space, or rather, *booth complex*, complete with an office area, executives milling about behind computers, a central meeting space with several four-top tables, bookcases, a long greeting counter, and an enclosed building at its center, a number of flat screens mounted to its walls, all rifling through images of Star Wars, Marvel, Mickey Mouse and Tinkerbell. Memories flood back of our freshman visit at BEA when Andreas had booked a small five foot by eight foot booth for us to exhibit my first book and our fledgling company.

Here's the journal entry I made that night, what seems like all those years ago:

When we arrived to set up the day before the show, we were delighted to learn that our booth-space was located directly across from Walt Disney's city-block-sized mansion. Trouble was, we couldn't find our spot right away. After making an inquiry, the convention tech pointed out that our booth was right where we thought it was, yet, regrettably, we couldn't see it because of the huge Walt Disney freight box planted on top of it. Talk about feeling small.

Andreas's optimism, "At least we get to be near their foot traffic," he said. "You know, like those little fish that swim with sharks."

"You mean pilot fish?"

"Yeah," he said.

"So we eat the parasites off the shark? I don't think I like this metaphor," I said, wondering who was going to move the massive wooden freight box so we could put our booth together.

Andreas laughed. "No. I see it like we'll end up being the shark's pilot. They'll go where we're going to take them."

Andreas is awesome.

I'm smiling, staring at one of the Walt Disney flat screens. An X-wing banks and dives into the Death Star trench. I love X-wings. Another pilot fish, I guess.

Pulling out my phone, I tap out a text message to my friend, Harvey Pepper, a former New Yorker. He has been urging me to make time for a New York pastrami sandwich.

Me: At BEA. I'm going for a pastrami sandwich today.

I met Harvey a year or so ago at The Art Spirit Gallery in downtown Coeur d'Alene during a busy art opening. The meeting I will never forget. Harvey, late sixties, white haired, neatly trimmed beard and bright smile, was introduced to me by the gallery's owner, Steve Gibbs. Steve dropped these accolades about Harvey: *writer for Laugh In, Saturday Night Live and wrote and toured with George Carlin for years.* Harvey reached out, shook my hand and said grinning, "So you're a writer? Poor bastard."

We both laughed. For the next hour, we talked about words, comedy, and books while the gallery bustled around us. I felt a rare and immediate connection to him. A week later, we met for coffee to continue our conversation—and the conversation continues to this day. Belushi, Goldie Hawn, John Cleese, life in New York in the 70s, in Hollywood—the Business—story after story—and his take on events is intoxicating. While tales of these monumental figures and formative times are compelling, he often says that when he was in the thick of it, writing with George Carlin or writing with SNL, *it was all about the moment.* All of the mythology came later. "At the time, we were just a bunch of kids writing funny shit." It was about the writing—the process— the doing of it. Of late, Harvey has been immersed in writing a documentary in development for HBO on what he calls the *Real History of the United States,* focusing on the darker, more sinister realities of our country's past—the stuff left out of history books and the New York Times.

Executives for HBO have been giving him grief. "Nothing unusual," he's told me, "but it just never ceases to be frustrating. They're all no-talent fuckers." Apparently, as soon as he gets a little too close to a hot spot or a political hot button, or if the historical truth is too real, these *reptiles,* he calls them, want him to "tone it down." A veteran of the art vs. commerce wars—he is in constant battle with the *lizards.*

My phone vibrates. Harvey's response:

Harvey: BEA—Book execs—Beware of those reptilian vampires! And don't you dare put mayonnaise on that pastrami. It is considered sacrilegious.

I laugh. My stomach growls.

I move on. More authors signing. More executives cutting distribution deals, networking. I imagine secret handshakes and back room agreements with scotch and cigars. Big plans for big cash, big books with big ideas. Big names stay big, little names get bigger. Big money. Big dreams.

A Rush lyric by Neil Peart cues up in my head:

> *Big money got a heavy hand*
> *Big money take control*
> *Big money got a mean streak*

Big money got no soul[7]

I'm dizzy. My feet come to a stop. I pivot in a circle. Again. And again.

"Yo, Michael," a voice says.

Turning around, I see a short, bald-headed man in a leather jacket, a collared white shirt, blue jeans. Slung across his chest is a grey strap attached to an overlarge, very heavy looking document bag.

"Yo, Michael." A muted smile on his face, "You okay?"

I chuckle. "Yes, yes. I'm fine. Just admiring the main nerve of the *booky-monster.*"

"Yeah, right?" In his hand, extended out to me, of all things, is a book. "Take a look at this," he says. The book raises up a little.

"Me?"

"Yeah, I see by your lanyard that you're an author."

The BEA blue and white, bar coded lanyards are emblazoned with both name and book vocation. In my case, in bold letters it shows my name and below it the word: AUTHOR. I glance at his chest and see that he doesn't have a lanyard.

I take the book. "Wow, thanks," I say.

"I've been writing for a couple of years and this is my first book. I'm here just networking and getting the word out." He reaches into his bag, then hands me a business card, a bookmark and a sticker.

"Thanks," I say again. The three hundred plus page volume is called *Trudge*. I deem it to be a murder mystery. The cover art is a high contrast black and white photograph of a man extending a knife toward the camera, much like the book was just extended to me. A second later, I notice that the man on the cover is the author.

"Is that you?" I ask.

"Yeah," he answers, "I do my own art, too."

---

[7] From Rush's, *The Big Money*, lyrics: Neil Peart. ©1985. From the album, *Power Windows*, Mercury Records.

I study it a moment. A slight chill plinks down my spine. I can hear what Sheree would say if she were here: *weird, weird energy.*

"Thank you for sharing."

"It's about a killer—a mystery. You'll dig it. Really fun."

I nod. "Cool."

"You think you could pass it on to your publisher?"

Without a moments hesitation I say, "Sure." The man's face is tired. His open case is full of his books. I add, "I'm not sure this is the kind of thing he's looking for, but I'll take a look at it and pass it along."

He smiles. "Thanks, man. Thanks." After a moment he says, "Hard business, getting people to pay attention to your stuff, right?"

I nod. "Yes."

"I was gonna get a booth, but I figured I'd just network on my own. Payin' my dues."

"I know the feeling," I tell him.

He starts back into the vortex, "Take it easy, man," he says.

"Thanks for the book," I say again.

"No worries. Have your publisher call me. Enjoy the show."

Just a few yards away, he engages another fair-goer. This time it's a rather stoic, older, suit-and-tie, not-to-be-trifled-with executive. His lanyard description: AGENT. *Lizard,* I hear Harvey in my head. I watch and feel anxious. The book is extended. Lips move. For a split second, the agent pauses and regards the man. His eyes move to the book, to the man's face and then an expression appears that I've come to know quite intimately. It says: *No. Thanks but no—this is not how things are done. Are you crazy—you poor bastard?* A moment later the agent is gone, halfway down the midway, and the author of *Trudge* is standing there, watching the agent walk away—the book still held out like a weapon. There's a slight trace of frustration—a simmering defiance in his face.

Bless him, I think as I start back into Bookcity. He's right. Do everything you can. Fortune favors the bold. But most people don't realize that writing the book is often the easiest part. Getting someone, anyone, to take the time to read it, consider it, or give it a chance in the marketplace is another work of art in itself. And the agent is right, too. It is impossible to engage with every hungry author. There are prescribed ways of getting into the back room with the scotch and the cigars—though the odds aren't generally kind.

I'm still working toward my invite.

Bless him, I think again. I know the uphill climb well. I know the tenacity. How you must take each rejection not as a failure, but as one more step toward your goal: another reader. And another. And another. Until, of course, you can get to the ultimate success: writing the next book.

A memory flash to when my second novel came out, *Leaves of Fire*. Before my national author tour was being planned, I was offered a short tour of regional grocery stores. That's right, *grocery stores*. Super One, Albertsons, Safeway—a few other chains that slip my memory (gigmentia).

Bless him, the author of *Trudge*.

I know how to trudge. I know how to trudge, indeed. I'm still trudging. . .

THE BOOKMAN DOWN THE AISLE

GREAT FALLS, MT. ALBERTSONS, 2016.

So, I say, "Something to read with your—" I pause—glance into her shopping cart. I see seven gallons of 2% milk, four different kinds of breakfast cereal (one is Captain Crunch), a package of Pasta Roni Alfredo, nine frozen pizzas, a bag of family-sized Chili Cheese Fritos, the weird, goldish glow of cheese dip in the jar (I love that stuff), glowing gold fish crackers —*then* I see it—the spaghetti supper pouch microwave dinner with garlic bread included, frozen mozzarella sticks, a box of wine—*there it is—the connection*. I pick up my invitation, "Something to read with your wine—with your Italian dinner— this book takes you to Italy." I raise my first novel, *The Invasion of Heaven,* so she can see the cover.

The first thing you look for, when offering your latest book to a grocery shopper (note, they are shopping for groceries), is simple acknowledgement—do they see you—then you must guess if they enjoy reading and, finally, if they are comfortable with a complete stranger suggesting a book for their reading list —if they do indeed have a reading list. You have maybe four seconds, and all you've got is their appearance, the contents of their shopping cart and what the mythical *Itonalya* of *Wyn*

Avuqua would call *Elliqui*—or maybe, your ability to sense what Brian Wilson called *Good Vibrations*.

The woman wears glasses. She's round-faced and slightly shorter than me. Her hair is dark and straight. By her eyes, I think late forties. I imagine that if she smiled, she'd glow. But she is not smiling. The book is still hovering between us. I finish out my four seconds "My second book, *Leaves of Fire* is out now, too —are you looking for a summer read?" I break off.

Three children gather near to her cart—around her skirt. They look at me. Then the woman's answer is something I find impossible to riposte. She says, "We *don't* read books. Nope, we don't." Then with a wave of her hand, adds, "My father didn't like us readin' books." My eyes tick to her kids—their faces opaque, blank, lost. "Come on!" she calls them as she pushes passed, "leave the *Bookman* be." The children linger a moment, staring, mouths partly open until the woman's order registers. They flinch and follow after her.

The Bookman. No one has ever called me the Bookman before. I want to take it as a compliment—but I'm sure it was not meant as one. And, I'm not sure what just happened.

An announcement, barely audible, begins a moment later: "We have a special guest today here at the Great Falls, Montana, Albertsons, Michael Kee-oop, Kow-eep, author of the books *The Invasion of Heaven* and *Leafs of Fire*." (*Leafs* of Fire? *Leafs?* Really?) "Visit him near the beer and wine and he'll sign his book for you."

I sigh. The high florescent lights sting. I can smell the detergent aisle a few feet away, and the alarming reality of too much plastic, the otherworldly colors of processed food, the refrigerated troughs, no, *trenches* of carved meat—reminds me yet again why I loathe shopping—my pathetic anger at humankind's cooperate, exorbitant, wasteful—hey, wait, there are some of those yummy goldfish crackers.

I turn to look at my book display. It is a discordant vision—a facade—as if a magical porthole has opened upon an Italian villa right next to aisle eighteen, near the beer and wine. Within this florescent wilderness, I call it my campsite. It consists of an antique wood table, a backdrop art piece filled with velvet, old swords, maps, leaves, books, quill and ink, records and joints, tobacco and leather. Two stacks of books dominate the center. I designed the display to provide a potential reader a view into the aesthetic of the books—an invitation to a place—the way I intend the books to feel once you're a few pages in. And amid the rattle of shopping carts, the beeping barcode readers, the aisles of canned logos and disposable packaging, my campsite is calming, so I stare at it. A lot.

"So what's this?" a friendly voice says. I turn to see another woman who could be my mother—gentle smile, sparkling blue eyes. "Are you the author?" She is scanning the artwork, the leather chair, the ink bottle, the ink splattered desk.

"Hello," I say, "something to read with your—" I resist the urge to look into her cart. *One shouldn't profile*, I caution myself, but I see vegetables, and that's encouraging. I smile, raising a book. "Something to read this Spring? Perhaps a summer read?"

"What's the book about?" She takes it from my hand and studies the cover. She turns it over and scans the synopsis. And it is at this point I give her the elevator pitch—the speech that's spilled from my lips countless times since the book's release. Memorized like a pop song—quick and to the point—Goes like this:

"It's the story of a painter and a psychologist. His paintings have this supernatural element that makes them dangerous to look upon—dangerous to the point of *death*. The story goes from the mountain lakes of Idaho to Italy and back—it is a murder mystery wrapped in political intrigue, international travel— there's a little bit of mafia, art curation, madness, and mindbogglingly fun twists. Oh, and there's even a sword fight."

A minute or two later, I am signing: "To Elanor, I hope you enjoy the story. *Michael B. Koep*." I thank her. She thanks me. Faith is now, somehow, restored. Maybe this grocery store thing isn't so bad. A little awkward, sure, but here in my campsite, I defy the chili cheese Fritos aisle and the Super sized Red Bull slushy machine. I feel as if I'm on a righteous path.

Before she turns away, she asks, "Why did you write the book?"

I smile and shake my head slightly. There's no time to convey all of the influences, the emotional yearning, my love of stories or the hopeless reach for meaning—not now, not here, so all I can think of to answer her is something author Jess Walter told me once—so I used his line: "I wrote this book so I could write the next one." I then added, "The ultimate success."

Twenty-four books sold during the two hours I stood there beside the display. A case of books.

"That's FANTASTIC! How magical!" my publisher, Andreas, jubilates when I report over the phone as I drive back to my hotel. "You just got twenty-four more readers. Three thousand titles released in the US everyday, and you just got twenty-four new readers. Wonderful! Just wonderful!"

"Yes," I agree. I can still smell detergent.

"So, you've done two readings at Barnes and Noble, now there's three more Montana grocery stores, one more Barnes and Noble reading/signing and that little indie bookshop in Missoula left to go until New York leg, right?" he asks.

"That's right," I agree.

"You okay?," he asks.

"Of course," I assure him. I smile, hoping he can sense it over the phone. "You bet. It's just a little strange—signing books in a grocery store—it's not like a bookstore where people visit to search for a book. . . "

"True," he says, "but who cares? You just got twenty four new readers!"

"Right," I agree, trying to force that woman's weird phrase: "My daddy didn't like us readin' books," out of my mind. I share the experience with him and the strange stab of sadness that followed.

He laughs. "What did you say to her?"

"I was speechless. I wanted to tell her, 'I'm sorry,' but I couldn't bring myself to say it."

"Get some rest," he says.

GREAT FALLS, MONTANA, SIP AND DIP MOTOR INN reminds me of a Canadian hotel / rock club that my band played in the late eighties on my first Canadian tour. The decor frozen in the 1970s—golds and wood accents—the aesthetics of Butch Cassidy and the Sundance Kid and 2001: A Space Odyssey mixed. The menu is classic diner faire—burgers, steaks, deep fried goodness—Folgers coffee. But the Sip n' Dip's defining element is the swimming pool adjacent to the bar, and from 7 to 11PM, two large glass windows allow a view into the secret and mysterious habits of mermaids, mythic beauties drifting in slow-motion just behind the scotch bottles. Truly, it is unlike anything I've ever seen. I scribble into my journal:

The etymology of mermaid, if I remember correctly: mer=sea, maid=girl. Seagirl. So, currently, above the rim of my glass is a spellbinding siren, a mermaid, in graceful, weightless dance—she flirts with patrons through the glass, smiles, makes funny faces and enchants us weary drinking bookmen as we consider the reality of the myths we know and the myths we've yet to write.

My friend Rebecca Zanetti, a New York Times bestselling romance novelist, was the one to enlighten me on the number of titles released in a given period. I thought it was 3000 new titles a month. Over coffee, her sweet smile curved tighter as she waited for me to finish talking about the challenges of getting a title noticed. She put her hand on my wrist and said: "Not three thousand a month. Three thousand a day, Michael. Roughly, three thousand a day." And here I was thinking that all you had to do was write a good book—as if that's the easy part.

I scribble the number *3000* in my journal and I look up from my seat at the bar. A beautiful mermaid glides across the window.

Seriously. Her sparkling tail glitters in the blue water. Tangles of her hair wave like coils of ribbon in a breeze. She crosses her eyes at me. Wonderfully weird.

I think of my new twenty-four readers and wonder if the still to be completed *Part Three of the Newirth Mythology* should include mermaids. I sip my scotch. I nod determinedly. "So it should," I say aloud.

SUPER ONE GROCERY IN WHITEFISH, MT. Same awkward position, but a little more bearable now that I've done it. I notice a kind staunch belief today, rising up from my chest to my smile and eyes. After all, I really like these books, this story (despite my desire to rewrite it again, and again—just rework a few more sentences)—I'm not at all pretending that this is interesting stuff —*it is!* And if it seems sort of complex—*it really is not!* my goodness, if I can get it, so can these people, so can you. . . *right?*

These are the thoughts rattling through my mind as I encounter the incredibly varied personalities of a grocery store. Hunters, loggers, teachers, hairdressers, office accountants, mothers, insurance salesman, soldiers, construction workers— wait, I'm profiling again.

I'm positioned next to the shopping carts this time, so every person that enters the store will see my campsite. "Hello," I say handing out a bookmark and a flyer. "A book for the summer?" Some take the card and smile. Some refuse eye contact. One tall man in a camouflage vest and high boots says, "Fuck off." I hand him a flyer anyway. I notice that just outside the doors is a group of girl scouts. They are stacking boxes of cookies. I sigh. Competition.

Another man stops before me, "Mythology, huh?" He lifts the book and examines it. I note his T-shirt: *Don't be so open-minded your brains fall out.* Beside the saying is a tall crucifix. "So this is about *God*, right?" His eyes are slightly crossed.

"Well, not exactly, it is about a painter and a psychologist, and how stories can change our behavior—about how the psychologist uses a story to trap a murderer. And from that, he causes a kind of supernatural change in history."

"Hmm." He looks down his nose at me. "That doesn't sound very *believable,* does it?"

At that moment, a couple swaggers up to me clad in black leather, chains and long necklaces. They look like '80s rockstars. "Cool hair," the dude says to me. Like me, he, too, has very long hair. "Seriously, you look like Lennon."

"And Ozzy," the girl joins.

"Totally. You a writer?" I want to say I'm a *bookman,* but instead I grin and hand him a flyer.

At the mention of Ozzy Osborne, the prince of darkness himself, the cross-pupiled fellow hands the book back to me, says, "I don't like mythologies, God bless," and walks away.

"Um, I, wha, huh?" I sort of say—words fail sometimes. "Have a good day," I offer.

I love the look of the smiling couple before me. People I know, somehow. Music folk. Rockers. Pot smokers. I bet they've got records and a turntable at home. I tell them about the book— and I even include that the famous guitarist from Led Zeppelin, Jimmy Page, is a character in *Leaves of Fire.* (*I share that fact because I am blatantly profiling. Or am I marketing?*)

"Far out, bro," the dude says. "Jimmy Page. Pagey in a Mythology. Awesome! Why Pagey, bro?" he asks.

It's a favorite question. "It was a *must.* I had to include Zeppelin in my mythology," I answer him. "Zeppelin was/is *mythical*—after all, they are the *Hammer of the Gods*, right?" I notice my vernacular shifting into musician speak. "Check it out, I think you'll dig it."

"We're in, bro," he says giving me a stoney grin. "Sign one up for us."

I have been a rock musician for most of my professional life. I've waited tables, yes. I've written, yes. I've been a university educator, yes. But mostly, I've hit things with sticks for money. Wonderfully weird. So the day the great musician/wizard Jimmy Page showed up *on* the page in my second book, opposite Loche

Newirth's deliciously dangerous wife, Helen, it seemed quite natural while it was happening. As the sentences stacked up, so did my excitement—and why not? I suddenly realized that it was right: Jimmy Page should be in the book. How often have my band mates in The RUB, Cristopher and Cary, and I shared memories, admiration, the things we've learned, et cetera, from our musical influences—Zeppelin, certainly a god among the others. It seemed right to include rock history and the sometimes seedy side of the rock experience. To simply pay homage. Plus, I know a little about the rock musician's lifestyle. A little about the circus. A lot I'll never admit. It doesn't mean I know about everything that goes on backstage but, let's just say I've the inside scoop on a thing or two. I hope those two shopping rockers will dig joining Helen in 1972 at the Continental "Riot" House on the Sunset Strip.

BACK AT THE HOTEL, I pour a scotch and call my son. I tap out a few emails. Then I practice a couple of sentences in my journal. I try a few more and scowl at the paper. All fragile tropes, colorless platitudes, fucking rubbish. After a few minutes reading and rereading, I switch gears and start the old exercise of writing about the difficulty of writing, which I find all-too-easy— especially the lines where I refer to myself as a dough-headed uncooked ink-leaker, a queasy wanna-be user of big words, and "Hey scribble-dork—just go play your drums! And oh, parenthetically, you best keep practicing that, too."

Pausing to read it over, I regard it as some of my most accurate work to date.

This kind of self deprecation isn't healthy—but at least now I know who I'm dealing with—and that makes for a better conversation. I quickly scribble out a memory to cleanse the palette.

Cold sprinkles of rain. Lime green shoots weaved in the grey grass. A stripe of clean blue sky is low in the East. I do the dishes. Wash some towels. Michael and I build Lego speeders. We

duel with lightsabers in the backyard—shoot arrows at his castle-
fort—We walk to Hudson's for a cheeseburger.
       Writing is hard.

I put the pencil down and think: cheeseburger. Yes, time for a cheeseburger. And on the way to cheeseburger, I call my publisher: "Twenty-one books today," I tell him.

"That is fantastic!" His voice is filled with encouragement and joy. "Twenty *more* readers! You're making my job easier by the day."

"Yeah," I agree, balancing on the edge of sarcasm, "Between yesterday and today, six thousand books have been released and we have *forty-four* new readers."

"Fantastic. That's forty-four more than we had two days ago! You're doing good work out there. You're going to be out all summer long. Maybe even into the fall. Be ready." *All summer?* I think. I open my mouth to respond, but words fail. Writing is hard. He senses my silence. "Don't worry, only a few super markets—mostly bookstores."

I look to the west. The sunset is a phantasmic red. A forest fire has started somewhere out there.

"I'm ready," I say. *But am I?*

"Good," he says. "Now go eat."

From my seat at the counter, I can hear my cheeseburger sizzling in the kitchen. As I wait, I read. I stumble upon a poem by Tony Hoagland titled *Special Problems in Vocabulary.*

At the moment, it means everything.

SPECIAL PROBLEMS IN VOCABULARY

There is no single particular noun
for the way a friendship,
stretched over time, grows thin,
then one day snaps with a popping sound.

No verb for accidentally
breaking a thing
while trying to get it open
 —a marriage, for example.

No particular phrase for
losing a book
in the middle of reading it,
and therefore never learning the end.

There is no expression, in English, at least,
for avoiding the sight
of your own body in the mirror,
for disliking the touch

of the afternoon sun,
for walking into the flatlands and dust
that stretch out before you
after your adventures are done.

No adjective for gradually speaking less and less,
because you have stopped being able
to say the one thing that would
break your life loose from its grip.

Certainly no name that one can imagine
for the aspen tree outside the kitchen window,
in spade-shaped leaves

spinning on their stems,
working themselves into
a pale-green, vegetable blur.

No word for waking up one morning
and looking around,
because the mysterious spirit

that drives all things
seems to have returned,
and is on your side again.
　　　　—*Tony Hoagland*[8]

My sandwich arrives. The first bite tastes like blue sky July—
like summer evening bbq smoke. I am nine years old—I'm with
my parents—at the Wilma Theater, standing in line to see Star
Wars—where all this goddamn trouble began. I set the burger
down and study it a moment, feeling certain it will be the subject
of my morning writing. A cheeseburger. Am I doing this right? Is
that mysterious spirit really on my side, or am I just hungry?
Maybe both? I'm thankful that writing is hard. Thankful I love to
practice. Grateful for cheeseburgers.

ANOTHER DAY, ANOTHER SUPERMARKET. Again, much
easier than the two times prior. The accosting doesn't feel like
accosting any longer. Connecting, I decide, is really about
sincerity. If someone isn't interested, no big deal. Can't please
everyone. At least tomorrow I will be reading from *Leaves of Fire*
at a bookstore.

A woman about my age approaches, pushing a cart. She is fit,
long dark hair, thick-rimmed glasses resting on her nose. Just by
the way she carries herself, I sense that she's educated. A student
or librarian, maybe? Perhaps she'd be interested in a new book.

I say hello, I hand her a flyer, I explain, I give her the simple
synopsis, and I wait as her eyes race across the story's description
on the back of the press card. A moment later, she hands it back
and tells me, "No thanks, I read things based in reality. I don't
read thrillers. I read non-fiction," She holds her palm up between
us (the old *talk to the hand* move) as she rolls her cart around the

---

[8] Tony Hoagland, "Special Problems in Vocabulary" from Application for
Release from the Dream. Copyright © 2015 by Tony Hoagland. Reprinted by
permission of Graywolf Press.

corner of the aisle. "And by the way," she says over her shoulder, "you need to work on that *pitch*, too,"

Three years ago I attended my first-ever writing conference in Los Angeles. It was the Writer's Digest Story World conference —an event that gathers writers to learn from experts the strict guidelines, the dos and don'ts of how to pitch a story to an agent. "Without the literary agent," as one of the presenters sermoned, "you are doomed to obscurity." Maybe that's true.

The three hundred plus of us were herded into a hotel board room. Around the perimeter, sitting at small desks, were fifteen to twenty literary agents, all with specific genre interests. The brochure guaranteed writers would get one-on-one time with a literary agent. And so it was true. Only the brochure failed to mention the *60-second* time limit. The waiting lines were partitioned like a TSA airport nightmare. I suddenly marveled at my place in the world. The utter desperation of it all. The room was stuffy. Claustrophobia crowded my lungs. The fellow in front of me was searching the herded writers, asking over and over, in a panic, "Am I in the *mystery* line? The *mystery* line!? Am I in it?" The woman behind me was stoic—her eyes closed and her lips whispered what I assumed was her pitch—rehearsing word for word, again and again, like a solemn prayer. Suddenly everyone appeared to be in trance, mouthing silently their pitch, their plea, their hope. I was simply confused.

I stood in line for forty-five minutes. When I finally sat down before a literary agent, Jill, I think her name was, and started my pitch (which, truth be told, I was making up on the spot, because, after all, it is really about sincerity, isn't it?), she stopped me ten seconds in and said: "No thanks, I don't read thrillers. I represent non-fiction and mysteries." I was shocked. "And by the way," she added, "you need to work on that pitch, too. Next."

I stared. "With all due respect, I stood in line for a long while and you don't read mystery-thrillers?" I raise my brochure, "It says here—"

"Mysteries, not thrillers. Next," she said, without looking at me.

I continued to stare, out of sheer amazement. "Next!" she said sternly. The fellow behind me tapped my shoulder. I could feel him vibrating for his shot at this freakish literary version of American Idol. I felt sick. Writing is hard. I rose, thanked Jill politely for her time and weaved my way out of the feeding lines to the less crowded room downstairs where there was scotch. My notebook, too.

I shake my head at the memory. I scent a new spicy detergent in aisle three. "Thank you," I say politely to the non-fiction woman now far down the aisle.

Another shopper carrying a heavy, oversized bottle of wine passes—she has three small children in tow. Again, *We don't read books,* drifts across my mind. The thought tongue-ties me. "S-S-S-psychological thriller?" I manage.

She grins. Friendly and quite likely very funny—she points the throat of the wine bottle to the three parading littles, "Behold," she says, "my psychological thriller." We both laugh as she passes.

Behind me, a short, middle-aged man with glasses and mustache, looking sort of like my science teacher from junior high school, is holding up *Leaves of Fire.* "I love this shit," he says. He taps the synopsis on back of the book, "Can I expect dimensional quantum physics and theories of the afterlife. All wrapped in art?"

I see he's read the flap-copy. I nod. I keep my mouth shut, not wanting to screw his excitement up with a verbal pitch that may need some work. I nod again.

"Well, I want one," he says.

A WEEK LATER, ON THE WAY TO NEW YORK[9], (I have now completely lost count as to how many books have been released into the market place), I tell Andreas the, *You need to work on that pitch,* tour story. He laughs. After a moment he says, "The pitch is marketing and I love marketing—the magic of it—

---

[9] Our second BEA.

especially with something you believe in. If there's no substance behind your words, your pitch, there's no sense in even opening your gob. It's really just a set of words that invite people to share in something magical, right?" He shrugs, "And of course, folks can join in or not. There are some people that just don't read thrillers. We're gonna find the ones that do!"

The magic of it. Words. In *Leaves of Fire*, the six-hundred year-old William Greenhame shares a little about the magic of words. He says to Loche (with a little *Hamlet* echo that I couldn't resist):

William says, "Words. Words. Words. They are made of magic, are they not? The arrangement of little marks, characters —letters—vowels, consonants. Language. Amazing isn't it? You know, that is why they call the construction of words *spelling*."

"Spelling?" Loche asks.

"Yes, my boy. Spelling. Spells. The casting of spells. Wonderful, yes? And the use of spells, words bring about change."

I mention the excerpt to him and he nods approvingly. "And that is why you're touring. Sharing the work. Spreading magic. That's why we're headed to New York, to meet the people who will help us spread the magic." He laughs again. "Think of it, you're a traveling magician."

"Magician, huh?" I say. "I prefer *Bookman*."

"Oh, very well. . ."

Since I've begun touring as a Bookman, I often compare the travels to my continuing career as a touring rock musician (Rockman? No. Not *Rockman*.) There are obvious differences of course—my hands don't hurt after smashing the drum kit, my ears don't ring after a reading, and I don't share a room with my bass player, Cristopher. But the single most similar characteristic is the *reason* to tour—and that is to share the work—to see if it resonates. To hold up something that you love and share it. To connect. Share the music, share the magic—share the story.

Three thousand new releases a day is a little tricky to get your head around. One should probably accept that if a title does get noticed, magic must, in some way, play a role. But magic isn't governed solely by mysterious forces—by magicians, artists and writers. It is most potent in those who love and support the arts. There is a glorious wizardry in simply saying *hello,* and then incanting the ancient and mystical spell that goes something like this: "Check this out; you're gonna dig it."

My goals as a writer are not uncommon ones—to suspend disbelief, to entertain, to connect, to find that elusive thing called meaning. (And more than often fail in the attempt. That's a big part of the job, too. Writing is hard). To inspire. I think it is safe to speak for every *bookwoman and bookman* that with every new cluster of letters, with all the new words that string into sentences, into graphs and finally into stories, there is the desire to get better at connecting—with ourselves—with you. To cast a better spell, we practice it, erase it, try it again, rethink, rewrite, over and over until we have something worth sharing. And for a short time, we raise it up as high as we can for you in bookstores, the occasional supermarket, at bus stops, at readings, in these magical, fantastical rooms called libraries so that in the end, we can carry on practicing. So we can get back to our desk at home and write the next one.

—mbk 2016

So here I stand, a few years later in the middle of the BEA chaos still attempting to raise a flag for all to see—just like everyone here, I suppose. The massive, billboard-sized book covers suspended in the rafters of the Javits Center, the authors signing books, the executives brandishing their pens and contracts, and me and the author of *Trudge*—we're all waving our flags.

I heave a sigh and trudge into Bookville.

My cell phone vibrates and I see that Harvey has texted me back.

CHAPTER 8

PASTRAMI

Harvey's text:

Harvey: Mike can you please call right away

I check the time. In twenty minutes, I am to appear for an online video talk about the Trilogy at the IBPA booth—a first for my work here at BEA. Nervous energy vibrates in my abdomen. I raise the phone and dial Harvey's number.

Harvey's life partner, Vicki, answers. As she speaks, my eyes latch to the escalators that connect to the main lobby. Long lines of people glide up into the event, long lines slide down out of sight, back into the city.

After a moment, the sight blurs.

When I arrive at the interview, I am greeted by a woman named Angela, the IBPA representative. After we shake hands, she pauses and asks, "Are you okay?"

I had hoped to have composed myself—but tears are tough to erase. "I am. Just a few minutes ago, I was informed that a dear friend has suddenly passed."

The woman places her hand on my upper arm, "I'm so sorry. I'm so sorry."

"Thank you," I say. "My apologies, I—I am struggling a bit here. Do you think I could have a few minutes before we do the interview?" Her video tech steps up to us and offers his condolences.

"Of course," she says. "Let me see how we might shift the schedule." Concern shadows her face. "I'm so sorry."

"Thank you. Quite sudden." Tears well. "Thank you." I turn toward a cluster of chairs a few yards away and sit.

Not an hour ago, Harvey sat down at his desk in Northern Idaho to write, had a massive heart attack, and is now gone. His partner Vicki was barely able to communicate the discovery. I am the last one to share words with him. Something about a pastrami sandwich. And lizards.

Tears.

Andreas arrives at my side. He listens. He comforts. He immediately begins planning and moves to postpone the interview.

"No," I tell him. "I'll do the interview. I don't want to throw a wrench in their schedule."

"I'm sure they'll be more than willing to accommodate—"

I shake my head. A weird, teary determination takes hold. I think of the *Trudge* author, I think of grocery stores, I think of the million book flags flying around me—our multiple visits here at BEA and how we've gone from a single book and no identity to signings and video interviews. I think of Cristopher and Cary—the show must go on. "No," I shake my head and wipe my eyes and cheeks. "I can hear Harvey now, 'Keep on keeping on.'"

Andreas studies me carefully. "You're sure? You look like shit."

I offer a pained chuckle. "Nothing unusual about that."

While Andreas confers with Angela and the video tech, I lift my phone and call Dad. I share Harvey's passing, how he was a mentor and a teacher—and through tears, I tell Dad I love him, adding with pained laughter, "And don't die." Dad listens, consoles and manages to get me on my feet and focused. After we hang up, I place a call to my dear friend, mentor, and business partner Mark and share the same sentiments. He, too, emboldens me. Then my college professor, another beloved mentor, Dr. Michael Herzog.

"Don't die."

They all steady me, strengthen me, nudge me forward.

I considered later that those calls were a way of saying goodbye to Harvey—a way of making sure that my group of mentors knew, from my heart to theirs that they have filled my life with light, thought, and the will to reach beyond my grasp. I didn't get the chance to tell Harvey those things, but somehow I think he knew—even if we were discussing the best pastrami sandwich in New York. And lizards.

A half hour later, I am sitting across from Angela. We each hold wireless microphones. My books are displayed on a table between us. I can't sit still. I struggle to smile with tears just below the surface. Then she asks the expected: "Can you tell us what your story is about."

I know that one. So, I vault into the answer—an answer I've spoken to countless people. The pitch I've thrown more times than I can remember.

"It's the story of a portrait painter and a psychologist—and the painter has a supernatural element to his work that makes his paintings dangerous to look upon. Dangerous to the point of death. . ." And so on. I'm smiling too much. I'm not focused. I'm overly emphatic.

We discuss characters and life experiences. We talk about writing, and future projects. How I got started, where I want to go. I give my best shots at telling stories—hoping I'm not boring —believing that I am, indeed, boring.

By the time the interview is over, I am exhausted and the memory of our conversation is hazy. Andreas and I thank Angela, her tech, and the others at the IBPA booth, and cross back into the hustle and bustle of Bookcity. The escalators gently pull us out and set us down into the lobby.

My phone buzzes. A text from Cristopher lists a number of new show dates that have just hit the calendar. My eyes blur.

Outside, we hail a cab.

The driver asks, "Where to?"

Climbing in, I say, "The best pastrami sandwich in town. 2nd Avenue Deli."

CHAPTER 9

THE DESK DOOR

During the interview I was asked the kinds of questions that I love to hear answered by other authors, musicians, and artists. One of my favorites revolves around the idea of origins; the *how did you become, or how are you becoming what you are now?* variety. The backstory. With the loss of Harvey weighing on me, I couldn't seem to find a solid answer for anything. I couldn't seem to remember.

Gigmentia.

Returning to my hotel room later that evening, I pour a scotch and stare out at grey buildings, yellow-lit windows, and the river of traffic below. The tears come again. Gratitude waves over me for that hour at the art opening where Harvey and I met—the several times we had coffee—the long phone conversations we had discussing stories, history, the trials of writing—the trials of living.

Then, I'm angry. We barely scratched the surface, Harvey and I. I didn't get the chance to learn his origin story—ask the *how did you become what you are now?* kinds of questions. And I didn't get the chance to share mine.

With the booze easing the shock of the day's news, I open my laptop and I pull up a short article I had posted on Goodreads a few years ago that dealt with some of my origins. I sit down in the chair beside the window. I say into the shadowy room, "Hey Harvey, here's a little about me that maybe you didn't know— just so you know."

WRITING ON THE DESK DOOR

Every wall is a door
   —RW Emerson
Every door is a desk
   —MB Koep

One should be open to the use of doors.

A few years back, my friend Agamon (Scott Haynes) gifted an old oak door to me. Walking me out through tall gold grass, wild flowers and aspen trees to one of those classic red and white, North Idaho barns, Agamon explained that when he saw the door hanging way up in the rafters, he thought immediately that I should be the one to have it. After some difficulty lowering it down from high above, he leaned the heavy rectangle against the side of the barn to await my next visit.

So, door use number 1: a door can be a gift.

My visits to Agamon's home were usually coupled with session work. A few yards from his house, he had constructed his recording studio to keep company with the aspens, the gold grass, red barns and the like. A beautiful setting to be asked to visit, and better still, to be invited to play drums. It is a flattering thing to be the "first call" drummer for studio engineers and friend audiophiles—and certainly a privilege when doors open to such beautiful places where you're asked to join in a creative process.

We stood before the barn, both of us with a steaming cup of coffee, and he said, "Well, what do you think? I found it for you in the rafters." I scanned the scene: red barn, white trim, pink and yellow flowers along the foundation, heavy steel farm decor, a stout wood door, and I shrugged. "The door," Agamon said, "I think you should have that door." I looked again and there it was. A large oak door. Brown. Small hole where the knob was supposed to fit. Heavy by the looks of it.

"You're serious," I remember saying. Then I smiled and thanked him while in my head I rattled through a series of past conversations—did I tell him I needed a door? My place doesn't need a door, does it? No. Do I know someone who is in need of a door? Well, I suppose I could replace my front door with this door.

Door use number 2: a door can be a door.

"No, no, no," my friend said, noting my confusion. "You need a desk, right? I thought you could use this door as a desk top." I had mentioned that I was looking for a desk in order to have a proper place to sit and type—and strangely, I'd not once thought about balancing a door on bricks, milk crates, or boxes to use as a desk. But then, it suddenly seemed like a very good idea. Who needs to purchase a desk when you can fashion a desk out of a door and some well placed cinder blocks? One should be open to the use of doors.

Door use number 3: a door can be a desk top.

I agreed enthusiastically. We loaded the door into the back of Samwise (my VW van) and then began our recording session. When I arrived home that evening, I managed to fit the monolithic slab opposite my bed, setting it on concrete blocks, and milk crates. An old coffee cup filled with pens and a small thrift store bookshelf filled with favorite books, and my computer rounded out the desk top necessities. I wrestled a chair into place, and *voila*, a desk door. Now, to write.

Between the ages of nine and fourteen, that magical crux between fervid boyhood imagination and that impossible to escape attraction to girls, I was hunched over a desk in my bedroom, month after month, scribbling stories into notebooks and keeping tabs on my day-to-day dealings. Being hit at nine with *Star Wars,* with my parents, and then shortly thereafter, my Uncle Stan pummeling me with *The Lord of the Rings*, I was set on an obsessive lifetime course of imagination—of operatic proportions. I read. I wrote. I thought about making movies every day. I even wrote plays for my friends to perform at recess (particularly *Star Wars* based scenes). To be a part of the working machine that produced an event so people could come and lose themselves was, to me, the ultimate achievement. A way of sharing magic with others. That was where I wanted my life to take me.

Little did I understand the distress that my Mother felt when she would knock on my door on late July, ninety-three-degree afternoons, and in an effort to engage my enthusiasm, she would suggest (or plead), "Michael, don't you want to go outside and ride bikes with your friends? They are going to ride down to the beach. . ." She'd crack the door open and find me leaning into a desk full of pages with weird scribbled symbols. "Not now," I remember saying to her once. "I'm trying to work out this new language I'm making up for the Elves." Then to myself: "Because I shouldn't name things on the new map of their world that I made without the names *meaning* something. I mean, that would be stupid." Then to Mom: "So I'm working out the lexicon and. . ." Mom closed the door before I could finish telling her about the runes in the letter system. *No matter*, I would think, and carry on with my monkish duties. She told me much later that she had considered making an appointment with a child psychologist to learn if there was something wrong with me.

The occasional neighborhood sword fight would get me out for some exercise, but not without my pad of paper and pencil. Sword fights with sticks and trashcan lid shields would often turn to choreographed fight scenes for the new movie I was going to make. I would sketch out storyboards (though I didn't know to call them storyboards back then), and direct the neighborhood kids in dramatic battle scenes. There was always a horde of orcs and a group of battle hardened knights battling over the front lawns of my childhood kingdoms. My best friend in those days, Morgan, will remember many of these raging clashes, along with the stories and drawings we both made.

But it wasn't solely the sudden notice of girls that postponed my writing obsession, as one would expect of a boy in seventh grade. With girls came another seduction that would enchant and frustrate me to this day: music—and my vehicle, the drum kit. The new desk.

It was my older brother's love of the Beatles that started it. From Bob's room I heard those timeless, magical songs through the wall every day. *Sgt. Pepper's Lonely Heart's Club Band, Taxman, Elanor Rigby, Please Please Me*—enter the rest of the catalogue here. The melodies haunted my room and my imagination as I threaded my weird little stories together. One day, I asked Bob if he would make me a Beatles mix tape of my own. He said that he would, but weeks went by without it appearing. Whether it was laziness or older-brother-syndrome, my requested tape remained absent. I asked again, and again, until I had to take my boon to the higher powers of Mom and Dad. Returning to my room the following day, a 90 minute TDK cassette was on my bed. The spine read, *The Beatles*.

I popped it into my cassette player and the first song was *Love Me Do*. I learned later that Bob had taken two or three songs off of each chronological Beatle record to make a decade-long greatest hits of his choosing. The last song on the B side of the tape was *Let It Be* (which, not long after, became my first record).

But my brother's sorcery was far from concluded. The day Canadian rock power trio Rush's 1976 record *2112* was placed on my parents' wood paneled RCA console stereo, I leaned over the edge of the cabinet and watched the Mercury Skyscraper label rotate while the opening sci-fi, keyboard swirl opened a supernova-lit porthole to my future.

When the band kicked in with tight, punctuated power chords, then to a riff akin to a starship catapulting through the stars, to the unforgettable high-pitched voice wailing over the frenetic rock odyssey (Male? Female? Child? Cat? What the fuck?), then the sweetness of a waterfall to the oppressive weight of a future dystopia, to the compelling theme of the individual against an evil collective government with music and art as the weapons of rebellion—a Shakespearian suicide end, concluding with nod to a war-of-the-worlds proportion battle for power in an unstable galactic society. . .

Did I mention the masterful musicianship?

And that was just side one.

Mind bomb. Paradigm shift. It all made complete sense. I was enraptured. There was nothing but music and words from that day forward. I would learn later that hundreds of thousands of would-be musicians would fall prey to this spell, too. But as such moments happened, I saw my future.

Music, words, and, well, *drums.*

As the epic work of *2112* played, something beautifully strange transpired with my hands. By the third track, both were raised up before me and moving in rhythm to the music. I began to memorize the drummer's patterns. Quick and determined drum rolls festooned across the music's intricate architecture. Complicated and thoughtful grooves, quite different than any I'd heard before, burst in and out of the songs like fireworks. My arms and hands tried in vain to follow along, while pounding an invisible battery of drums and cymbals before me. I later realized that this was my first time ever air-drumming. (I have since become a professional air-drummer.) I would also spend the rest of my life reaching for the high bar that drummer Neil Peart (the Professor) demonstrated.

It was settled. I would be a drummer. I would write. I would play. No more questions.

Because I didn't have any money to buy drums (or cymbals), becoming a drummer became an exercise in creative carpentry. When my partner in all things swords and sorcery, Morgan, received an electric guitar as a birthday present, and he needed a drummer, I was the obvious choice. I gathered together several coffee cans, set them up on a board at just the right angle, and with a pair of number 2 pencils (pencils being the literary bridge from the desk to the drum kit—just sayin'), I began my career as a drummer. My older brother took some interest in my kit one day and managed to fashion a snare drum (snare can) by putting a few tiny wads of tinfoil in the bottom of the container. When I hit the plastic lid, the tinfoil balls would vibrate, giving the can a snare-like, *crack* quality. *Pretty smart*, my brother.

Again and again did I find myself on hot summer days, cloistered in Morgan's basement recording our strums and tappings onto cassette tapes, and listening to his Dad's records on breaks. Rush, Frank Zappa, The Beatles, Pink Floyd, Kiss and Cat Stevens and more. Morgan and I were so completely mesmerized with the sounds we were hearing and making that our sessions became daily, eight hour basement jam sessions. It wasn't long before Morgan's frazzled mother was forced to negotiate with my mother and make arrangements for us to play every other day at my house. So, on Tuesdays and Thursdays, Morgan and I would pack my coffee can drums up in a box, along with his guitar and amp and haul them up the stairs, out the door, to lug it all down the block three houses to my basement.

My first experience with touring.

It wasn't until after Morgan moved away to Montana (the archetypal *childhood best friend separation* story I'll revisit at another time) that the coffee cans turned to real drums[10] and the pencils, well, the pencils turned to real drumsticks. It was when I found myself playing in my first band (Anthem) with my dear friend Sean Jackson (Tetpon), that my beloved desk bounded back through the door of my life. Music should have words, I thought, so I'll write lyrics. With my drum kit set up in the basement, and my desk upstairs in my bedroom, I would go from one desk to the other, smashing out rhythms and beats at one desk (or both) and scribbling out lines at the other (or both). And as weird as it may seem, very little has changed to this day. Certainly, I've gotten a little better as both as a writer and drummer from having practiced for over thirty or more years, but what keeps me truly fascinated is that I feel that I can never learn

---

[10] For the drummers—because drummers love this sort of thing—the first real drum set I *played* was in a dilapidated Idaho barn (really), while sitting on a hay bale for a seat (truly). My Uncle Stan made that happen for me. I was 13. My first purchased drum kit was a lovingly cared for, rare, 1964 Gretsch tangerine sparkle (22",13", 16"). Mowed many a lawn to buy it from my dad's good friend, Pat. Regrettably, I sold the drums a few years later to a person that promised he'd offer them back to me, first, if he were to ever sell them (that didn't happen—damn it). My next set was a TAMA Superstar I named Rebecca—almost a replica of Neil Peart's 1982-85 kit with the same candy apple red finish. (Two 24" bass drums, 13", 14", 15", 16", 18".) I later sold that drum set, too. From what I've heard, Rebecca is currently on display in a Canadian fan's Neil Peart museum, along with several other of the Professor's refitted kits.

enough about either activity. Simultaneously, the more I learn, the less I understand, as the saying goes. I can swing from a place of confidence and joy to utter frustration, and back again in a single sit-down session.

Door use number 4: a door can be a creative portal.

I sometimes imagine that I can stand up from my chair, reach for an imaginary door handle fastened to the desk door top and pull it up and open. Gazing down through the door, I can see a mysterious light bursting from the opening, illuminating the room behind me. Stretching out from the doorstep is the next adventure, the next road twisting out into the distance—the next line, and I need only open the door, move through it and let the experience turn into words. I like to think that I am working atop the lid of a chest full of secrets and, when I want to be reminded of how to start my pen wandering, I need only open the door and peek inside, or hurl my mind into the treasure. One should be open to the use of doors.

The memory of a book cover from my childhood always comes to mind when I think of falling through the desk door. *The Forgotten Door,* by Alexander Key, is a book my brother, Bob, had lying around his room when we were growing up. I don't recall the story as well as I remember the cover. I was very young when I first saw it, and the image of a boy falling through a door and into the unknown has always intrigued, and mostly, scared me.

This weird little tool has been useful to me over the years when I find myself stuck and unable to get into the right frame of mind to write. Most writers have ways of getting the ink flowing. I guess mine has been the idea of hurling myself down into the abyss beneath my desk door and getting good and scared.

For the longest time, I had myself talked into the notion that I could only write *seriously* (whatever that means) at my desk. I suppose if I look back at some of my most creative work, written at my desk, the notion holds. Perhaps not solely because of the desk but also because of the things on the desk, the quiet room surrounding the desk, the shelves filled with the things I've collected through the years that provide some kind of experience-echo. There is a lot of time spent staring down onto the desk as if it were some translucent memory generator flipping through lifetime colors and feelings cross-fading across its flat surface. Years ago, the ashtray that cradled the smoldering red bead of a cigarette, or the lacing braids of smoke that would tangle up through sunlit beams leaning in from the window were hypnotists. Getting in, sitting down and falling out through the door, was to me, paramount to prolificacy.

These days, I yearn for that kind of time, because it is no longer available to me, at least not in this season of my life: a family, teaching, recording, performing—all at the speed of life. And being wise enough to know that I must adapt or perish, I am becoming much better at what I call *line writing*. Yes, that is a kind of short hand for scribbling single lines whenever they come along—but more accurately, I mean, I write standing *in lines*—at the grocery store, waiting for a street taco, for a frighteningly ice cold gin martini—I've got a pen and pad, or my hand held device, and I'll write. I am reminded that I must change in order to keep producing. If there's one thing I *don't* enjoy, it's waiting in line, so, I am forcing myself to do what I love to do where I would be least likely to do it. And for me to do that—that's serious business—and I guess, serious writing.

Door use number 5: a door can be a wall.

Then there's writer's block. Or, as one of my writer friends tells me: "There is no such thing as writer's block. One is either a writer or a block. And *you're* a block." I think I agree (sometimes). Then there's Emerson's "Every wall is a door." When I'm stuck and can't produce, and the desk door won't open no matter how hard I try, I'll look at the walls and turn them to doors—the doors to relationships, responsibilities and recreation (the 3 Rs). Have I been inattentive to my friends or family? Am I not having enough fun and working too much? Or vice versa? You know, the simple questions. The kind of questions that are so simple that we seldom ask them—and when we do, we're suddenly surprised at how closed off and isolated we've become because we've not noticed the doors slamming around us. Have I been open to the use of doors?

I'm no fan of closed doors, nor do I like closing them (unless it's cold out side, of course), though it is certain that some doors should be shut, locked and the keys destroyed: meth, mainstream media, war, etcetera. And it is also certain (and unfortunate) that doors get closed between people. Sometimes with an unexpected slam or a slow, creaking pivot. Closed doors turn people away. Locks become mechanisms of fear. Doors become walls.

Door use number 6: an overused metaphor

A closed door can keep the cold out, and sometimes the pain. But a closed door also shuts out a point of view. Sure, the metaphor is an old one, and has certainly been explored by a lot of people smarter than me, but I'm finding that its relevance is no less potent no matter how many times I'm reminded not to shut things out. Even those *hard to deal with* sorts of things. One must try to stay open to the use of doors.

But still, tired metaphor or not, my desk door is cool.

The *door* and the *road*, both tired and well used symbols for transition, change and the life journey. Professor Tolkien's Bilbo Baggins's use has always been my favorite: "It's a dangerous business, going out your door. You step onto the road, and if you don't keep your feet, there's no knowing where you might be swept off to." The very action that makes for good tales: exiting or entering, depending upon how you're seeing. Doors represent hope, opportunity, transition and transformation (makes a great band name too). The point on a circle from which the journey both begins and ends. I've often wondered if that is why

Tolkien's hobbits preferred circular doors—the *there and back again* portal, the ring that is everlasting.

Door use number 7: both the entrance and exit

And here, while I type upon my desk door and glance around my office, I am thankful for the weird and unusual things that make up my life. Fencing swords on the wall, a library of books and records, guitar in the corner, paints and brushes, sticks and a practice pad, photos of dear friends, family, and my lady and little boy, and this gift of a desk-door beside my newly constructed *round hobbit door*. That's right. I built a round door to my office. Something I've always dreamt of doing since I first read the books all those years ago. And each time I go into my office, I am reminded that a journey *should* take place. Doesn't always happen, but still. . .

But of all the uses that a door has to offer, I think my favorite, to return to the beginning, is that a door can be a gift—a gift to be used as, say, a desk, a creative outlet, the exit from old to new, the entrance to a creative adventure, or just as the covering to the hole in your house. And now, it's become a kind of journal entry. So this short collection of paragraphs on desks and doors I gift to you, with the hope that it has somewhat transported you out and away for a spell, and the wish that the seemingly mundane, boorish doors you go through everyday might become as interesting as the passage to a dragon's treasure horde—even if, after all, you're really waiting in line to enter the DMV. If either of these things have happened while you read this, we've both achieved something wonderful and magical. Something came knocking at the door, and we let it in.

—mbk 2014

I close my laptop. "So there you have it, Harvey," I say into the empty hotel room. I rise from the chair and get ready for bed.

CHAPTER 10

OCTOAPALOOZA

Walter is waiting by the house. He has obviously changed his look while we were gone. Small, pale green leaves now waggle from his long fingers in the high breeze. As we heft our bags out of Finn and into the Burrow, Sheree waves at the old sugar maple and says, "We missed you, too, Walter."

Sunlight glows amber from the Burrow floors. The scent of coffee and wood and home greets us. I pull a stack of envelopes out of the mailbox and set them on the dining room table. Sheree sits at the counter and starts a grocery list. I start a to-do list.

We're home.

Our remaining days at BEA were productive and inspiring. My two signings put me in contact with hundreds of new readers, many of whom, surprisingly, had read book one. Andreas felt confident that he had laid the necessary ground work for the new book and says we're ready to start the machine moving toward the publish date of October 1st, as well as the planning of the book launch celebration in Spokane.

On the plane we discussed ideas for the event's aesthetic and potential venues. Like our past launches, *The Shape of Rain* celebration should reflect a scene from the story. I suggested that the obvious choice would be to create the masquerade ball setting from the *Shape of Rain's* climactic ending. Andreas was delighted with the idea and we began drawing the blueprints for the fast approaching date.

Then Andreas fell asleep on MJ's shoulder, and I leaned into Sheree. I thought about Harvey while the white noise of 600 miles an hour through the troposphere lulled me into some needed rest.

At home over the next few days, Sheree and I visit family and friends, we do laundry, we watch movies with my son, Michael. I go with Michael's fourth grade class on a downtown field trip. We stop at the 1950s styled Roger's ice-cream parlor on Sherman Avenue and the kids get ice-cream cones and fudge bars. I shake my head at the thought that I have a nine-year-old.

In the evenings, at home, Michael and I take two wooden swords into the yard and fence until we're tired. Sheree makes homemade pizza. During the day I go over the lists, tackle tasks, journal, begin formatting Michael Herzog's book, *This Passing World,* for publication, and keep one eye on the upcoming Friday RUB performance at an event called Octopalooza.

We're home.

And here come the gigs.

On Facebook, Octopalooza describes itself as *a most excellent outdoor rock party that happens in Spokane every summer.* This will be the first time The RUB has played this festival.

However, this year, Octopalooza is being held at a much smaller venue on the grounds of what was a much larger, now defunct festival called Elkfest.

Elkfest had a thirteen-year history that began with the simple idea of closing down the street beside a popular restaurant called The Elk in Browne's Addition, Spokane, gathering a few bands, and throwing a party. As any good party should, it grew. Through the efforts of its founders, Marshall Powell, John Grollmus, and Brad Fosseen, Elkfest became the Inland Northwest event to herald the summer, winning seven *best music festival* awards and hosting regional and national soul, reggae, folk, rock and blues bands. Best of all: *free.*

While its great success was unexpectedly above and beyond, the neighborhood was too small. Audiences grew. Revelers reveled. Drink was drunk. Lines were crossed. Damage was done. As the complaints came in from the surrounding homes, The Elkfest organizers had to bring the overflowing party to a reluctant close.

After all, people don't like strangers peeing in their yard.

That was last year.

For The RUB, Elkfest has been an exercise in endurance. When the prospect of us performing at the event came up four years ago, Cristopher negotiated a rather unique position for us that to this day makes my entire body sore at the thought. Instead of The RUB simply taking a slot on the performance roster, arriving, setting up our stage gear, playing an hour set, tearing down, and rolling into El Que Tequileria beside the main stage to watch the next band, Cristopher came up with the idea of The RUB acting as hosts for the entire event. He proposed that another stage be erected beside the main stage, just for us, and it would house our gear for the entire three days. In order for the festival to have nonstop performance music, The RUB would perform in between the main stage acts while one band moved off and another set up. In other words, when a band stopped playing, The RUB jammed until another band was ready to go.

While we thought this was a great idea the first year, we hadn't taken into account the effort, time, and sheer endurance it would take. Over the three days, The RUB would play over thirty sets, thirty to sixty minutes long in the direct summer sun from before noon to late in the evening.

Revelers reveled.

It was a breakneck, not-for-the-weak, do-not-try-this-at-home musician marathon. Broken sticks, bleeding blisters, snapped bass and guitar strings, beer sprays, shredded vocal chords, instrument stage destruction The Who might have considered worthy—all of that multiplied by a wonderful and uncanny three day audience relationship to the band—to say the least, the hosting of Elkfest was a career highlight.

So, we did it all again the following year. The experience had become our pre-summer workout, as well as giving us the modest permission to live up to our tongue-in-cheek, *not-to-be-trifled-*

with reputation. Elkfest toughened callouses, got us a little muscly, and sharpened our focus.

Then, sadly, the aforementioned party lines were crossed, and neighborhood complaints brought the event to an end. The news wasn't a terrible surprise. We could portend that the event was growing well beyond what the venue could handle. Vandalism, a few rotten apples, and clogging traffic were all telltale signs.

But when we were asked to play a show called Ocotopalooza, we were delighted to learn that it was taking place at a private residence just yards from where the Elkfest main stage had been. A miniature version of the former, it is to be a backyard party with the feel and excitement of a festival. Small enough to stay under the neighborhood radar and big enough to sate that music festival need and excitement for all. Perfect. We're in!

We're home.

Overcast.

Drat.

From the edge of the Burrow's porch, I watch warm rain fall. I scan the horizon, hoping to see a blue break in the grey. Nothing. But there is a brighter steely light to the west. Maybe it is not as wet in Spokane.

It's 3PM. I pack my gig bag. I tuck my rain parka down into the bottom and fold my necktie. My stomach is nervous. Up in Walter's limbs, a squirrel is perched—seemingly still, but looking closer—the little creature is staring directly at me, gnawing at something in its paws—almost frantically. Strangely enough, I can identify. Calm on the outside—hyper and frenzied on the inside. *Must be the show to come,* I think.

At 5:30PM Sheree and I pull into Taco Bell just off the freeway in Spokane. Traffic is heavy. Rain falls. We see Cary's truck in the parking lot. I laugh and tell Sheree a story that when Cary and I carpool to a show, which we've done countless times, we almost always grab a Taco Bell burrito en route.

Today it takes way too long for three bean and cheese burritos to arrive—nearly a half hour. While we wait, Sheree and I have the pleasure of watching several groups of glitter-splashed, rainbow dripping stragglers from the day's Pride parade. I learn later that thousands had gathered earlier in the day to march, sing, dance, eat and drink, all costumed, festooned, and lit up with smiles in support of LGBT+ causes. Sheree and I are a little disappointed to have missed the spectacle. Red, blue, and violet hair, tutus of pink, face-painted hearts, white fur boots, and kind faces cross the street and parade up the South Hill.

"How fun," Sheree says.

"I want those boots," I say.

What was once a three-day music festival has transformed into the quintessential backyard party. Elkfest may have ended, but its spirit has endured. Just feet from where the Elkfest main-stage used to sit, a medium-sized, four-foot high platform, bookended with a cranking PA system, is positioned beside a craftsman style home. A huge tent covers nearly the entire event. People crowd the wraparound porch, the doorways, and the sidewalks. With my hands on my hips, I scan the grinning gathering. Performing is Indian Goat, a local Spokane guitar and drums duo—heavy riffs, infectious grooves, loud—some of my very favorite things. The audience has their hands in the air. Many are dancing. In nearly each person's grip is a plastic cup of beer. Beside the gate entrance, a small group smokes a joint.

Octopalooza.

I shake my head and grin at the sight, thinking, *I hope their parents don't return from vacation in the middle of our set.*

I meet Cristopher and Cary at the backstage area. We lean into hugs, a few brief stories and try to connect the dots between our last show three weeks ago and now. Cary had just flown in from LA. Cristopher vibrates with anticipation (or is it tequila?). After some show logistics, we begin to prep.

There is a tingling in the air.

The audience is loud, moving, waving, grinning.

Before hauling my drum kit over from Finn, Sheree and I stand to watch and listen. Indian Goat hits hard. They grab hold and don't let go. The drummer is a delight—focused, intent and completely in. Now *I'm* grinning.

Then comes a series of handshakes, hugs, and greetings from a number of friendly folks that I have met a few times before—some I've seen at shows or shared a word or two, others are long time friends. Some I know by name, others by face only. I try to keep my head down and focus in on the assembling of the kit and the show ahead. There are more hellos and kind greetings. I do my best to smile and shout-converse with each person while the band on stage hammers into another tune just feet away. I lift hardware out of cases. In a few minutes I construct a small enclosure for myself and the kit by lining my cymbal stands like a wall. From behind the barricade I finish with the preliminary set up without interruption. Standing nearby, Sheree nods to the small Tequilieria, El Que. "Let's go," I say.

We sit in the tiny bar sipping Patron. The music blasts outside. Fine rain falls. I try to relax and enjoy the short time with Sheree, but I am distracted and nervous—quite a normal thing for me on a show-day. Sheree notices my fidgeting and orders us both tacos as if they might be medicine. When they arrive, we squeeze limes over the top and eat, watching the line to the venue lengthen. My feet tap at the table base—my fingers play beats on the bar.

When the music ends, a roar goes up outside. I pay our tab and we thread our way through the crowd to the backstage area. Indian Goat's gear is nearly struck. Drums are moved off by the drummer and a couple of stage hands. The guitar player's amp tilts toward the stairs and is hefted down. Once their gear is completely cleared, our friend, Conrad, the front of house engineer, repositions the stage monitors for our performance and gives us a nod.

I turn toward my kit and my stomach sinks, as I realize that I had forgotten to pack my drum carpet into Finn that morning. A drum carpet, if you want to know, is just what it sounds like: a carpet that goes underneath the drum set so the kit doesn't slide around. *Damn it*. I quickly mention my absent rug to Conrad and he tells me that they have one on stage already. Boom. Good. Okay.

The kit is lifted onto the stage, pieces at a time and positioned on the carpet: kick drum first, then the bass drum pedals, then snare and hi-hat stand, floor tom, rack tom, cymbal stands, and finally my vocal microphone stand. Each part of the kit is arranged into my usual office. Glancing up into the audience, I note that people are already crowding the front of the stage, excited for the show to begin. Their energy is infectious, and vibrating, I make adjustments to the cymbal stands, clip my stick bag to the floor tom, place the fog machine pedal down beside my left foot—and I then feel a hand on my shoulder. It is Cristopher. His smile is slightly lazy, his eyes are a bit red, but still bright. He leans down and says quietly, "Hey, don't be in a hurry. You look like you're in a hurry. We've got as much time as we want to make this stage ours."

I'm suddenly aware that he's right. All day I've been feeling out of sorts. I am moving way too fast—too frantic—too focused. In other words, it's not very cool for the headlining drummer to be so amped up and bustling about the stage. I look down into the drum set and grin, embarrassed. "Sorry about that," I tell him. "Old habit, you know. Kinda nervous today."

"I know." He smiles at me as he moves toward his amp, leisurely uncoiling his guitar cable as if strolling through the park on a summer afternoon walk. Cool.

That old frantic get-onstage-quick-setup habit emanates from the myriad multi-band shows I have played over the years. When a band comes off the stage, it is preferred by all involved: the stage hands, the other bands, the audience, and the venue owners that you get on—fast—play your show—then get out of the way. For me, it has always been about not inconveniencing anyone, and striving to be amicable and easy to work within the chaotic rock show environment. While those might be noble pursuits, there's nothing wrong with being *cool* about it, I guess.

I'm not very cool.

It is also the New York trip. The passing of Harvey. My mother's ill health. The book I need to finish. The summoning of energy it will take to perform at my best for the band—for the audience—for me.

I take a deep breath. I now make slow, conscious adjustments to the drum set. Satisfied, I step off stage and wait for soundcheck. It isn't long before I am again seated behind the kit and rounding through each drum. Conrad, the show's engineer and a drummer himself, dials my kick drum into a thick, hit-in-the-chest tone from out of the PA. The toms are warm and responsive. The monitors are clear and cutting. Both Cary and Cristopher check their instruments and appear pleased. Conrad asks if we would like to run through a song before the performance. We decline, trusting that he will make the proper modifications as the show progresses.

We leave the stage to change into our performance clothes. I cross the street to Finn, open the back hatch and rifle through my gig bag. *Slow down*, I think. The misty rain is strangely warm. A quiet chuckle comes from the thought of not having a proper greenroom to change, so I must do it on the busy street beside my car, as people pass by. I wonder, *how many fucking times have I done this?* The droplets feel cool on my skin.

Once I am dressed, I lay hold of the violin case.

The violin case is yet another important piece of gear that I'm surprised I've not yet mentioned. A gift from my dear friends Eric and Laurie Wilson, the case is a fashioned portable cocktail bar containing nearly everything a rock band might need when there isn't a hospitality rider to deliver a pre-show, nerve-easing drink: bottles of tequila, scotch, and vodka, three small metal goblets, and three cans of club soda. Additionally, a cigar (just in case a cigar is required), a notepad and pencil (if a random thought must be recorded), a candle and a book of matches (if it is dark or there is a need for ambiance), a deck of cards (if there's a long wait-time before the show), an M80 firecracker (if a diversion is called for), a bottle of cucumber oil (to smell nice), a drum key (if I lose mine), a copy of Hamlet (in case anyone wants us to prove where the band name comes from), and finally, a clip-on bow tie (if one is arrested and must appear before a judge).[11]

I cross the street to the backstage area where Cary and Cristopher are waiting. I open the case and pour us each a shot of tequila. We drink. We hug. I close the case, set it at the side of the stage, blow a kiss to Sheree, and we walk up the stairs to our gear.

The people cheer as we take our positions. Sitting down behind the drums, I can see a gathering of nearly two hundred faces, all grinning, all slightly buzzed, and all warmed up for the last performance of the night in someone's backyard. Intimate. Wonderful.

I press my foot down on the fog machine activation button at my left and stretch my hands. I breathe. Cary begins the opening drone for *The Boys of Summer.* A moment later, another rush of applause erupts when the audience recognizes our version of the song.

Conrad's handling of the sound is a joy. Monitors are loud and present. When we hit the three-part harmony in the chorus, we can feel the notes buzz and weave together.

As we near the end of the song, Cristopher calls the next tune, *What I Got,* by Sublime. I drop into the infectious drum loop—a groove that Sublime guitarist Michael Happoldt told *Billboard*: "Sounds so dope that when people hear it, they just want to get up and jump around." And he's right, though, I think I play it quite differently. In any case, the people begin to move to the beat (a few jump around). Cristopher begins the hooky first verse:

---

[11] Requiem for a Violin Case.
As of the time of this writing, The RUB violin case has been lost. It was my fault, alas. While preparing for a show this last year (2021) and moving too fast, I placed the case on the top of Finn while organizing the drums in the back compartment. Interrupted by a phone call, I failed to return the case back into the car and drove off with it on Finn's roof. I realized too late. But when I did discover my blunder, I backtracked vainly, hoping to find the case at the roadside. I did not find it. So, let this short footnote serve to be the notice and offer of reward for the return of our beloved case. If found, please email info@willdreamlyarts.com. My publisher guarantees me that the reward will be a delightful surprise.

Early in the morning, risin' to the street
Light me up that cigarette and I strap shoes on my feet
Got to find a reason, a reason things went wrong
Got to find a reason why my money's all gone
I got a dalmatian, and I can still get high
I can play the guitar like a motherfucking riot[12]

I cast my gaze around the venue. Hands go up. Beers spill. People hoot. Side stage, the monitor engineer's head is bobbing along with my hi hat, his eyes trained on Cristopher's perfectly delivered vocal: sarcasm veiled in emotion—an ever-so-slight tequila slur. I lower my head down and stare into my snare drum. I try to make my heartbeat match the tempo of the song. I imagine myself dancing.

When we reach the chorus and the audience sings along, I am reminded of a couple of things. First, it is obvious why this song became a certifiable number one smash hit record, selling over 5 million copies in 1997. It is packed with hooks, vibe, groove, and wit. Secondly, like so many other hits from Elvis to Zeppelin to the Stones, the chorus's hook, words and melody: *Lovin' is, what I got, remember that,* was lifted from another artist, dancehall Jamaican singer Half Pint from a 1986 song called *Loving.* I learned later that eventually Sublime awarded the originator royalties and credit. As the audience's voice croons the melody, I marvel at how a song can have so many lives and versions. Even Sublime's version is a cover. I wonder where Half Pint found his inspiration. As Elvis Costello says brilliantly, "It's how rock and roll works. You take the broken pieces of another thrill and make a brand new toy. That's what I did." Either way, a great tune all the way around. Currently, the song is The RUB's.

Vamping through the final measures, I glance over to Cristopher. His gaze is trained on the swaying crowd while he

---

[12] From Sublime's, *What I Got*, lyrics: Brad Nowell ©1996. From their third self-titled album, *Sublime.* MCA Records.

chooses the next song. After a few moments he nods to me and I read his lips: *"Whole Lotta Love."* The selection feels like he just gave me my favorite candy bar. I twist and lean toward Cary, *"Whole Lotta."* He nods, takes a step toward his pedal board. The custodian at the Spokane Fairgrounds plinks into my memory: "You're doin' a *whole lot a* good hitting those drums. . ." It makes me grin.

Led Zeppelin's *Whole Lotta Love*, like *What I Got*, is yet another burgled tune. Parts of Wille Dixon's *You Need Love*, recorded by Muddy Waters in 1962, found their way into Zeppelin's catalogue. Robert Plant's lack of a lyric resulted in nicking the old blues song. Famously, he said later, "It was decided that *You Need Love* was so far away in time and influence that. . . well, you only get caught when you're successful. That's the game." Zeppelin eventually awarded the originator royalties and credit, but Jimmy Page's opening part to *Whole Lotta Love* was all his.

And now a single spot light flashes onto Cary as his guitar grinds out what the BBC has deemed the number one guitar riff in rock history.

I admire how Cristopher's song choices were as if he had simply turned the energy volume knob up for the crowd; our weighty, emotional take on *Boys of Summer*, up to the mid-tempo, feel-good Sublime hit, to all-out, frenzied rock classic, and we were simply three songs in.

While the riff growls to my left, I grab hold of my mic, wipe the sweat out of my eyes, and scream:

> *You need coolin*
> *Baby I'm not foolin*
> *I'm gonna send ya*
> *Back to schoolin*

A wave of cheering, hooting, whistling.

> *A-way down inside*

A-honey you need it
I'm gonna give you my love
I'm gonna give you my love[13]

I push my mic away and lay into the classic Bonham drum fill—
the sound of a car rolling end-over-end down a steep hill—as the
band smashes into the chorus. The crowd meets our volume with
howling and singing. We feel the connection.

Somewhere in the middle of the set, Cristopher hurls us into
one of our medleys—this one is a mash-up of Stevie Wonder's
Superstition, Flo Rida's *Low*, Eminem's *Shake That*, John
Denver's *Take Me Home, Country Roads,* climaxing with Bon
Jovi's *Livin' On A Prayer.* A seemingly strange grouping,
certainly and, quite accidental, as it turns out. At one of our
earliest shows, we somehow glued the songs together and they
stuck.

Following the *Low/Shake That* section, the band has a short
respite as I keep a four on the floor kick drum and Cristopher and
Cary march a thick E chord cadence. We let the audience breathe.
Allow a minute or two for groove and bearing. As the music
pushes and pulses, a sudden melody floats across my memory—
and before I know it, I am singing it as well as I can muster. It is
terrifically high in register— and I'm suddenly fearful I might not
pull it off. I double down. I lean in. My eyes squeeze shut and I
hope for the best.

For future reference, I think, *Bono is not easy to imitate.*

I want to run
I want to hide
I want to tear down the walls
That hold me inside
I want to reach out
And touch the flame

---

[13] From Led Zeppelin's *Whole Lotta Love* lyrics: Willy Dixon/Robert Plant ©1969.
From the album *Led Zeppelin II*, Atlantic Records.

Where the streets have no name[14]

After I hit the first two lines, both Cristopher and Cary are in support—their instruments follow the left turn, and in moments we are performing U2's *Where the Streets Have No Name* almost as if we've rehearsed it (well, maybe). The crowd begins to hop in place to the heavy downbeat. I'm thrilled and grateful that my cliff-jump turned to flight (or a glide, at least). In the corner of my eye I can see Indian Goat's drummer watching—he shines a huge smile as if feeling the spirit of our improvisational moment (or he's bemused and hoping we don't fall too terribly flat on our faces). We make it through to the second chorus when we turn toward charted territory and the Bon Jovi song takes over.

Perhaps here I should point out that part of our joy as players resides in our collective courage to attempt a piece of music in front of an audience that we've never played before. We either get close to rendering it or fall flat on our faces—and accepting the success or the failure is a part of the show. Both outcomes typically bring laughter.

This practice has brought its fair share of criticism from folks that have a kind of religious tie with a particular tune or band. If the song isn't played like the recording, with reverence, et cetera, we may be regarded with a kind of stuck-up distain for not rehearsing the said piece. If a lyric is missed or a bridge is ignored, we have occasionally been marked as lazy, or disrespectful or worse, as if we're making fun of the song we're attempting. I don't think any of those accusations are valid.

A substantial amount of any serious musician's time is spent practicing. In many of the bands I have played with, we have rehearsed far more than we had shows. These days performances are more frequent than practice time. And while I believe rehearsing is important and necessary, there are times it can constrict and smother a performance. *Over-rehearsing*, especially

---

[14] From U2's *Where the Streets Have No Name*, lyrics: Bono ©1987. From the album *The Joshua Tree*, Island Records.

when it comes to hit songs, seems to diminish the spirit of the medium itself, not to mention the song. Given that a majority of the greatest songs were written and recorded within hours of their inception, many artists contend that to capture a genuine performance, melody or lyric, one must lay hold of and render it before it becomes stale or overworked. There is something magic about that first take—the first flight—the first ride. Therein is the sorcery that makes a hit rock song. After all, rock music isn't rocket science—it is feeling, vibration, attitude, and should never be taken too seriously.

There is of course another school of songwriters and musicians who are meticulous, searching, demonstrative, and veritable scientists when it comes to attaining the perfect chorus, tempo, sound, production, mix, performance, and so on. In my early years, I was just the type to overthink, overwork, and overplay. It served me in some ways, to be sure. Such attention (obsession) to detail helped to nudge me closer to mastering my instrument (still a long way to go). I've learned my limitations. I discovered the elemental ingredients to a good song or performance and what might spoil an attempt. To this day I appreciate the hard-wrought care artists put into their work to attain their desired effect. How could one not love the sonic craft and performance-driven Steely Dan, or the perfectionism of Rush, Queen, and Prince, or the countless others that have labored to make their respective masterworks.

That said, there is certainly something remarkable about setting up a few microphones, strumming three, maybe four chords, a catchy melody, and voila—a hit. In one take or three— The Beatles, Eminem, Radiohead, Cheap Trick, Johnny Cash, Bruce Springsteen. . . It took me the longest time to learn the beauty of simplicity.

For us, performing the great works is about trying to capture the spirit of the song when it first crossed over that empty void of silence and into the air. The moment the artist(s) heard and felt the magic for the very first time. When the fingers found the right strings, the voices discovered the melody and the words, and the heart and head joined together.

And truly, just being able to play a song on a whim with a degree or two of accuracy and the very real possibility of falling on your face is a cause for gratitude. Music is that magic of free flight.

That same fearless spirit has also kept The RUB from performing with a set list. A set list, if you want to know, is an ordered list of songs that a band will play over the course of a show. Sometimes you might spot an eight-and-a-half-by-eleven sheet of paper with song titles scribbled or printed across it at the feet of the vocalist or guitar player. A set list enables a band to play a prescribed set of songs so they might dial up the audience energy (much like Cristopher's first three song choices at the beginning of Octopalooza).

While set lists have their place, we feel as if they constrict (there's that word again) and limit the energy and spontaneity of a show. Every venue is different. Every audience is different. So, therefore, to us, every song choice and where they are placed in the show should match the vibe of the party. Most of the time this job lands in Cristopher's able judgement and he must observe, listen, feel, and decide just what will make a room listen, dance, shout, and ultimately, giggle and scream for more. A big job, to say the least. His duty is the chooser at the jukebox, the disc jockey on the radio, and circus ringmaster all in one.

No two RUB shows have ever been the same—so it follows that each show is a new challenge, and both the audience and The RUB never know what's around the corner. This has served to keep us on our toes and prevent mundanity.

Cristopher penned a wonderful little poem that appears in our social media that I think is accurate and quite funny:

The RUB does things that have been done before, like never before. Before The RUB did things like that, those things had not been done. The RUB likes that those things have not ever been done the way The RUB does them. Do The RUB, then be done.

All of that, and the show at hand is nearing its end, three encores and two hours later, Cristopher is showing signs of a little too much drink. We had been passed several shots of various spirits during the performance, which is a common occurrence, and a couple of mine still await my attention down on the drum carpet to my left. However, Cristopher's collection of plastic shot glasses look emptied. Yet, his energy level is seemingly full. He steps to the mic, thanks the audience, the crew, the hosts and gives a shout-out to the surrounding neighborhood, "And thank all of you, neighbors, for allowing us to come together and celebrate the start of another beautiful summer." Both Cary and I watch him, waiting to read what his choice will be. "Thanks for letting us play longer than we were supposed to. We've one more song for you tonight. We'd like to leave you with a slow, love song. . . ."

I tense. I crouch my body forward and prepare. I know what's coming—

Cristopher screams: "KICK IT!"

We're home.

Thus, we crash full tilt into the Beastie Boys' *Fight For Your Right To Party.* Loud, nasty, snotty, heavy, and mean. The audience explodes and begins to bounce. I can feel the rumble of their feet shaking the stage.

At a pause in the song, I throw a stick up into the air. As it falls back to me, it tumbles across a cymbal edge and escapes my grasp. I laugh. We crash back into the heavy groove. I pull another from the floor tom stick holster. Next pause, I try again. I miss and it flips away from the kit. I'm laughing uncontrollably now. Cristopher notices. By the third throw and miss, Cristopher is in on my personal challenge. When a fourth chance arrives, I throw, and Cristopher reaches down, quickly seizes a handful of sticks from my bag and tosses them skyward. They rain all over the kit. as we plunge down into the train-wreck section: a long, resounding A chord like a winding engine. With no sticks left, I resort to bashing the cymbals and toms with my bare hands as my feet pound single strokes as fast as I can muster into the kick drum. Coming to the final punctuated end, I kick my bass drum over. Cristopher bashes my toms to the side. They topple. He marches like Godzilla through the center of what is left standing, hoists his bass guitar, and chucks it high into the air, over the back of the stage. Hitting the ground, it clangs, howls and groans as the amplifier fuzzes and nearly blows. We're done.

"One more song!" the people shout over and over.

You know you've done an excellent job of entertaining an audience when you destroy the stage on which you've been performing and they aren't able to understand why you cannot perform another song. Instead, in delight, they rally and plead. Puzzling, sure. But it's happened a great many times. So wonderfully fun.

Bright red blood is streaming from my left hand. A low rumble of feedback cycles through Cary's guitar amp. We all step down the stage stairs and through a gauntlet of hand slaps, hand shakes, smiles and well wishes. A huge number of *fuck yeah(s)*. And, of course, much laughter and head shaking.

Passing the drummer from Indian Goat, I stop and take a breathless moment to tell him how much I enjoyed his performance. I introduce myself, and he tells me his name is Travis Tveit. He kindly returns the compliment and we both share a few words about our love of the drums. Sweat beads along my cheekbones. A little blood trickles down my fingers. I raise my hand and tell Travis, "I love drums this much." We both laugh. He adds, "I know the feeling."

We are thanked by Conrad— and we return the thank-you. We are also thanked by Levi, the evening's host.

I cross the street to Finn, open the back hatch and change out of my soaking wet shirt and tie. From out of my gig bag, I pull out my small First Aid kit to bandage my hand. The rain has stopped. A cool breeze blows gently. Across the street, the party is slowing down. Several people file out of the gate and disappear around the block. Some pass me and extend another kind word or two. Others cross the street to the Elk Restaurant and bar. The street lights shine wet white rectangles in the black pavement.

An hour or so later, I move the last couple of cases back across the street. I heft the rolling hardware case into the back of Finn.

I'm thinking of the eighteen drum stick throws and eight catches (worst ratio so far—yikes), but I'm including Cristopher's added handful of raining sticks. The shot at the U2 song makes me smile. Then Cristopher's mention of my moving too fast during our set up. As I lift my old grey Anvil case up and rest it on the lip of the bumper, then tilt it into the car, I suddenly notice that I am again moving too fast—in a hurry. Perhaps because the band has been invited to a nearby pub where our friends Brooke and Jay are performing their new punk rock record. Is that the hurry? The idea of a noisy bar and a loud band doesn't seem to align itself with what my head currently needs. Meanwhile, seemingly still in a rush, I slide my hand under the Anvil case edge and roll it up on top of my K Sub speaker. As I do this, my feet slip on the rain-slick pavement and I fall forward. My throat smashes into the sharp corner of the case. I quickly regain my balance and reel backward from the impact. "Damn it!" I croak. My voice sounds as if it is being crimped off. Heated tears fill my eyes. Both of my hands go to my throat. I turn and sit, hoping the pain will not last—hoping not to go into shock. Sheree rushes around to the back of the car and steadies me.

"I must've been in a hurry," my voice creaks. "Feeling a little after-show clumsy."

She immediately rummages through her bag, looking for an essential oil that might ease the pain.

A few minutes later, starting to recover, I stand and finish securing the final pieces of gear into the back of Finn.

"You sure you want to go hear the band?" she asks.

"Of course," I manage to say. I pull my jacket on. "I mean, isn't that what I'm supposed to do? Drive to a town, play a rock show, and afterward, tear the gear down, change clothes and go punish my hearing that much more at a punk rock show?" I check my hand to see if it is bleeding through the bandage. I swallow gently to learn if my esophagus is okay. *I'll live*, I think. *Singing at the next show might be a trick, however.* I take a deep breath and offer her my arm as we walk a block to a bar-pizzeria.

I ask, "Are you sure *you* don't want to go home?"

In her best Penny Lane impression from the movie, *Almost Famous,* she grins, waves her fingers before my eyes, and says, "We are home."

CHAPTER 11

THAT WORD

It's Wednesday. Mom watches TV.

I've been sitting beside her in my parent's living room for about fifteen minutes. An episode of M*A*S*H is nearly over. Dad asks if I'd like a cup of coffee. I say yes.

As he readies the Keurig machine, I study Mom's expression: distant, as if she's staring through the screen. Benjamin Franklin "Hawkeye" Pierce says, "I'm not sleeping, I'm inspecting the inside of my eyelids." I hear Dad chuckle at the line. I smile. Mom stares.

She suddenly says, "Do you have any gigs?"

I tell her that our summer is booked up and about Octopalooza, my throat injury, the loud punk rock band afterward.

"Did you play Elvis?" she asks. Her eyes sparkle.

"Not this time," I tell her.

"Oh, that's a shame." Her sparkle dims. She stares. "What's that word, *Octopalooza*?"

"It's the name of the festival."

"Oh," she says. She looks back at Hawkeye.

A little while later, Dad helps her stand up and he walks her down the hall to the bedroom for a nap. "I love you," she says as she passes by. "I love you," I tell her.

I sip my coffee. When Dad returns, he sits down and takes a deep breath. I do the same.

"Frontal lobe dementia," he says after a beat.

"What's that?" I ask.

He takes another deep breath.

What's that word?

Growing up, I've asked that question many times about Mom's health. Words like, *tumor*. Words like, *depression*. As the years went by, a storm of new words: *anxiety, shock treatments, Nardil, Xanax, Prozac, diabetes, fibromyalgia, dementia.* One of Mom's earliest physical maladies was described to me by a combination of *tumor* and *softball*. The thought of a softball-sized lump growing inside her abdomen obviously led to more and more questions. How did that happen? Softball? Why? How do you get it out?

What's that word?

Surgery. Biopsy. Cancer.

Tragedy is a cruel teacher. One of its many tangible lessons is the hasty building of a medical vocabulary. Nothing will enhance your physician terminology faster than the tragedy of a loved one's illness.

Mom has suffered from severe anxiety and depression her entire adult life. Meeting her, you would never know it. It is true what they say about how a manic depressive can hide her condition. Mom has been known for being bubbly, generous, funny, and the brightest light in the room, until. . . I was eleven or twelve and I began to see behavior I did not understand. One afternoon she appeared at my bedroom door. Her face was a blur of teary mascara and fear. She said, "I have to go to the doctor. I have to go to the doctor right now."

A few minutes later, we were in the car, driving downtown. She cried all the way there. I asked her what was wrong. All she could say was, "I don't know. I don't know."

That day I learned *anxiety attack,* and what those words meant. It was the first of an incessant number of attacks that she would endure for the rest of her life. Days later, I learned the word *tumor*.

Over time her mental distress manifested itself in more tumors, acute depression, spinal issues, fibromyalgia, vertigo, and dementia, inevitably forcing her out of a normal lifestyle. She spent more and more time seeking refuge in doctor-prescribed, high-powered medications until another word found its way into my growing armchair medical argot: *addiction.*

Attempting to grapple with Mom's manic affliction, I penned a lyric in 2006:

Up To The Dark

Mother, you were always strong
Like the dark yellow light on Autumn afternoons,
Letting us see how black depression could be,
Then you'd warm us in your arms
With your eyes full of moon.
    Mother, you said you'd be okay
    Even as your defeated face, pale as bone,
    Smiled between those blurry pills above the sink.
    Where the doctors said for you to go
    When you're feeling alone.
        Me--
        Up to the dark
        And down
        Downward like a stone
            In the sea--
        One and the same
        Waves in the middle
        In the middle of me.
Mother, no one wants to know,
No one seems to care, they say it's in your head.
Their eyes lit like lanterns on a stormy sea
The little blinking lights of ships
High on a crest, lost in a valley.
    Mother, you worry that I
    Might be like you, caught beneath the waves,
    Sinking day by day or rising up like a desert
    Flower only to wilt when no one

Is around to save me. [15]

That's the short version. None of it happened overnight. There were times of relief and times that Mom was quite able and sure of herself. So sure and bright, in fact, that she became known in our community during the holiday season as the one and only Mrs. Claus. It is not often that the jolliest of elves, Santa, is eclipsed by his doting, mostly behind the North Pole scenes wife, but my mom's magic was uncanny.

In 1986, Coeur d'Alene's mostly timber-driven industry began a long needed shift to tourism with the construction of visionary Duane Hagadone's *Coeur d'Alene Resort*. The five-star hotel caught national and international attention and sparked a new era for our sleepy little town. And since then, at Yuletide, the Resort has hosted a Christmas parade, a lighting ceremony, and a world-class holiday firework show. For over ten years, my Mom was at the center of those holiday seasons. She rode in a bell-jingling sleigh in the parades, ran an old-world caroling group each afternoon, and made appearances all over town at schools and retirement homes. Through December, lines of children stood in line to see Mrs. Claus. Thousands of wishes whispered in her ear —and I like to think that somehow, Mom can still remember every one of them. Sure, Santa was there, too, but it was evident that Mrs. Claus was the brightest star.

Concurrently, Mom's real gig was the Resort's lead concierge. Her kindness, bubbly personality, and genuine smile became the *Coeur d'Alene Resort's* high bar of hospitality excellence.

Mrs. Claus was one of Mom's claims to fame—one of her favorite memories—one of her proud accomplishments.

"Frontal lobe dementia," I ask, "what is that?"

He's about to speak when Mom's voice calls out. "Ken? Ken?"

---

[15] *Up To The Dark*. Lyric: Michael Koep ©2006. From KITE's album, *Sleeping In Thunder*. TreeARC Records.

Dad lets out a sigh of exhaustion. He disappears into the hallway.

Another episode of M*A*S*H is beginning. I hear the opening bar of the show's theme—the acoustic guitar hook—the clatter of helicopters—then that sad melody rushes in on woodwinds and horns—then a 70s trap kit lays down a groove. And, still moody, the version attempts to wash away the painful tones of its original form. After all, what suited television executive wouldn't take issue with a situational comedy's theme that's title is *Suicide Is Painless*. One can almost hear the television control group second guessing a 1970's primetime audience. "Let's make the theme a little brighter, shall we? Peppy. Peppier. Not so, not so. . . what's the word? *Heavy.* That's it, not so *heavy*."

Originally written for Robert Altman's feature film M*A*S*H, staring Donald Sutherland as Hawkeye, Elliot Gould as Trapper, and Robert Duvall as Frank Burns, the original lyric is woeful and dark. I pick up my phone and Google the song. I learn that Altman was said to have attempted to write the lyric but gave up claiming that he couldn't write "stupid enough," so his fourteen-year-old son Michael took up the task and penned it in five minutes.

I feel a smile coming on. We can spend a lifetime grappling with the existential dilemma and, somehow, a fourteen-year-old can capture it in five minutes. *That's so rock and roll.* I scan the verses. A couple-three stand out:

> *The game of life is hard to play*
> *I'm gonna lose it anyway*
> *The losing card I'll someday lay*
> *So this is all I have to say*
> > *That suicide is painless*
> > *It brings on many changes*
> > *And I can take or leave it if I please*

and

The sword of time will pierce our skins
It doesn't hurt when it begins
But as it works its way on in
The pain grows stronger watch it grin, but
    That suicide is painless
    It brings on many changes
    And I can take or leave it if I please

and

A brave man once requested me
To answer questions that are key
Is it to be or not to be
And I replied 'Oh, why ask me?'
    That suicide is painless
    It brings on many changes
    And I can take or leave it if I please[16]

I set my phone down, lift my coffee, and sip. Fourteen and hitting Shakespearean vibe—suicide—choice. What's the word? *Heavy*. That's it, *heavy*.

Dad sits down.

"What is that, Dad? Frontal lobe dementia?"

He takes a breath and tells me about Mom's latest doctor appointment, the results from the MRI, and an outline of the condition. I nod along, not quite sure what I'm hearing. He describes it. I nod. He shows me a couple of images supplied by the doctor.

According to the Alzheimer's Association: "Frontal lobe dementia, also known as Frontotemporal dementia (FTD) refers to a group of disorders caused by progressive nerve cell loss in the brain's frontal lobes (the areas behind your forehead) or its

---

[16] From Suicide Is Painless for the 1970's film M*A*S*H. Lyrics, Michael Altman ©1969

temporal lobes (the regions behind your ears). The nerve cell damage caused by frontotemporal dementia leads to loss of function in these brain regions, which variably cause deterioration in behavior, personality and/or difficulty with producing or comprehending language. Frontotemporal dementia inevitably gets worse over time and the speed of decline differs from person to person. For many years, individuals with frontotemporal dementia show muscle weakness and coordination problems, leaving them needing a wheelchair — or bed-bound. These muscle issues can cause problems swallowing, chewing, moving and controlling bladder and/or bowels. Eventually people with frontotemporal degenerations die because of the physical changes that can cause skin, urinary tract and/or lung infections."

I ask a few more questions. He offers what he can. The outlook is not good.

"It is terribly aggressive," Dad says, sadly. "It's a matter of time before her memory is completely gone."

I nod.

Two words: *time* and *memory*.

The sound of studio audience laughter.

Colonel Potter says, "I gather you drink."

Hawkeye replies, "Only to excess."

CHAPTER 12

FIRE TRUCK

The next morning, I sip coffee as I double check my hand-scribbled list.

—storage unit

—meeting with Andreas

—stage/backdrop/lights/monitors to venue

—pick up xtra PA from Mark

—Michael swim lesson

—hardware store/light bulbs

—set up

—repair fog machine

—call Mom

—try to rest.

I feel certain I've forgotten a thing or two. I look at the clock: 6:42AM. The sun is bright. A squirrel scales the fence and runs along the narrow top. It stops and stares at me for a moment through the window. A walnut is clamped in its jaw. Its tail jitters.

"Busy, are you?" I ask. "Me, too."

Each year, for a couple of days mid-June, our small town transforms into a museum of sorts—a rolling, rumbling, cruising, leather and oil, rubber and road museum of classic cars, car aficionados, and automobile motor heads. Even the town name transforms from Coeur d'Alene to *Car d'Lane* for the event.

The RUB will perform four times this weekend. The first will be in the Car d'Alene parade, while riding the back of a Coeur d'Alene Fire Department fire truck. With our PA system strapped to its sides, we will play over the two mile route that ends in front of the venue where we will perform later that night, the night after that, and finish off Sunday afternoon with a show before teardown. The venue is our home bar, our primary Coeur d'Alene performance residence, The Iron Horse on Sherman Avenue.

Sigh.

The squirrel is gone. Then I notice it busily scrabbling in one of Sheree's raised garden beds. I finish my coffee and resolve that I, too, should get to work. I rub my eyes and study the to-do list. The coming days will be challenging mentally and physically, and right in line with our full throttle summer season. In order to make the shows work, I need to begin my prep a day early. My right shoulder aches. The gash across my knuckle from Octopalooza still stings, but it is healing. My voice is still weak from the throat injury.

I think of Mom, likely still asleep this morning. I wonder if she's dreaming. I wonder if she can still dream.

Samwise is necessary today given the staging pieces that need to be transported. The VW bus starts on the first try and we rattle away from the Burrow. On the way to the storage unit, Michael describes a massive underground bunker he is creating in a video game called Minecraft. He describes a vast cavern lit by torches, a waterfall elevator, and chests full of weapons, food, tools, books, and rare minerals. "I can't wait to see it," I tell him. "We should build that for real."

He nods, "Can we?"

"Of course. We just need to find the right spot to start digging."

At the storage unit, I see my portable, personal drum stage buried beneath a few boxes and a couple of monitor speakers.

"Looks like we'll start digging here," I say to Michael.

After a few minutes, I wrestle the stage base and its plywood platform out and load them into Samwise. I locate the massive cloth backdrop, the stage lights, and a few other pieces of gear and pack them into the van. We drive to the Iron Horse and load it all, piece by piece into the stage area. A half hour later we're at Mark's house (KITE's bass player) to pick up some extra PA speakers. We return to the venue and drop them off. Back at the storage unit, I load up The RUB drum kit, cymbals and hardware. We drive back to the Horse and I lug it all inside.

I notice Michael wearing only one flip-flop.

"Where's the other one, buddy?" I ask.

He shrugs.

Ugh. I look through the gear. I search the stage, Samwise, and the path between. We return to the storage unit, where I discover that he had somehow dropped it into a plastic bucket beside a tower of speakers.

The sun is bright. Sweat beads on my forehead. Must hurry. *Slow down*, I hear Cristopher in my head.

With a close eye on the time, we make one more stop, to purchase a couple of light bulbs for the stage light rig, and then we rush to Michael's swim lesson.

While Michael learns how to float on his back, I phone my aunt Mel to ask if she can watch him for a couple of hours so I can return to the Iron Horse and begin setting up the backdrop, center stage, and light rig.

At 1:00PM, I arrive back at the Horse and find Cary about to raise his own light rig above his personal stage. He threads the power cable down through a hole in the plywood base and asks if I might assist in raising the high pole from which hangs a chandelier with five multicolored bulbs. He produces a 1980s boom box and hangs it just below the bulbs with a wire hook. A tap on a foot pedal, the lights wink on, and the boombox begins to slowly spin. It is perfectly LoFi unique. Very RUB.

"I love that thing," I tell him.

"Yeah," he says. "Me, too."

"What's the cassette in the player?"

He grins, "*Moving Pictures*."

"Perfect."

In short, my next couple of hours at the Horse tick down the below task list:

—drape the 10'x30' red cloth backdrop

—hang the RUB sign.

—set up my personal drum stage

—repair a broken fog machine

—re-head a snare drum

—fix a broken hardware stand

—assemble the drum riser light-rig consisting of five overhead lights, eight floor lights and various special effects—all of which route into a foot controller that sits down beside my high hat stand.

—set up The RUB drum kit.

—wire microphones to each drum.

—hook up two fog machines and line the controllers beside my hi hat.

—order a Coke.

—drink the Coke

—try to make sure I've not missed anything.

I call Mom. She doesn't answer. I call Dad. He tells me that she's taking a nap.

Several times I am interrupted by passersby commenting on the scale of the set up. Phrases like, "Wow, that's a lot of gear for a bar gig," and, "you guys sure have a lot of shit," and, "must be a pain in the ass with all that stuff," et cetera.

A mildly buzzed baseball-capped guy stops and compares our set up to his buddy's band that plays all the time. "You really need all that shit to play?"

I hear Cristopher suddenly as he rounds the corner with his personal stage hoisted on his shoulder. "We're The RUB." There's that edgy tone in his voice.

I jump in before Cristopher cuts him, "Well, we like to think that all this effort makes for a better show—for you. There's no stage quite like ours. We've hand-made everything you see here —its a kind of sculpture. An art project." I grin. A droplet of sweat trickles down my neck.

The guy takes a sip of his drink and studies the steam-punkish design of my kinetic light bar, Cary's rusted antique sewing machine guitar stand/incense burner, the 1970s salon dryer lamp that hovers over Cristopher's stage—the glittered RUB sign flown above it all. He takes another sip.

"Looks like a pain in the ass," he says.

"Well," I say straining for patience, "so is a Christmas tree, but the kids really like it. Are you coming in to see the show?"

He shrugs. "What's the name of the band?"

Cristopher mutters something under his breath that I don't catch.

Cary, with his head down, working on wiring his pedal board, chuckles.

I turn and look at the huge RUB sign. I point to it.

At that moment a group of RUB friends enter the bar and start shouting, whooping, and cheering that we'll be playing tomorrow. "Can't you play tonight, too?" they call out.

The guy still stands there. He sips. He sways a bit.

"We're The RUB. I hope you can make the show," I say as I turn from the pain-in-the-ass to the pain-in-the-ass set up.

At 7:30AM the next morning, that same squirrel eyes me over the top of the fence. His little head is as still as a statue.

"You again?" I ask, "Don't you have some work to do?"

It whisks away, clawing over the fence and up Walter's trunk.

Michael and I eat breakfast on the porch. We listen to NPR. Some horrible news from the Mexican border—children being separated from their parents. Our current acting commander in chief, blames others for the debacle. The stories are heart wrenching.

Visibly moved, Michael asks what it all means. I shake my head and feel the overwhelming complexity of it all. Then the cruel idiocy of separating children and parents.

"I know for certain," I answer him, "there doesn't seem to be good leadership handling the problem. Seems to me that instead of blaming, our President should be taking all the blame and working toward a solution. He has every resource to handle the problem instead of blame. . . Great leaders don't blame others,

Michael. Great leaders own the situation and lead. At least that's what all the leadership books teach."

I watch him chew his french toast. I am grateful for what we have. I am grateful for the moment: syrup, butter, morning, squirrels, and him.

After breakfast we head again to the storage unit where we load Finn with yet another drum kit. This kit is a red Yamaha Rick Moratta Hip Gig drum kit specifically designed for compact spaces, low volumes, and simple set up. I use this kit for smaller venue shows and dinner sets. Three small cases and a cymbal bag and that's it. Simple. And simple is needed right now.

Michael and I talk about how a hover board would be a good thing to own as long as you've got a parachute. "And a helmet might be important, too," I add. He nods.

I drop him at Aunt Mel's and make the quick drive down to the Iron Horse parking lot, where I pull up beside a retired Coeur d'Alene Fire Department pump truck. Huge, white, and complete with all kinds of dials, pressure gauges, chrome levers, and hoses; I marvel at the mechanics and what it took to design such a vehicle.

Cristopher has already arrived. As he rounds the back of the truck and glances up at my arrival, I wave. He is scowling. *Uh oh,* I think. In his hands is a mess of cable, tangled and knotted. The cable could be the reason for his scowl (a tangled cable is certainly not one of his favorite things), or it could be the oppressive heat, or maybe he's simply considering the next steps on how he wants to put the band on a firetruck. Could be all three. Our friend Eric Halliday is assisting in lifting a speaker. Cary is unloading his truck. He hoists a smaller amplifier off his tailgate. I wave to him. He returns a nod and slightly forced smile. *Uh oh*, I think again—*something is up*.

When I step out of the cool air within Finn, the summer heat smashes into my patience. I take a quick peek at the clear blue above. The sun, not yet high, is already cooking the parking lot concrete—and sizing up the look of Cristopher and the sweat in his eyes, I take a deep breath and prepare my resolve for a long day.

We strap PA speakers to the side of the fire truck and string cables from the generator to where the band will be playing on the upper deck. Cristopher barks orders at Cary and me. He is abrupt and rude. The chaos of such a set up, the incessant heat, and the weight of the looming five-hour show later tonight has obviously pushed his disposition into what we've come to know as his *captain mode* (like an autocratic leaning, no nonsense construction foreman, maybe). Albeit, bossy, but it gets the job done.

Nevertheless, I bite my tongue. I try to smile. It's a parade, after all.

Cristopher snaps at our driver Mark about some part of the set up. They exchange a few aggravated words. Visibly pissed, Cristopher walks away and enters the Iron Horse. Cary and I lock eyes for a moment. We keep working. It's clear that I'm not informed of everything going on with this set-up and, given the tasks at hand, I've little time or energy to seek understanding. Mark asks me a question about how we might position a side speaker. I smile and work the issue out with him. He then says, "From now on, I'd like *you* to be the primary communicator for today's ride."

I nod, "No problem," knowing full well that it could be a problem.

Obviously, I think, *I must have missed something—always more to the story.*

Mark starts, "Because that guy—" Before he can utter what I am expecting to be a complaint about my partner, I head him off. "It's going to be a long day for all of us. It's awful hot, and that makes things tough." I point, "Does your truck have one of those mister hoses? A fine mist of cool water will solve everything." He tries a smile. I then begin asking him questions about the fire truck and its gauges and levers. He brightens and happily falls into talking about what he loves.

When Cristopher returns, he hands Cary and me day-glow green T-shirts. He puts on one himself and climbs up onto the upper deck and begins prepping his rig. We join him. After a quick sound check, we climb down and slip into the Iron Horse to finish our evening stage setup. With the entire three-stage sculpture electrified and cranked up, we soundcheck for the approaching performance. A small crowd gathers before the band and there are requests and a couple of dancers.

Gonna be a long day. A long hot day.

Rock bands and parades are a strange combo. The first time I played a parade was in the late 80s, on the back of a huge flatbed trailer, raised up on a drum riser (which put me and my kit some ten feet above the pavement—yikes). It was the Fourth of July. The trailer was packed with PA speakers, red, white, and blue balloons, shiny dollar-store Independence Day decorations, and my candy apple red TAMA drum set. And me, too. The bass player, Daryl, and guitar player, Lane, with their wireless units, were free to orbit the moving trailer, running and jamming and doing their rock n'roller moves, jumps, and poses. Oh, and our singer, Kevin, who had recently suffered a terrible back injury, unable for the time to run, jump, and pull high-kicks and whatnot was strapped to the front of the trailer with his mic on a stand.

An odd thing, a moving rock band. From an audience point of view (or point of hearing), the band approaches and a snatch of music floats on the air—the song is recognized—the band gets closer—louder, until there's a momentary rock-show front-row view—the music pounds through the speakers—the kick hits the chest—the band passes—the fume of exhaust—the music slowly fades—then a block away the guitar player kicks, jumps, and whatnot to the clip-clop of horses—yes, horses—horses of the 4-H Troop that has suddenly appeared. Odd.

And while a passing rock outfit might make a spectator's toe tap for a few measures, said spectator will likely give little thought to what the band's next song might be, if there is one.

After all, why should a band run down a set list when no one at the parade save the band, the band's driver, the float ahead, and the float behind (and maybe the 4-H Troop) will know the difference or hear more than thirty seconds to a minute of music. I mean, isn't that what marching bands do in parades, play the same bloody song?

It eludes me as to who in the band had the sudden revelation that we should only play one song for an hour or longer while meandering down the parade route, but I do remember being completely against the idea. In the end, I was outvoted 3 to 1. That seemed to happen a lot to me in that band (probably because I was the youngest). Nevertheless, having to play an overly extended tune under a punishing July sun, struggling for balance, ten feet above the searing asphalt, one might think I'd remember what the song was. I'm pretty confident I could simply give Lane a call and he'd remind me, but for now I believe gigmentia happens for a good reason. Therefore, suffice it to say that the song, as well as the performance and the pain of the experience, should remain lost.

From atop the fire truck,I can see that the sidewalks are packed with people, some standing, others in their own portable living room views with folding chairs, small side tables and coolers—sunglasses, flip flops, straw hats, and arms in the air, waving.

Thankfully, Cristopher's mood has improved, for the performance, at least. As the truck pulls out of the parking lot, he calls the song *What I Got*. Thankfully, too, over the course of the parade Cristopher will call the songs, *American Girl* by Tom Petty, Zeppelin's *Ramble On,* James Taylor's *Steamroller Blues, My Best Friend's Girl* by The Cars, and *The Boys of Summer.*

Though it is a parade, it feels a little like a lethargic car race. Classic cars jockey for position to be close to us, as if trying to keep their place in the front row at a performance. A red convertible stingray corvette, early sixties by the look of it, with an older couple pull, up beside us from time to time. The driver is a white-haired man and his passenger a white-haired woman. They grin up at me. Another car just behind us pulls alongside, too.

In a few of the songs, I attempt a few high stick throws. I manage to catch five out of seven. One stick I lose over the side of the truck—it drops into the back seat of a convertible. The other clips the railing and flips out to the sidewalk where a little boy of maybe ten years picks it up and waves it at me with a huge grin.

In spite of the punishing heat, the knowledge of the teardown coming next, another show following hard upon, and the generator's exhaust fume wafting over the band as we belt out rock vocals and three part harmony, the drive is strangely calming.

After the last lap, the truck parks in front of the Iron Horse and we prepare to deliver a preview of the night to come. Cristopher calls for The Beatles' *Don't Let Me Down.* In moments, the sidewalk crowds with bodies, and the folks on the patios, with drinks in hand, stand and sing along. After a fine round of applause and smiles, our driver wheels us around the corner and back to the parking lot, so we can begin the tear down.

The heat leaves its mark. My arms and face are burned. Hauling speakers down and winding up cables, I feel dizzy. Captain Cristopher is again barking orders at Cary and me. I check myself, knowing that he, too, must be suffering the same frustrating heat, the same fatigue. I bite harder into my tongue and keep my eyes from meeting his. I know he is just trying to get the job done, but growls vibrate under my breath anyway.

After Cary's amp and my kit are off the truck deck and the last of the cables are coiled up, we enter the relatively cool Iron Horse where the next stage waits for our attention. I make a few adjustments on the larger drum set. Cary checks his guitar. Cristopher continues to rant about how we could have made the tear down from the truck easier. He tells us that our removal of gear was in the wrong order. I wonder why he is transfixed—seemingly trapped in some anger feedback loop. I'm simply wanting to get on with the next task, but I know this is the way his mind works, so I try to listen and understand. When I find a moment to speak, I inform both him and Cary that I must leave to relieve my aunt Mel who has been watching Michael, see if I can rest for fifteen minutes, shower, eat and get back to make the 9:30ish show time.

Cristopher waves his hand, "Whatever."

I wipe sweat out of my eyes and head for the door. I cough. *Carbon monoxide*, I think.

I quickly run down a list outlining my next few hours:

—rest —eat —shower
—dress
—call Mom

Bursting out the back door of the bar, heated curse words hiss out of my mouth. The interior of Finn is a boiling four million degrees Fahrenheit. I try to control my anger. A kind of chorus rolls through my mind, over and over: why wreck a day, an experience, a mood over mindless *coulda-shoulda-wouldas?* Each of us have our stressors, challenges, puzzles—why the rudeness? Why bark orders? What happened to kindness? Fuck.

I growl. I spit. I curse.

Then, just as the air conditioning within Finn drops the temperature a few million degrees, I pull in a deep, deep breath. *Let it go,* I think. *No sense in perpetuating and trying to fix what you can't control. Let it go. Your anger is your choice. Choose differently. Don't blame. This is on you. Own it.*

A few minutes later, I am standing in the Burrow kitchen searching frantically through a cupboard. *Pasta*—my mind cries out—*where's the pasta?*

I lean my weary head against the wall and realize that I must now run to the grocery store. . .

I growl. I spit. I curse.

Then, thankfully, I laugh. Better choice.

To the grocery store I go.

CHAPTER 13

THE HORSE

The Iron Horse on Sherman Avenue in Coeur d'Alene, Idaho, opened its doors in 1972 and has since been at the literal center of our small town's nightlife. For The RUB and for our family and friends, the Iron Horse has been the room where the funniest, seediest, strangest, and freakishly memorable moments have staggered by, most often during a smudged, giggly, tequila hazed euphoric gathering. Queue the sitcom *Cheers'* theme song (with Frank Zappa on guitar), the bar is just that (maybe a little darker) —filled with friends, gossip, hilarious characters, and the wobbly sentimental toast, or the occasional overly-dramatic booze-induced conflict. And sometimes it's the perfect place for a quiet meeting with a scotch on the rocks, a friend, and talk of art, missions, and world domination. Our pub.

As for live music, The Horse began hosting country musicians on a tiny, smoky stage tucked in the back around 1973. Countless solo musicians playing folk, blues, and some rock haunted the club until about 1991. Speaking with the bar's owner, my friend, Aaron Robb, I learned that one of his most memorable artists of that time, and perhaps the one with the record of the most Horse appearances was a fellow named Three Chord Dave. If I scrunch my forehead and try to push the gigmentia to the side, I think I can see Dave strumming out the classics on a weatherbeaten guitar, a cigarette smashed between the strings in the headstock, and a line of empty beer glasses on the wet table beside the mixer.

A remodel of the back room in the early nineties brought live music to a close for nearly a decade. It wasn't until sometime just around the turn of the century, 2002 or so, that the bar hosted live music once again—and as fate would have it, I was in the band that rekindled the Horse's live music fire.

All those years ago, my original band, KITE, was returning from a west-coast tour, feeling rather defeated and tired. The tour had been wearisome, our audiences had been small, the pay excruciatingly low, or rather, nonexistent, and our spirits matched the journey's overall theme: sad. Nevertheless, our enthusiastic and unshakeable manager, Shokie (Craig Shoquist), got in contact with our girls at home and put together a kind of homecoming show, and the Iron Horse was gracious enough to move some tables around to accommodate. Posters were made, word of mouth spread, and before we knew it, we were setting up our instruments in our favorite bar, as an audience of some two-hundred-plus people assembled to hear what we'd been up to over the last few weeks.

The show was a joy. The crowd was riveted on the performance, and we felt jolts of electricity and appreciation as we ticked down the set list of our complex and carefully crafted songs.

Post show we huddled around our usual table—long branded *The Corner Table,* and toasted with a tray full of *tacos* (our name for a tequila shot with an orange wedge sprinkled with cinnamon) to a rough journey and its happy ending.

Aaron, hearing about the night a few days later, got an idea. The following week he decided to start a live music rotation through the bar, given the successful bar revenue from the KITE show. He told me that the first cover band to start the now nearly twenty years of music at the Horse was a group from over the pass called *Back For More.*

"Back For More?" I said with an ironic lilt. "Really?"

"Yeah," Aaron said.

"Well, if that just doesn't seem just right."

Below the Iron Horse kitchen, there is a basement. It's an old, untidy rectangular, cellar-like space cluttered with water heaters, a furnace, retired tables, broken furniture, shelves of miscellaneous cups, plates, old beer bottles, and a layer of twentieth-century funk (maybe even nineteenth-century funk).

There's a slight tinge of mildew and a faint reek of something dead in the far, dimly-lit corner. The concrete walls are stained with an unsavory yellow-brown leakage. It isn't the first subterranean bar underbelly I've been in. Strangely, there's something comfortable about it. Only the best bars have basements like this.

From the mess, Cristopher and I have assembled a make-shift table and pulled in three chairs that can still sustain weight. It's hot down here. My vodka cocktail sweats on the table beside a shot of tequila. I nervously tap out rudiments on my knee while Cary tangles together a flurry of notes high up on the neck of his guitar. Cristopher texts furiously on his phone. We don't speak.

Above us we can here the tramp of footfalls. The crowd is gathering. Dust glitters from the ceiling in the florescent light.

Cary coughs. He mentions something about the generator's fumes from the firetruck.

"Did you get some rest?" I ask.

He shakes his head, "Nope. You?"

"Nope."

I'm exhausted. At home there was little time to rest, if any. When I had returned to the Burrow from the store with a box of pasta and a jar of marina sauce, I rushed inside, showered and, with a towel around my waist, I put water on to boil, started coffee, chose a shirt and tie, and checked the contents of the gig bag. While I slurped noodles, I tied my shoes. While I tied my tie, I finished my toast. I sipped coffee on the drive down.

The basement door swings open and in walks our friend Tyler Davis. Tyler is a local promoter and the owner of Coeur d'Alene's summer concert series, *Live After 5*. His kind eyes look lit-up by the half full glass of whiskey in his hand. He is tall, bald, and handsome. He's got a fair amount of TVs Kojak about him.

"Let's go, boys!" he says, "Hit the stage!"

Suddenly, Cristopher raises his tequila and says, "Let's do it!"

I like the sound of this. I like his smile.

We raise our shots, shoot, and move toward the stairs to the back kitchen. Tyler holds the door for us to pass through.

The place is standing room only. It's hot. People shoulder for positions in the front. At 9:35PM, the venue lights dim and we thread our way through the crowd to our stages. There's applause and then a roar when we step up onto our platforms and prepare to start. It is a wonderful feeling. A favorite feeling—a rock show about to begin.

A couple of people reach their fists out to me as I get settled behind the drums. I bump them with a smile. My left foot presses down on the two fog machine switches and a low, white vapor rises out of the stage area. A few seconds later Cristopher and Cary vamp a hypnotic drone as lights fill the weighty mood with reds, golds, and greens. Off we go.

A few songs later, all is a blur. Between numbers I take a moment to sip from a glass of water and check the status of my pedals and the control switches at my feet. Adjusting the light board, I nudge my high hat stand back closer to the kit. The audience is howling. Screaming. Laughing. Grinning. One fellow, just feet away, yells, "Fuck yeah! Fuck yeah! Fuck yeah!" His fist pumping—his legs wobbly. We're doing our job in spite of my failing voice and fatigue, and I'm all-too-aware that gas fumes from the fire truck generator earlier in the day has done some damage. The stuffy venue is vexing. I glance up and see the sea (okay, *lake* maybe) of people stretching out into the next room and spilling out of both the back and front entrances. Roughly three hundred, I guess. Well-over the room's capacity. By the end of the night at least six hundred will have passed through the venue.

My throat hurts from scream/singing—still sore from smashing it into my trap case. When I get Cristopher's attention, I point to my monitor and gesture for more volume, hoping the adjustment will make the rest of the night easier. He frowns at me and shouts, "It'll feed back!"

I shrug. "Okay, just having some difficulty hearing myself."

He frowns again. Then, with a begrudged lean down to the mixer, shaking his head, he twists a knob.

He's right. There is a chance that adjusting the monitors at this point may start a chain reaction of annoying high pitched squeaks through the PA. I know it can be tricky. Ordinarily I wouldn't ask —but. . . *I gotta be able to hear.*

"Thanks," I shout over to him with a shrug.

He returns a determined nod. I notice he's in complete *captain mode*—fixed upon the job at hand, planning the next few songs, and enveloped in his role as bandleader. He stands up straight and yells another couple of orders across the chaos before we launch into another cluster of songs. His next song choices are all high energy—or more accurately—extremely physical drum numbers. I lean in and focus. Frenzied, the audience smashes ever closer to my kit.

Here we go.

Sweat stings my eyes. My vocal chords feel cut as if with a razor. Arms are numb. Four songs later we come to a loud, train wreck ending and I sense a relief, for we've been playing an overly long set, a little over two hours, and a break must be near. After all, we've three more sets to go. Before I can reach for my water, Cristopher shouts over to me, "*In Bloom!*" The crowd is fevered and screaming. I look at my hands. Bright red blood has splattered from my split knuckle on my left hand. Tiny blood dots have misted across the kit's white drum heads. *Not again,* I think. I look at Cristopher. "*In Bloom!*" he shouts again.

It is time for a break, I'm sure my face says. I'm shocked he wants to keep going, but machine-like, I nod and count the song in.

Nirvana's *In Bloom* is a powerfully dynamic piece that tacks from soft, controlled verses to loud choruses, and it takes an enormous amount of concentration for me to perform the song well. What is more, I have been given the high harmony on the choruses to sing. The *"He's the one / Who likes all our pretty songs / And he likes to sing along / And he likes to shoot his gun / But he knows not what it means / Knows not what it means"* part

— quite a trick while I smash out the bombastic, highly energetic Dave Grohl drum part while I'm starving for oxygen.

But the audience loves it. I strain to hit the vocal. Black spots appear in my periphery. Ignoring the very real possibility of passing out, I hit harder. I grit my teeth, leaning into the song's climax. Cary's guitar growls the heavy riff, and we round into the ending with a resounding boom.

More blood splatter on the heads. The air burns. I set my sticks down on the floor tom and I'm about to stand and leave the stage when Cristopher barks: *"Ob-la-di, Ob-la-da!"*

I stare at him. He glares at me. I open my mouth to protest but I refrain, lift my sticks, pull my mic forward and prepare to sing yet another high-in-register vocal. I'm dumbfounded. *Why a two hour set? The audience is completely satisfied. Why is Cristopher pushing us, or rather, what seems like, me?*

Half-way though the Beatle song, I can barely hear my vocal. My chest is tight and my throat squeezes for every note. Thankfully the crowd sings along with me and I'm able to let a line or two slide.

As we come to the triumphant ending: *And if you want some fun / Take Ob-la-di, Ob-la-da,* and the stage lights black out, I again set my sticks down on my floor tom, lift my water and twist around to leave the stage. *Absolutely break time,* I think.

Then I hear Cristopher's bass vamping a slow progression that I recognize as U2's *With Or Without You.* Surely, I think, we should take a break after the energy of the Beatle song. Looking up, I can see that he's intent on not leaving the stage yet. My head shakes in exhaustion, frustration and not a little anger.

The U2 song is not one we know or have played with any kind of seriousness. Like many RUB songs, we often approach an unknown song with our respective voices and interpret the parts how we see fit. Unfortunately, those agreed-upon protocols at this moment are nonexistent. As I start in with a drum part, Cristopher growls that my tempo is too slow—that I'm not in the right place —that the part is wrong. I feel my eyes widen and a sudden jolt of fear floods through me at the thought that I must have missed something. Then, I'm pissed, knowing that there is nothing accurate about our attempt at this song—countless parts are missing: the Edge's delay effects and impossible-to-miss melodic hooks, Bono's impassioned delivery, and Daniel Lenois's masterful mix—but never mind the drums. I turn my eyes into my drum set and focus on playing with extreme accuracy and feel —deep pocket—serving the song, performing it as if The RUB wrote it. I sense daggers from Cristopher when he begins to sing. (*He's not quite singing it right*, I think.)

But at this point, I care not. I'm fucking over it.

Those up front are at first baffled by the atmospheric shift to a ballad, but not enough to vacate their front row positions. They sing along completely unaware that I am devising ways to shove a drumstick through Cristopher's temple, and he is likely fantasizing about breaking his guitar across my skull. Whatever the reasons why, I can't wait to finish the song and get off stage. A *talk* is coming next.

And the U2 song does eventually come to an end.

As I stand and bend down to lay hold of my long-neglected glass of water, Cristopher turns to me and yells over the din of the crowd: "Downstairs!"

"Now!" I shout a stern confirmation.

Our eyes are aflame, yet we both turn to the audience with big grins and wave. A minute or two later, I am spitting curse words as I shove my way through the crowd to the back kitchen and the dungeon below.

This is the part where I could share what really happened.

But here's this instead:

Entering into the basement dungeon, Cristopher stands, marches up to me and without a word breaks a beer bottle over my head. Glass glitters into my vision and I buckle. Amazingly, I riposte with a right hook to his chin, knocking him to the scum-glazed concrete floor. With a shout, Cary rises from his chair and rushes in to stop the fight but Cristopher trips him and he falls forward, cracking his forehead on a sharp metal shelf. Blood gushes from a tiny cut above his eye brow. Enraged now, Cary grasps what looks like a two-foot pipe and thrusts it into Cristopher's ribs. Cristopher lets out a heave of wind and doubles over. Cary then starts in on him with a series of blows to his head, shoulders and back until Cristopher goes down. I can see most of this, but I've a shard of glass in my right eye. Wiping at it, I notice I'm weeping blood. Through a red blur, I can see one of Cary's guitars leaning against a chair. I lay hold of it, raise it above my head and let it fall like an axe between Cary's shoulder blades. The guitar snaps like a twig as Cary's body folds and drops to the floor.

Of course, the above is just silly and certainly not the truth. However, as we gather in that dismal crypt, the ensuing argument has a similar ugliness. Angry words are spoken, interruptions are rife, and misunderstanding is the main theme. Was it the long day? Likely. Are there some challenges going on in our respective personal lives that might be fueling this fire? Probably.

I suddenly recognize that I am emotionally unbalanced. My partners are not fully aware of the chaos in my personal life— especially Mom's recent diagnosis—and I am wishing I had shared my feelings before we started. Perhaps I am easily triggered. Becoming angry was wholly within my control—and I chose it. And what of Cristopher's trials? How did his day start? What triggers did he have to navigate today? *A great many,* I think. There's always more to the story.

It isn't long before one of us blurts out a sincere apology. Then there's another. Cristopher says something like, "I didn't mean to be rude, I'm just being the captain amid the chaos." And I reply with, "I didn't mean to take it personally, I'm just at my wits end." The mood softens. Then there's a flurry of kind words and statements like: "Oh, I see what you meant," and, "oh, I didn't realize that was happening," and so on. The cool balm of empathy.

Hugs follow. The three of us cluster with our arms around each other in that squalid cellar. Cristopher says, "That's better." I have to agree.

Cary: "Okay, let's rock."

We go up.

Knowing that I will be scribbling about this RUB misstep in my journal for use in the book that will eventually be called *Gigmentia*, I begin thinking about how to share our inner battles, our tough moments, and our idiosyncratic baggage. While I agree that a story without conflict is no story at all, and our occasional disagreements might have some enticing, if not delicious story arcs, I weigh the fairness of a single narrative (my narrative), and I feel a sudden desire to keep our more sour moments off the plate. These morsels should be ours alone.

All of this crosses my mind as I thread through the crowd toward the stage for the second set. Friendly faces blur as I pass. Several high-fives and eager comments erupt: "Fuck yeahs," and, "you guys are killing it," and, "RUB rules!" Heart warming, without a doubt. And just minutes ago, we three were engaged in a bloody battle to the death—or rather, arguing over something I can't quite recall. *These people and the feeling in the room are the why of all our effort,* I think, stepping up onto my drum stage.

The argument, like most arguments was ridiculous. In our long history we've only had a couple of brotherly brawls: a mild shoving match, perhaps—maybe a tackle or two. Like all relationships, ours have their moments. But as far as who's to blame for our discontent, or wrong or right, on this hot evening in early summer, is moot. Sometimes familiarity breeds contempt. Sometimes fuses can be short. Sometimes one of us has a rough day. What is relevant and worth a thousand mentions is how our shortsightedness can be brief, how our anger burns out quickly, and how our ability to forgive and learn from each other are the keys to our union as a group. There is understanding. And something my dear friend and business partner Mark has taught me as quintessential to progress, "Have short term memory and don't stop moving forward."

A cocktail waitress hands me a shot of tequila. With some difficulty she manages to weave through to Cary and offer a glass to him—her arm outstretched between bodies crowding the front row. He grins at her as he takes it. Looking over to my right, Cristopher's spotlight is on, his bass slung over his shoulder, and a glass of booze is lifted up high. The audience raises hands up.

"Here's to being together!" He shouts. He turns to Cary and me. His eyes say, *I love you*.

Oh, the Horse.

CHAPTER 14

THE RULES

Typically, the area just in front of the band is its own kind of ecosystem apart from the rest of the room. This three-foot space —sometimes mere inches, between us and the crowd—is often where very interesting, odd, and surprising things happen. Things that one might never expect could happen in a room packed with hundreds of people. In this space, during a guitar solo for example, grown men will bow down on their knees and worship Cary's skills, entranced by his divine delivery of pure electrified rock. Only a couple of people nearby will notice. Women, also seduced by the pounding music, will twirl, spill drinks, try to touch Cristopher's legs, Cary's legs—sometimes other body parts. No one save the band really notices. As I hit the kit, men will egg me on with fists out, rock n' roll fury in their eyes, grunting and growling as if they are themselves pounding the drums. There are the sublime expressions on faces that seem to be experiencing some distant memory that only a favorite song can conjure. There's a guy passing a joint down the line. There's a woman flashing her breasts to the band. There's a dude mouthing the words to the song on unsteady feet. Up front, there is pandemonium—and it is somehow sheltered from the collective attention of the room. You don't notice it unless you're in it—seemingly, no rules. It is in the throes of music that we become fifteen again. Arms, hands, legs, faces, grins, sweat, hair, whirling, twirling, singing, drinks spilling, voices shouting. . . It is, indeed, a spiritual experience. And to think that The RUB is the prime mover, the priest, the auctioneer, the ringleader, the catalyst—the wizard casting the spells.

It is the following night, a Saturday night, and the Horse is again, shoulder-to-shoulder packed. We are in the middle of playing Zeppelin's *Ramble On*. All systems go. After our basement battle, our reconciliation, and our somewhat healed return to the stage, we finished the rest of last night's gig strong. Despite a long sleep, a late rise, handling a few chores, and a band dinner/meeting to ensure that we covered last night's issue, it feels as if the two shows have simply been interrupted by an extended set break. The summer shows are now running into each other. One long show.

Down front are some familiar faces. I see a group of friends that joined our shows since our first few gigs. Sara and Rodd, Doug, Dennis, Perry, and Maggie have been with us so long that they've come up with a name for their gang: The RUBBISH. There's Amidy and Renee in the center of the crowd. My aunt Mel is dancing with Sheree to the left of Cary. But mostly, the front seems to be filled with several faces that I can't quite place. People I know I've spoken with, but names are just out of my. . . wait. . . I shove the thought aside and focus on the coming drum fill, and then as I syncopate the John Bonham groove in the chorus, I scream my best Robert Plant—the piercing:

> *Ramble on*
> *And now's the time, the time is now*
> *To sing my song*
> *I'm goin' 'round the world, I got to find my girl*
> *On my way*
> *I've been this way ten years to the day*
> *Ramble on*
> *Gotta find the queen of all my dreams[17]*

Yes. I'm back—faces, faces and names just out of my reach. We've met and performed for a great many people, sometimes it is simply impossible to remember everyone's name. *Gigmentia.*

I love this song, *Ramble On*. Reminds me of our local record store when I was in my middle teens, The Total Eclipse—then later, The Long Ear.

---

[17] From Led Zeppelin's Ramble On. Lyrics: Robert Plant ©1969. From their album Led Zeppelin II, Atlantic Records.

Just behind the front row is another line of faces that quickly register and I can feel my face light up with a surprised smile. Former co-workers and colleagues from my days as a college educator at the University of Idaho. As soon as they see that I've noticed them, they cheer and raise their hands up. I try to blow a kiss while hitting the drums. My friend Randy lets out a howl equal to the band's volume. I laugh. Beside him is Andrea, my former boss. She's grinning. There are a couple of younger guys holding positions in front of Cristopher. They both wear RUB T-shirts. With beers in hand and wide eyes, they watch Cristopher and mouth the words to the song along with him. There's a little bit of a sway in their stances.

Hold on—I need to focus on the upcoming chorus.

I'm back.

We take a moment between songs. I gulp water in the dark, kneeling down behind my kit. I let the fan cool my face.

Cristopher begins to talk to the audience about how nice it is to be back at the Horse. The crowd cheers. A few people shout out their favorite songs—their favorite bands. I notice Cristopher begin to process the next few numbers.

Then someone in the middle of the crowd shouts out: "*Sweet Home Alabama!* Fuckin' *Sweet Home,* man!"

Oops, I think. I smile and wait.

The noise of the crowd noticeably drops. I take a quick look at The RUBBISH and the many other faces that have seen us over the years and watch their humored expressions prepare for our usual handling of someone asking for *Sweet Home Alabama.*

"The rules!" one of the RUB shirted guys slurs out.

"Yeah!" his buddy joins, "the rules!"

The RUBBISH begin shouting, "The rules!"

I hop up onto my drum throne. My left foot clicks the stage lights up, and with a smile Cristopher says, "Time to tell you the rules."

"The rules!" is shouted again from different parts of the crowd.

"There are only five songs we do not play," Cristopher states in a tone not to be trifled with. Both Cary and I raise our right hands with our five fingers spread out. "We do not play *Sweet Home Alabama*," he continues. Cary and I close one finger leaving four showing. "A great song, but no." There's a couple of grumblers at this edict. "We do not play *Old Time Rock and Roll*." Another finger disappears.

I say, "We love girls and we love brown eyes, but we do not play *Brown Eyed Girl*."

Cristopher nods and repeats, "We do not play *Brown Eyed Girl*."

Cary: "What's the fourth song?"

I shrug.

Cristopher: "We do not play *Mustang Sally*."

Cary and me in unison: "We do not play *Mustang Sally*."

With one finger still showing Cristopher says, "And there's one more song we don't play, but we play everything else."

Then somewhere in the back, a voice rises up. You've probably heard this guy. A fellow likely wearing a backward ball cap. You know who he is. He is seemingly everywhere.

He shouts: "*Free Bird!*"

Cary and I lower our hands.

There's always that guy. He's usually the guy that calls out for *Sweet Home Alabama* in the first place.

What is it like to play the song, Sweet Home Alabama, 403,975 times? And why won't I play it 403,976 times?

Fair questions.

Sweet Home Alabama is overplayed by bands, period. From my first cover band up until fourteen years ago, the song found its way onto a set list almost every night. When you are out on the town, seeing bands, there is a 97.9 percent chance you will hear it performed—maybe three times. Sometimes twice a night at the same club, depending upon the group. The song is relatively easy to capture, people generally like it, and it will invariably fill a dance floor in a pinch. After playing it 403,975 times, I have somehow lost the magic of the song, if I ever really felt its magic. Don't mistake me, however; I do not dislike it. . .

The song itself, brilliantly performed by Lynyrd Skynyrd in 1974, is a masterful recording and smash hit single defining a time and place in rock history—specifically, Southern rock history. Recorded at Muscle Shoals studios in Alabama, home of the Swampers,[18] the song has the sound and feel of the greatness with the first notes of the iconic guitar picking—not to mention the moonshined voice of command that could be everyone's best friend sitting across the room muttering: "Turn it up." Every time it comes on the radio (which is quite often), I still *turn it up*.

The song had its controversy, too. Written in response to Neil Young's anti-racist songs *Southern Man* and *Alabama,* Lynyrd Skynyrd's Ronnie Van Zant called out Young for labeling the entire South as racist with:

Well I heard Mister Young sing about her
Well I heard ol' Neil put her down
Well I hope Neil Young will remember
A southern man don't need him around anyhow[19]

Young later agreed that his songs' sentiments were accusatory and condescending. Ultimately the seeming feud between the artists turned to camaraderie and a shared stand against racism in the South.

Oddly enough, no one in Lynyrd Skynyrd was from Alabama.

While there's mythology, controversy, and excellent writing and playing, it might seem peculiar that we decline performing it. After all, aren't those the very attributes that make a great song? Yes, I believe they are, indeed.

---

[18] Muscle Shoals studio house band, The Swampers, produced more than 500 recordings with almost a hundred of them achieving gold and platinum status.

[19] From Lynyrd Skynyrd's *Sweet Home Alabama.* Lyrics: King/Rossington/Van Zant ©1973. From their album *Second Helping*, MCA Records.

However, in my time, too many former band mates felt as if the song was a necessary part of *every* show. We played it, and played it, and played it until the very thing that made the song great to begin with, we lost. The song even found a new life with Kid Rock's 2008 hit song *All Summer Long* wherein the *Sweet Home Alabama* guitar hook makes its presence, yet again, known (I won't play that request, either). No offense, Kid.

The other songs in *the rules* occupy a similar overplayed status. All great works of art, of course, but to us they have simply found themselves on a growing list of songs that should be retired from the cannon—unless of course the original band plays them, or maybe a bride at a wedding makes the request.[20] Just my opinion, of course. No offense, *Sweet Home Alabama, Free Bird* guy.

"*Free Bird!*" The guy shouts again.

"We do not play *Free Bird,*" Cristopher concludes. "But we play everything else."

Then a request is made that makes nearly every musician jitter with either fear or joy—*or both.*

"Rush!" is the call louder than the rest. "Rush!"

Fuck.

I grin.

Both.

I look at Cristopher. He gives a sort of shrug. Cary looks at his fret board and begins to plot. I look down at my sore hands, my blood splattered drum kit, and I think about my earliest influential introduction to the Professor, perhaps the greatest rock drummer in history, Rush's Neil Peart. As mentioned above, I was twelve and my brother set the needle down on side one of *2112.* If you know the record and mastery of Mr. Peart, you may have an inkling of the gauntlet being thrown. Suffice it to say that

---

[20] We have broken our own rules a time or two—however, not before stating our case, pleading, suggesting alternatives, and finally demanding more money. Sounds rather hard-lined, I'm sure. We must have some principles, after all.

Rush is indeed a mighty challenge rehearsed, never mind, off the cuff—and for us, yet another musical realm we've not entered into, at least seriously. There was a time in my early years that I could play a number of Rush songs note-for-note, and it boggles my mind to consider just how much time and effort went into learning those songs way back then. As for us, well, Cary and I have dabbled a bit. Cristopher knows enough Rush to have a basic vocabulary. So, in the spirit of The RUB, we waste no time. And besides, we have to follow the rules.

I say over the mic, "I've an idea! Hey Cris, Cary—will you just play a massive, earth-shaking, E chord—loud and distorted? A single note?" They look at me questioningly. "Yeah," I nod to the left and right. "A massive E chord. You'll know right where we're going."

No further questions necessary, the two prepare their attack of a single power chord. Cristopher sets his feet wide on his stage and waits. Cary watches me for the cue. To the crowd I say, "Here's a shot at something we've not tried before." I squint a moment reaching for courage. "One, two, three, four. . ."

A thunderous E crashes. I slide into a mid-tempo beat, quick eighth notes on the hi hat— heavy kick and snare. At a full measure I sing:

A modern day warrior
Mean, mean stride
Today's Tom Sawyer
Mean, mean pride

With delighted grins, Cary and Cristopher add the well-known power chords that make up the brilliant hook. And we're off. We make it through another verse and through to a chorus before I decide that we should cut and run lest it all falls apart. Instead of leading us into the off-time of the instrumental and solo sections, I land on the last verse:

Exit the warrior

Today's Tom Sawyer
He gets high on you
And the energy you trade
He gets right on to the friction of the day[21]

What should follow is an arpeggiated 80s keyboard hook that leads the piece to its end. A melody enigmatic of the song and the decade itself. Of course we do not have a keyboard in the band, but when I hear the notes in the mix, I'm not immediately surprised (because when have we ever let a missing instrument stop us?). I turn and see Cary feigning playing a keyboard and singing the part. I lose it. Laughter comes rolling out of me. Tears, too. Cristopher is shaking his head, grinning. The audience, too, somehow gets the joke.

As we leave the stage to take a long needed break, I'm thrilled by having managed to scratch the surface of the epic song, *Tom Sawyer*. I feel delighted, as if I were twelve again, watching the Rush vinyl spin.

Rush *rules*, I think.

[21] From Rush's *Tom Sawyer*. Lyrics: Neil Peart/Pye Dubois ©1981. From their album *Moving Pictures*. Mercury Records.

CHAPTER 15

KITE, THE BAND

The following day, The RUB arrives at the Iron Horse near noon—certainly feeling a wee bit out of sorts given the chaos, drink, laughs, and pouring out of energy over the last couple of days. We have come to the Horse on a Sunday to tear down the gear, lights, staging, and leave no trace, but we are also ready for a bit of fun. For the last couple of years, our Sundays after playing the venue have become another kind of performance where we have a late lunch, a sip or two of our favorite spirits, and lazily play a few songs for whoever decides to join us. Eventually it builds in both attendance and fervor. In the end, Sundays invariably turn into a madhouse. Sundays are our favorite.

When Sheree and I walk in through the back doors, there's a cheer. We see Mom and Dad, along with Bob and his wife Bobbi, Gerry (my niece) and her husband Nic, and my dear aunt Mel in a booth across from our stages. They've ordered drinks. They're laughing. I'm delighted and astonished. Also in the club are three or four more tables of people that have heard about our Sunday teardown shows.

Cristopher is standing beside Dad. Dad is asking him if he knows any Everly Brothers songs. Cary is on stage tuning his guitar. A long necked Budweiser sits beside his pedal board.

Sheree says, "I think you're going to need food."

"Looks that way," I say.

Scrambled eggs, ham, sour dough toast, and hot coffee is arrayed before me. Mom watches me eat. The waitress stops and sets a drink down beside my plate.

"Thank you," I say.

She smiles. Mom raises a single eye brow. "What's that?" she asks. "It's pink."

"Yes," I reply. I crunch the toast. "Its a vodka soda with a splash of cranberry. Sometimes you just need to sip on something pink."

She takes a quick glance at Dad and then reaches for my drink, lifts it and takes a sip. "Mmmm." She looks good, although I can see the ghost of fear behind her smiling eyes. She's a little unsure as to where she is. She studies Cristopher and Cary and then turns to me.

"This is the band KITE? Where's Scott? Where's Monte?"

Dad inserts, "No, Dee Dee, this is The RUB. Kite was a long time ago." Mom looks confused.

"KITE hasn't played a show in years, Mom," I tell her.

"KITE," a friend from a nearby table says. His name is Benny. "I love KITE, man! You guys were killer. I've got two of your albums. What ever happened to you guys?"

I look down at my eggs. *Long story*, I think. "That's a good question," I say.

"Did you guys break up?" Benny asks.

"No," I say feeling my eyebrow scrunch. "No, we're still a band as far as I know. Mark, Scott, and me, at least. We're just in hibernation."

Mom continues her attempt to put my last original band and ten years ago together with my current band The RUB.

"Monte moved to Ireland," I remind her.

She nods. "I love that Monte," her eye brow raises again. "Sexy, sexy."

I chuckle. "I love him, too." I shake my head and count years in my mind. I've not spoken to him since the day he left, ten or more years ago. He and I were songwriting partners since the late 1980s, when finally our relationship broke—the tides of time, personal ambition, family, and wanderlust swept between us.

"What happened?" She asks.

Another lifetime ago. Yet it still seems strangely present. When we came to our end, we were working on a record that was to be titled *NOW*. Ironic, really, given that we never arrived.

I push my plate back and take a long pull of my cocktail. I'm reminded of an essay I wrote just after the band fractured. Another piece of time I've kept:

NOW

(As it appeared on the KITE website all those years ago.)

NOW, we've sat around this table for a lot of years. A 1970's, round walnut kitchen table we acquired through one of our close friends who had a knack for finding cool, old things. She had it delivered to our Coeur d'Alene recording studio (at that time called: The Room—*clever*) along with five matching chairs upholstered in light tan leather. Our love of music and camaraderie often leads us here to talk things over. Coffee, strong drinks, sketches and plans, cash, noodles, tea, spills, tools, saw dust, blood and a whole lot of talking have been supported by this table, so it's no surprise that we are sitting here right now.

NOW, it's November, 2008. Monte lounges across from Scott, and Mark is facing me. I am uncomfortable and nervous because momentarily KITE will begin a major transition, and my mind is flitting through the last couple of years, if not the last fifteen. Scott's voice breaks the weird silence and he casually asks me about the two newest shows that have been added to the calendar, and I blithely tell him that they are "inked" or confirmed—and then I mumble something about one of the venues being a beautiful theater that will be perfect for our rear screen projection work. But our exchange is strained, for we both are aware of the real discussion ahead—and the specific reason we've gathered together today. I shift in my seat and glance across the room at our instruments, poised and ready. The green drum kit crouching within a jungle of cables and microphones (newly refinished in a green natural wood stain by Monte and myself over a couple of beautiful fall days). Like a curved stone castle wall, behind the kit are planted the sable blocks of bass and guitar amps. The guitars are perched on their bent, *one-too-many-times-crushed-in-the-trailer* guitar stands. The floor is strewn with more vine-like cables zigzagging to effect pedal boards and more microphones, and finally connecting to the snake (a hub that joins many cables into a single, manageable cable. *Juss' so ya know*). As the fellows make small talk I think back to a time not too long ago when our rehearsal room was an outdoor shed with a dirt floor and gaps in the walls—a string of winter rehearsals on the schedule. A chill runs up my spine. These instruments and devices of ours have led us to a lot of different places—and their arrangement across our stage has been set up exactly the same for nearly 15 years. From left to right, Scott's pedals and station inhabit the far left, with Monte's amp behind him, then Monte's spot with Scott's amp just to his right and behind (a curious crisscross of amps due to Scott's unwillingness to be too loud [which he never is], but he seems to play with less inhibition if his amp is further away from him—so we can turn him up when *we* want to), then mission control with the drums and cymbals, and then on to the far right where Mark's rig looms like a bookend monolith. Since our earliest shows we've not deviated from this offensive line. I'm stung suddenly by how that line may look very different, depending upon the outcome of the impending discussion. My focus is brought back to our meeting and I wonder how our gatherings around the table are going to look after today.

NOW, since the release of *Sleeping In Thunder* (2006) we have been meandering between a number of challenging projects. The seemingly impossible to finish *Lost All Age* has found some new life with Mark's entry into the group. We began the tedious task of retracking the entire record, infusing the work with fresh arrangements and focused performances. Concurrently, Monte and I have been able to compose a set of new songs that are getting arrangement and studio time as well. Songs like: *The Proposal* (a kiss blown to the marriage of Scott and Dani), *A Ghosting Heart* (a love letter I had penned for Monte and his new girl friend from Ireland), *Tissue Like Winter* (a cocktail napkin scribbled lyric) and *Leaves On Stones* (another of those "undiscovered country—what dreams may come" pieces that I'm wont to vainly pursue), among others. A string of future performance dates are booked out on our calendar into 2009, and the show itself has not only been accommodating our love of making music but it has also inspired us to make our own films, to be screened behind the band during performances. In many ways, creating and performing with our own original film projects is a dream come true—something that we have talked of achieving since our very infancy and planning sessions around the Hope Tree (the red leafed maple in Monte's yard in Hope, Idaho). So we are making progress with both the old and the new; a sort of swerving line between now and a future release, but progress nonetheless. The new songs are settling themselves into a theme that we've titled, for the time being: *NOW*, in which, as in our previous albums, each song is a part of a larger idea—and this time it is about living in the present and celebrating the Now.

NOW, of course, at this very moment, here at the table, I feel like the *big three* (past, present, and future) are simultaneously racing away in different directions, and being *present* at the table is, I'm afraid, beyond my ability. For *now,* anyway.

NOW, I suppose some of the irony of this tentative title, *Now,* resides in the amount of time it is taking us to compose and record—which is a lot. But we've always operated under the dictum: *we can do it all,* meaning that we are capable of creating and living complete and full lives. In the two years since the release of our last record, our writing and studio schedules, and performances ran parallel to Scott's back injury and then getting married, me becoming a new father, Mark becoming a father to his second child, and Monte nurturing a new relationship—all of that combined with an occasional date night with our wives, the weight of our "other" jobs, the daily *get stuff done at home,* very little sleep, paying the bills, and so on. It has certainly brought us to question our idealistic *we can do it all* modis operandi (all worthy of a run-on sentence). But when I consider the amount of life that's been lived these past two years, I am astonished at the good amount of work that KITE *has* accomplished. And what's more, delighted that our experiences will be captured in our work, as they always have been. Under the circumstances, our concentrated force has prevailed—and as the Buddist quote goes: "Do not dwell in the past, do not dream of the future, concentrate the mind on the present moment," and all seemed to be going as planned. Though, suddenly the word *concentrate* seems to stick out. If there's one thing that's certain right now, sitting here at the table, I sure ain't concentrating—I know this because I can feel my mind drifting from heady dictums to weighing our current state to wondering just where this table was made. Wisconsin? Seems right.

NOW, I can tell that we're about to begin, and as I've said, today is a day of change. A moment of change, one single moment—and very soon, everything will be different. Before anyone speaks, I think back to the completed projects that we've worked so hard on, and are consequently so proud of. Our debut album *Gravity* in 1997 with its ambitious theme and packaging. A record we made, I recall, *for ourselves*. We had no plans of playing live—we were going to be a studio band—studio cats, that sort of thing. The theme for the project was centered around those weighty subjects of the human condition: love, death, freedom, coming of age, hope, war and so on. Far reaching for me as a lyricist, to be sure. But thinking back on it right now, it feels like we just released the thing. That record is, in many ways, the overture to our work that followed. Our bass player at the time, Doug Smith, became a first time father just after *Gravity's* release, and with that life-changing addition, he felt that we should look for another member—someone who would have the time to be present. Very soon thereafter, the three of us decided to change our route and we found ourselves being led to the stage, and on to touring, so we switched our lives around to do just that. Bassist Darren Eldridge (D Rock) entered the group and, on Valentines Day 2002, KITE, played its first show. A string of performances later, we arrived at our second release: a live EP called *In Memory of the Sketch* which contained live versions of some of the songs to be included on our next studio effort, *Lost All Age*. Yet again, KITE practiced its o'er-reaching talents with the fourteen track, sonnets for lyrics, *slightly* overcooked epic on the end of innocence: *Lost All Age*. A couple of years, a couple of tours and a couple of nearly complete studio versions later, we eventually shelved the album, unsatisfied with our ability to render the thing.

NOW, because of our bottomless tenacity, and the addition of a fearless manager, Craig Shoquist (Shokie), we were able to land a few high profile gigs warming for national acts. One particularly memorable one was a New Year's eve show warming for the pop group Smashmouth at the Fiesta Bowl in Arizona. Moments before we took the stage, Monte and I nervously chatted about anything that might take our mind off of the fact that we were about to play one of our ten minute, odd-time signature and thick-worded works before a gathering that came to hear, "*Hey now, you're a rock star, get your game on, get paid.*" Part of me reveled in the overblown, self-important, integrity of it all. Another part of me took note of the location and distance to each and every exit (escape route). But luckily, as with most audiences that we'd the pleasure of playing for, they appreciated our work, and even made the effort to meet us afterward. Better still, the sound and video company hired to capture the headliner's set presented a nearly full length VHS tape of our performance. The director told us smiling, "After your first song I asked the camera men to take their places and shoot. If you don't mind, I'm keeping a copy for myself." That was nice. We drove north through the desert late that night with a little bit of money and some free promotional material. I smiled, thinking that two out of three wasn't bad: at least we got our *game on and got paid*. Not too sure about the *rockstar* thing.

NOW we'd had our run-ins with record companies, executives and potential big-time folks, and as most stories of that kind go, each time we got close to some substantial break through, things just didn't work out, for one reason or another. Whether it was our stubborn nature to make our music *our* way, or our resolve that we wanted to live lives filled with family, friends, children, travel and everything else we wanted to experience individually, and not just the dangerously obsessive path of music and music business (*we can do it all*), somehow we steered clear of any sort of traditional music business success. *Now, aren't we clever.* Maybe that lack of success is due to what another friend of mine was fond of saying about KITE: "You guys suck." Maybe.

NOW, whatever the reason(s), we've let our love of what we do lead us to years of writing, recording and playing to full concert houses to playing to three stoned guys at an empty sports bar, as well as filling our lives with all the stuff that makes the work worth it in the end. To us, something wonderful was going to happen, and sometime soon our financial futures would be affected by our hard work (because that's what happens when you work hard, right?), and we would be able to spend focused time on future projects, and tour Europe and Asia, and from all of that more heady thoughts and experiences would inspire more and more interesting works, and so on. Our love leading the way.

NOW, ultimately our financial futures were affected, and not in a good way, unfortunately. As I've said, we reach pretty far, even so far as to occasionally roar out a manifesto: "We will rule the world" (quite a different tune from *Gravity's*, "We want to be a studio band"). Not that we really thought that *ruling the world* was our destiny, but when you're headed down the road to accomplish any kind of success in the music industry, any battle cry less potent is futile. You don't want to meet a record executive and lamely say: "We really want to just garner an audience that allows us to tour for a couple of months in the states and maybe a six week tour in Europe, and then come home and have enough money to survive while we record the next album. Oh, ahem, and *roar*." But the truth is just that: we wanted to write and perform and still make rent, and maybe take our families along with us sometimes. And though humble but rewarding tours and two to three months to write and record was realistic to us, reality had another view point. The balance between a harmonious family life and the pure and simple lack of money began to cause some difficulty. A common story. Over time Darren and Shokie departed, and we found ourselves again wondering where our love would lead us. But just like with every other obstacle that KITE has experienced, our stubbornness would push us along and we made compromises in order to keep the journey alive. It might take longer, but so what. We want it all, right? And "all" meant a full life. Not saying no. Opening every door.

NOW the release of *Sleeping In Thunder* brought a new energy. With bassist and vocalist Mark Rakes filling out the group, we felt that we could carry on chasing that elusive present moment. And it is the love of that very feeling of *what's next* that enabled us to create elements in our live show that we didn't think possible with just the four of us. Lights and originally filmed, edited and projected video have become yet another aspect of our creative work, and their introduction injected our performances with a visual impact that would leave audiences wanting more (well, that's what they said). While creating the show, we had to accept that outside assistance, or rather, *roadies* were for the time, out of our budget. We have some dear friends that come in from time to time to aid us in times of need (Stroman, Chris, Cristopher, Cary, Jeff, Justin, Joe), but when it comes to the actual performance, we would have to do it all. Mission control, as Mark likes to call it, is behind the drum kit (*as it should be!*). From there I control all of the video transitions and projection. I also control a selection of lights and sequenced sounds by electronic drum pads dispersed around the kit and around my feet. As if playing the drums weren't enough—*sheesh.* Mark is also controlling a selection of light and sound with his feet, and between the two of us we round out the background vocals, the rhythms and the visuals. Monte's voice, feet and hands are busy with the complex dance of guitar pedal work and intense vocal performance, and so too are Scott's feet and hands, with the guitar textures changing several times over in a single song. All together, we've choreographed a powerful exhibition of content, sound, picture and light. Each show on the calendar seemed to be pulling more and more people in to see KITE—the show that was being called, "the big spectacle in a little room" (well, that's what they said). Yet again, our love was leading us right where we wanted to go. And our belief "that we could do it all," was proving to be a reality. And we *were* doing it all.

NOW, such a mantra can be a challenge, as you might expect: *we can do it all.* As I scan the table in front of me, I find myself realizing how many things are now crowding our space. Certainly, as the long fingers of time began to pull each of us this way and that, and children come, and marriages, and mounting debt, and well—life happens, we can all see that changes are on the horizon. Especially for Monte, whose newly-found love is currently residing in Ireland. For three of us, Scott, Mark and myself, life has become extremely complex, and we can sense that Monte's eyes are often gazing out across the sea. Several times over the last three years, we've communicated to him that we feel like he is distancing himself, and after these meetings, things would seem better. But only for a short time. Though KITE was about to embark on another mini tour and the follow-up to *Sleeping In Thunder* was progressing nicely, Monte's focus seemed to be drifting.

NOW, my thoughts are interrupted. Mark begins the meeting. He tells Monte that we've noticed his restlessness and tells him that we believe he should pursue his heart, go to Ireland, to his new relationship. The elephant is on the table. And with that, the now changes into something entirely different. The three of us wish him love and luck. He seems relieved. He reciprocates. We talk for a while longer about how to divide nearly two decades of a partnership. We come to terms with ease. And in a single moment, the stars shake loose, and that carefully plotted chart is obscured by clouds. A new now.

NOW, as the door shuts behind Monte and the three of us eye the empty chair at the round table, we don't speak. We listen to his descending foot steps fade away. In spite of all we've done, and have planned to do as a group, I am glad that we've finally opened Monte's path to leave. I'm happy that we have made it easy for him to do so. After all, we want his happiness, above all. That is the larger part of wanting it all. Yet, there is that undeniable emptiness now. Even though we've done the right thing in letting Monte go, we can't help but feel loss. I feel broken.

So what NOW?

I stand and cross the room to see if there's a drop of tequila left. The confusing patterns of letting go and mourning begin. Each of us deals with the change differently. Though I can guess at how both Mark and Scott are processing, I find it almost impossible to guess my own feelings. Though I know that this break is necessary, I wonder just how long it is going to take for me to recover—to truly feel confident about the work to come. I have invested my small family's entire future in this relationship with a man that so easily accepted the invitation to go. Can we do it without him?

And then the realization that such questions don't matter. All that matters is right now.

•••

KITE went on to record several new songs without Monte. We even played a show—unbelievably—at our local record store. But, inevitably, our momentum slowed, too busy with life, projects, and kids, the fervor and passion was disappearing.

Mark, Scott and I still flirt with each other about gathering to record a new song—a new record, but the day has not yet come. I have faith it will. Oddly enough, I still regard KITE as still together, rationalizing that we've simply been on a long, long vacation. As I push my plate back and lean over to kiss Mom, I think of Monte, Scott, and Mark and I feel sad. The era of KITE, the touring, the writing and recording, the original music, the blood, sweat, tears—the blind ambition—the pain—I cling to some hopeful, almost prideful, feeling that it was all worth it.

Another lifetime ago.

Another version of me, long gone. A me I can barely remember—but thankfully, a few words are still left from that time.

I join Cristopher and Cary on stage and we begin to brew sounds. An audience gathers and we play late into the afternoon. Before Mom and Dad leave, we sing an a cappella version of Elvis' *Love Me Tender.* Mom grips Dad's arm and mouths the words.

As the afternoon wanes, the room fills with familiar faces from last night. We play until it is dark outside. We tear down the gear slowly and load it into our vehicles. The moon is waxing crescent. I point to it as Sheree and I drive home. It looks like a thumbnail has cut a hole in the black sky.

CHAPTER 16

SHOWRUN

Michael rushes toward me, sword in hand. His feet come to a stop and they shift quickly into a steady base for his *en guard* pose. Menacing. It wasn't long ago that our fencing matches consisted of random, haphazard parrying with me landing a gentle touch of my sword to his arm, on top of his head, or along his forward leg. No longer. In what seems like a sudden storm, his motions now mirror mine. His speed has doubled. His accuracy and confidence has become, well, dangerous. Fierce eyes, sword at the ready, knees bent, ready to spring, I think it is about time to get him into some armor. Or, maybe its time I started wearing my armor.

The grass is cool under our bare feet. After a couple of matches, we catch our breath. We lie down on our backs and stare up. Walter's leaves sizzle. The sky is electric cobalt.

June is nearly gone. RUB shows run by one after another.

We play at the base of Silver Mountain for a private party just a stone's throw from where Cary ran track in high school. For most of the performance our audience are children. Maybe ten kids jumping up and down while their parents eat pizza, sip beers, and stand together in clusters. We jam through a block of Tom Petty songs—as many as we can remember.

We play a summer solstice party on Cristopher's family ranch in Rathdrum, Idaho, on the back of a slightly unlevel flatbed trailer. The power is inadequate and our PA and amps sound weak. We are situated at the bottom of a hill, the audience of maybe fifty people watching us from atop a hill, fifty or so yards away. Michael, Sheree, and I play frisbee in the green pasture on breaks. Michael gets a painful hornet sting. We tear down in the dark. All the way home I can feel that my back is out, due to the leaning stage.

One afternoon we perform a 50th Wedding Anniversary for sixty three people in the back yard of a house in Hayden, Idaho. The heat is maddening. Meatballs, brats, veggies, and coconut macaroons on long tables—beers in ice filled tubs. Cristopher complains of a stomach ache. We find some shade to try and rest before the show. We labor through.

Directly afterward we tear down the gear and drive to the Iron Horse to play an impromptu one nighter. We begin with an entire set of Pink Floyd: *Vera, Young Lust, Comfortably Numb, Another Brick In The Wall Part Two.* Dazed from the heat of the day and the rich food left in the sun, all we can do is plough through and try not to appear as if our tummies hurt or that we're hurrying to get home to rest.

We play a show at a huge mansion in Post Falls, Idaho, on the Spokane River. The audience consists of realtors from the Pacific Northwest. Good looking, well dressed, highly affluent—they clap politely, and resist getting too close to the band (I get the sense that we're looking a little spent). After a set or two, we've won them over and the dance floor fills with bejeweled women and golf shirts. And in perfect RUB fashion, things get crazy enough for an over-served fellow to launch himself into the swimming pool fully clothed. He is promptly shown the door. The moon peeks through a veil of ghosting clouds. Afterward, we find a nearby Denny's and discuss some band business. Cary counts out crisp hundred dollar bills and hands a stack to me, a stack to Christopher. I drive home with the window down. The air outside is cool. I follow the moon all the way to the Burrow.

Beneath a freeway overpass, we play the wrap party for Hoopfest, the world's largest three on three basketball tournament in Spokane, Washington. We're the headliners on a bill of great local bands. The stage is overly high above the audience and the PA is massive. We listen to friends perform. Sheree and I have drinks backstage with Cary and Cristopher. On stage, the lights are freakishly bright. Their glare distorts the view of the small audience. The RUBBISH is there.

We take a last minute job in a downtown park in Coeur d'Alene to headline a barbecue food show. The event is poorly planned with little or no promotion. When we take the stage there are maybe thirty people and the RUBBISH, occupying a sliver of grass in front of the huge festival stage. I wonder briefly if it wouldn't be better to move our gear down onto the grass—if intimacy would make a better memory. Instead, we grin, we imagine the first time we heard Boston's *Long Time,* and we play it like we wrote it (at least, that's how it feels).

A day later, Sheree and I rush over to Spokane to briefly join the 50th wedding anniversary of my college professor, Michael Herzog and his wife, Jean. We sip a tequila and chat with members of their family. Not an hour after we arrive, we're on our way back to Coeur d'Alene where I drop Sheree off and I head south to the next gig at a rather well-to-do gated community called Black Rock for the *Men's Member Guest Wyatt Earp Golf Tournament.*

Brown forest fire smoke crawls over the lake. Breathing is difficult. Dinner consists of sushi, calamari salad, prime rib, salmon and tiny red potatoes. Shrimp, too. An ice sculpture of the famous lawman presides over a hosted bar. The tournament winner reportedly takes home two antique Colt .45 pistols in a nice display box. We play well—loud—snarly. We remain a rock band despite the surrounding pomp, circumstance, and polo shirts. One of our stage props, a beat up football helmet with our RUB logo on its side, is lifted up by an audience member. It is none other than John Elway. Cristopher, an avid football fan, watches with wide, almost starstruck eyes as the football icon dons the RUB insignia, pulling the helmet onto his head. We all grin. *Imagine that.*

The following night we play a private backyard party for a small family in Spokane. Gear is hauled uphill over fifty yards of grass under the afternoon sun for set up beneath two pop tents. We eat homemade mac and cheese. We change our clothes in an office study in the back of the home. Three sets are performed in front of maybe twenty people, then we haul the gear down the long lawn, load the vehicles, and journey to our homes. A smoke-red moon hangs in the passenger window.

We set up our gear with a couple of roadies on one of the Coeur d'Alene cruise ships for an evening performance. We are told, while loading our stages up the narrow staircase, that the show sold out.

A long line of people stretch down the dock and out to the parking lot as the sun falls. At sunset we start motoring south toward Beauty Bay. We play *Boys of Summer* as the lake washes to reds and golds. The air slowly cools. Activating the smoke machine at my left foot, I notice several people panic seeing the white vapor—as if the boat is on fire. Cristopher eases their fears and points out the special effect. I tell the audience that they are seeing *love smoke*. *Love smoke* becomes the phrase of the evening. We hear later that our friends Paul and Shannon could hear us from their lake cabin as we passed by. I throw seven sticks high into the air. I lose only one over the side.

Halfway through the show I lift my phone between songs, activate the video camera, and say to the audience, "My mom says hello, will you say hi to Mom?" A wave of joy explodes from the crowd as they wave and send Mom kisses. I pan the camera across the front of the stage catching as many faces as I can. I text the movie to Dad.

On a rare night out, Sheree and I stop off at a quiet bar and order drinks. We sit close together in a corner table and try to make sense of the speed of the summer days, the pace of show to show, work day to work day, and we consider pulling up our phone calendars to see if there's a slight chance we can escape up to Priest Lake for a couple of days before the season ends. It's hard to find a group of days that work. The curse of the musician's life: we work weekends.

A couple of old friends pass by our table to say hello. One of them, a guy I went to high school with, asks me, "Hey, you still playing drums?" As he poses the question, he raises his hands up and does a little air-drum pantomime with a bemused grin. When I tell him *yes*, he shakes his head with amazement. "Man, *that's fun*, right?" He sits down with his drink, "But what are you doing for work these days?" Sheree stirs slightly in her seat. I raise my hands and do a little air-drum-roll as an answer. "No shit?" he says. His tone is skeptical.

I ask him, "Are you still an accountant?" I lift my hands and pantomime tapping on a computer keyboard. Sheree giggles. He giggles. "Yeah," he says.

"What are *you* doing for work?" I ask.

We both laugh.

Sundays are often blurry—a thick, heady mix of fatigue, hangover, and lack of sleep. I try to rest between weed eating, mowing the lawn, or repairing a broken air conditioner. Mondays I'm studiously back at my desk from early morning until late afternoon editing, journaling, and compiling scene ideas that I believe will eventually be a pilot script for the Trilogy. Andreas and I meet to discuss the advanced reader's copy (ARC) of my third book, *The Shape of Rain*. We start sketching out plans for an event to celebrate its release. For most of each week my hands are stiff. The joints of my fingers are sore—a condition coined as the musician's bane, *swollen hand blues* in the song *Nobody*

Home by Pink Floyd (at least, that's how I've always translated that line). I do, indeed, *got those swollen hand blues.* I can still type without any issues, of course, but it is vexing when I must pause every couple of paragraphs to stretch. Michael, Sheree, and I make dinners, watch movies in the evenings. We take bike rides whenever possible. We shoot arrows at a makeshift target in the back yard. Some afternoons we sit on the porch and stare up into Walter's leafy limbs spreading out a blanket of shadow over the house. I tell them both how much I am looking forward to autumn.

"Autumn is coming," I whisper.

Then it's showtime again.

CHAPTER 17

SHADOWS

In early July I receive a call from Dad. He tells me that Mom fell on top of him in the garage while he was assisting her out of the car. It is not the first time she has taken a tumble. On this occasion, her ankle twisted, leaving her unable to walk. Dad sustained a minor strain to his back trying to keep her from the fall. While Mom's balance has been a subject of conversation for over five years, the newly diagnosed frontal lobe dementia and its aggressive symptoms have now kicked in. Things can only get worse. At the hospital Dad talked with the doctor and had to make the difficult decision to move her to an assisted living facility. The family rushed in to support. Over the following days Mom is checked into Guardian Angel Retirement Community.

The walls in her room are a fading-rose pink. The carpet is ash grey. Dad has moved in her comfortable burgundy recliner from home. He's brought a few framed pictures of family—her makeup kit—her bathrobe.

Mom is angry, scared, and confused as to why she cannot be in her house. She has forgotten about her fall. She's forgotten about all of the falls she's had. This of course is a terrible problem because when she stands up intending to walk to the kitchenette, the bathroom, or over to her bed, her knees buckle and she falls again. Residents have been experimenting with pressure alarms on her chair and her bed that go off with a high pitched squeal when she rises. So far the horrible siren hasn't done anything but frighten her more.

Sheree and I visit. Dad sits beside her, looking spent but focused. His skin is grey and I'm struck that he's not had a good night's rest for what seems like years.

"What time did you get here today, Dad?" I ask him.

"Breakfast time, I stay until lunch. Then I come back before dinner and we eat together. Once we get her settled back into her room, I head home."

We try to have a conversation with Mom, but she is irritated and resentful. Out the window a huge maple tree sways gently with the summer breeze. Across the street is a summer-abandoned middle school.

This isn't the first time Mom has had to face an assisted living situation. Twice before we had to make the difficult decisions to move her into a facility due to similar circumstances. In short, Dad simply cannot lift her if there is a fall. But amazingly, twice, she found her way home by regaining her strength.

While we hope for a similar outcome this time, the latest dementia diagnosis looms black over our thoughts.

Dad rises and leans down to give her a kiss. "I'll be back in a couple of hours," he tells her. Fear claws at her eyes as he leaves the room.

When the door closes, I attempt to distract—I try to tell Mom about the new book coming out and the craziness of our band schedule. Squinting at me, she tries to follow along. Sheree's phone buzzes. She steps out into the front lobby to take the call.

Mom looks around as if to make sure we're alone. Tears in her eyes, "I want to go home," she whimpers. "I want to go home. I'm not supposed to be here. Tell Dad to get me out of here. I'm not old enough to be here. Everyone is old here. I'm not that old."

"Mom, I—"

"You have to do this for me. I don't want to be here. I don't want to be old." She reaches for my hand and squeezes.

Suddenly, I'm twelve. I'm sitting on my bed in my childhood home.

"Mom," I say, tears rising, "I don't want to grow up. I don't want to get old."

A poster of the band Queen blurs in my vision. The Beatles, too, are distorted through my wet eyes. Above, in the corner ceiling, a Kenner toy X-Wing banks and positions behind a TIE

Fighter—both ships dangle from thumb tacks and fishing line. On my desk beside the closet is an open notebook filled with letters of some ancient language I am inventing. Rush's *2112* sits motionless on the turntable. Tolkien's 1970s boxed set of the *Lord of the Rings* presides over the scene on the highest shelf. My first toy drum set, the Galaxy 3000, is huddled beside the door.

Mom sits on the bedside. She is healthy and bright—blue eyes, long limbs, and fair skin. I hold her hand and squeeze.

"What's this?" she asks gently.

"I don't want to be old," I tell her again.

"Oh sweetheart," her fingers touch my wet cheeks. "You're not old. You have the whole world out before you. You're just beginning."

"I don't want to change," I try to explain—tears streaming. "I want to do *that*." I point to the bands on my wall, to the open notebook on my desk, to the spaceships dangling in the upper atmosphere of my bedroom.

Her smile is like starlight. Lowering herself down and leveling her eyes with mine she says simply, "You *are* doing it. You don't have to grow up, you only need to grow. Never stop doing what you love and you'll never be old."

At that moment, it all seemed possible. My interests were valuable, worth pursing, and most of all, worth living. My desire to create art wasn't kid stuff. Her words and comforting had translated into possibility and hope.

Now I sit at Mom's bedside again. Her hand is clamped to mine—hot tears of frustration stream down her pale cheeks.

"I don't want to—"

"What's this?" my voice quavers. I lie, "We're here just until you get stronger—until you can get your strength back. You're not old. We've got a lot yet to do. . . there's a world of things to —" Her eyes are empty and sad. I attempt to remind her of that time when I was a kid; when I told her I didn't want to grow up. "Do you remember that, Mom?"

She stares with a hollow expression. She squints at me and says, "No." Then, she pleads, "I don't want to die here. I can't remember how I got here."

Her two sentences appear in my mind as black and white text.

A shadow covers us.

A shadow I cannot lift.

CHAPTER 19

MEMORY

I don't speak much for the rest of the day. Back at the Burrow Sheree asks if I'm all right. My answers range from, "Sure, I'm fine," to "not in the slightest," to "meh," to "I'm losing my mom. . . not much more to say right now." The memory of sitting there beside my fading mother at Guardian Angel—that childhood bedroom moment juxtaposed with her pleading for her life, has left me stunned and ungrounded.

I pace in the backyard grass. The sunshine is vexing. I try to trace where Mom began to lose her ability to remember things. Has it been in the last year? In the last ten? Why can't *I* seem to recall? After an hour or so I go back inside.

It's not long before I realize that I've been standing at the window staring up into the summer leaves for too long. My mind is a haze of grief and confusion. What it must be like to forget. What it must be like to lose one's memory. What torture.

I conclude that it is a kind of death—an end.

I move from the window and sit at my desk. A stack of old journals crowding a lower shelf on the bookcase grabs my attention—an armload of volumes that I had excavated out of my storage unit sometime after I had built the new shelves in the Burrow's back office. Maybe ten or so, all of them worn, beaten up a bit, and used. I scan their spines, trying to remember their ages by their case color and binding style. Many of them are tour journals—a couple are daily records filled with bullet point descriptions and sketches. A good number of the journals are missing, or rather, they are still boxed up and buried somewhere in storage. There are a few that I wish were at my finger tips at this moment.

I lean toward the shelf and randomly tilt one journal out into the light. A few moments later I'm thumbing through its pages. Pencil scratched, messy, and the occasional sophomoric drawing, this one is from the year 2000.

It is strange to recall that almost a quarter of a century ago I earned an English Literature degree from Gonzaga University. A lifetime ago. Bulleted notes in the journal remind me of when, donning my academical cap and gown on graduation day, I sat with hundreds of the *first* twenty-first century GU grads and searched the crowded bleachers to locate Mom and Dad, my fiancé Lisa, my brother Bob, and my two beloved KITE bandmates, Monte and Scott. As the long ceremony wore on, the temperature in the hall rose to the nineties. Seated there, I tapped a drum beat on my knee, wondering vaguely what the humidity on the Pacific ocean must feel like; for in a little over a week I would be leaving for a two month rock tour of Guam, Korea, and Japan with another of my bands during that time: Manito. Thoughts then squirreled to the unfinished KITE album, *Lost All Age,* and its myriad puzzles of studio scheduling, incomplete parts, and the one last sonnet/lyric to finish. Then to my fast-approaching September wedding, which was being formulated and imagined as a medieval ceremony surrounded by an entire village that Scott, Monte, and I would begin to construct immediately upon my return from tour. I mean, why not?

As the esteemed US bank executive, Phyllis Campbell, gave her commencement address on innovative business development and the importance of building upon the Pacific Northwest's community values (or something near to that—memory a bit foggy), my internal sketch pad scratched out 13th century high-peaked gables framed from fallen deadwood, walls of brightly colored canvas, and a massive village gate built from live-edge mill ends—a sword fighting ring enclosed by twelve chairs and twelve flag poles—a village pub, winery, and restaurant. Before long my fellow graduates rose and formed a line to the stage. I joined them and we slowly marched to the lectern where, eventually, an artifact representing my degree was placed in my hands.

Afterward, family, friends, and I celebrated at the old-world styled Clinkerdaggers restaurant, overlooking the falls on the Spokane river.

I remember ice crackling in the scotch—the beloved gift of a handmade wooden, green velvet lined writing box. Nestled inside was an orange feathered quill, ink bottle, and quill stand. I remember Mom holding my hand at the table and smiling—she said, "You come back to me. I don't like all this touring around so far from home."

"I will," I told her.

"What memories you'll make," she sighed.

The memory reminds me I'm alive.

Flipping through a few more pages, I see that days later, I scribbled this entry:

May 21, 2000

Leaving this time around was harder than any other tour departure. With my wedding drawing near, KITE's Lost All Age aging on the anvil, and being freshly graduated from college may have a little to do with the difficulty. But here I am, once again, looking out over the Pacific Ocean in the shade of a palm, and ice cold beer, a bag of pencils and a hammock to lie in— Blissful in truth. One thing is certain: Mom, you wouldn't want to know that I'm here.

JOHNSTON ISLAND—USO Military tour. We're playing for the troops again!

From the air, this little island looks like a cracker in an enormous bowl of soup. Simply put, it is a little mound of manmade acreage in the middle of the sea. The mission for the islanders is a bit complex, and certainly unusual—something that will take me some time to get my head around. At the northeast end of this island is a chemical plant belching plumes of white smoke into the sky. Its sole purpose is to destroy weapons of mass destruction by burning. The smoke is the byproduct of nerve gas, Agent Orange and blister bombs. Fortunately for us—and for those that dwell here, this unincorporated territory of the United States is positioned in the center of the Pacific air stream. The smoke goes one way (most of the time). The architects should get a serious high-five for their foresight—for after all: proper prior planning prevents piss-poor performance (P.P.P.P.P.P., or 7P). Best not get downwind of that bad-boy, me thinks.

The island has been a nuclear test site and has had its share of accidents and contaminations. They've experimented with chemical weapons here. Biological weapons, too. Yikes.

Stranger still, the island is a wild life sanctuary—a National Wildlife refuge for a variety of various seabirds. And why not? Again, another nod to the United States for this match up. This haven, located a little distance from the plutonium waste mounds, protects the lives of some twenty different bird species—each of which has become quite accustomed to humans, so much so that they're quite comfortable with the occasional roadblock for food, *the stalking of your front door* for food, *or the stop off at the local chemical weapon blister bomb plant for a tasty snack from the dumpster sweltering in the sun. The band has been told not to interact with the birds in any way. Also, if we are to harm one of them by some unlucky circumstance, we will be escorted to the flight line and flown away without any dinner. We were told all of this by Ken, a fellow that I thought for a moment had a vague neon glow about him. After the briefing I raised my hand and asked Ken who would be punished if the wind changed directions and the deathly smoke fell over the wildlife refuge. "Would we all have to leave without dinner?" I asked.*

Without a pause or smile, he replied solemnly, "No, no. If the wind shifts, put your gas mask on and keep your blister bomb antidote syringe handy. We'll direct you to the evacuation site." At that point he provided each of the band members with a gas mask, a long-needled syringe filled with some yellowish liquid, a bottle of water, and a map of the island. "Oh," he added, eyeing our facial hair, "You'll have to shave before we take you to your lodgings." Seeing the confusion on our faces, he said, "You don't want to fuck with the integrity of your gas mask's seal. Beards'll do that." At that moment, his skin seemed to pulse electric green. We all nodded and went to the restrooms for a shave.

"It's okay," I told Ken as I rummaged through my bath kit searching for a razor. "Mom hates my beard, anyway."

Leaning back in my chair, I close my eyes. I remember more about that day: the white bird that warbled to me from the branches of a tree just above the hammock where I wrote the entry—Cristopher and I walking to pick up snorkeling gear so we could explore the reef—barbecues wafting the smell of cooking meat—the crossing of a narrow strip of aquamarine chop to a nearby island and tip-toeing among a hundred-thousand birds nesting beneath the sky—bird shit on my shoes. Laughing and laughing and laughing with Dave.

I remember. I close the cover.

The memory reminds me I'm alive.

I reach up and randomly pull another down. More blurry pencil scratches and poorly executed sketches. This one is from 1996, chronicling another Department of Defense rock tour. I shake my head at the first inscriptions: *Post Desert Shield—Saudi Arabia—Kuwait—Bahrain—U.A.E.—Portugal, Azores.*

This was Manito's first overseas military tour. Over a month's time, the band played shows for U.S. soldiers still in harm's way after the relatively short Gulf War of the early nineties. I grin, thinking about how *not thrilled* Mom was concerning the still seething, war trembling region of the world that I was about to be catapulted into. "We're with the best of the best," I told her, "we're going to be just fine." It wasn't a surprise for her to be worried, but I when I noted a slight blench in Dad's reaction to the news, I realized I may not be internalizing the very true dangers I was headed toward—armed with only drumsticks and songs. Dad simply said, in his quiet authoritative way, "Mind your surroundings and be careful."

I scan a few entries. Here's one:

November 2, 1996

This morning we were met by Sgt. Chris and Sgt. Woody, both sporting serious crew cuts, and they ushered us into one of three gleaming black Blazers. These two men were much more serious than others we had met so far, as if they were dealing with a hidden pressure—in spite of their calm demeanor—and crew cuts —they were hard to read. Then the answer came. . .

They said hello. We said hello back. Then, they busted out some bullet proof vests and steel helmets. "Put these on," they said with weird smiles. "Your safety is assured, but these vests are just a precaution."

We nodded, trying to fit the idea of assured safety *and* precaution *into some kind of sense. Wrestling the heavy body armor, we laughed nervously. "Do you have a vest in purple?" I asked Sgt. Woody. He said, without a smile, "No."*

As we crossed the base, the two men informed us on some of the perils beyond the fences. Things like roadside bombs *and* snipers. *There was much more discussed, but something about roadside bombs and snipers seemed to eclipse everything else— that is why I'm scribbling only* roadside bombs *and* snipers *into the journal currently.*

Passing through the perimeter of the final gate to the outside, I noticed my entire body chill, a rush of excitement, and a strange comfort while entering into an uncertain future—like a childhood experience but with real danger attached. It was the way the focused gate guard said before he closed the gate behind us, "Good luck."

I think I loved that feeling. I think. . .

The memory reminds me I am alive.

I thumb a few more pages in—a few more collected moments, hours, days. Then there's this:

November 11, 1996

Sgt. Pat: "It is always advantageous to look as officious as possible."

Me: "Especially when machine guns are involved."

Security is doubly tight. We are in Kuwait—and since Iraqi forces have been driven north and out of the city, there are still real dangers to watch for. That's what Pat says. And I believe Pat. The more identification tags and official paperwork one wears stuck to one's forehead the better.

Yesterday we were invited to play at perhaps the most dangerous place in Kuwait during this time, Camp Buehring. From this northernmost U.S. post, the Sixth Brigade watches the Iraqi border some twenty-five clicks away (fifteen miles). Pat says its really the front line. Indeed, we weren't actually on the "wire" as Pat puts it, but we were definitely closer than any civilian can get. The mood was, to put it mildly, austere.

After another wrestling match with bulky body armor and helmets, we were loaded onto a tour bus with three heavily armed soldiers joining the band: one at the front of the bus, the other in back, seated next to the rear exit, and lastly, the driver, silent and focused. Pulling out into the courtyard we inserted into a convoy between two covered military trucks both filled with armed soldiers, and two Humvee (High Mobility Multipurpose Wheeled Vehicles), both with rooftop machine guns turrets. There was another good luck *offered by the gatekeepers, and we sped off at over-the-top speeds passing through stop-light intersections as if we were emergency vehicles, onto the six lane Highway 80 that ran north to Iraq. This highway, we were informed prior to our departure, had become known as* The Highway of Death. *Gulp.*

Here's what Wikipedia has to say about the Highway of Death:

During the American-led coalition offensive in the Persian Gulf War, American, Canadian, British and French aircraft and ground forces attacked retreating Iraqi military personnel attempting to leave Kuwait on the night of February 26–27, 1991, resulting in the destruction of hundreds of vehicles and the deaths of many of their occupants. Between 1,400 and 2,000 vehicles were hit or abandoned on the main Highway 80 north of Al Jahra. The scenes of devastation on the road are some of the most recognizable images of the war, and it has been suggested that they were a factor in President George H. W. Bush's decision to declare a cessation of hostilities the next day.

Five years later, the destruction remains. We passed hundreds of burned out, bombed, and bullet-pierced cars, trucks, and busses left tumbled and piled along the roadsides. It is beyond my ability to describe the feelings as our convoy sped by—on our way to sing songs—spread smiles.

And very few smiled or greeted us as we arrived at the base. Even as Sgt. Pat toured us through the command center, no one seemed to care that a band was about to perform that evening. They acknowledged us and were as gracious as they could be, I suspect, but it was easy to see that their thoughts were elsewhere. Gas masks hung from everyone's uniform. Weapons were in every soldier's grip. All were locked and loaded. We, too, were given gas masks and told to keep them close—even on stage. Gulp.

The wind was strong in the desert that afternoon and flying sand pelted us as we set up on the back of a flatbed trailer within a horseshoe enclosure of multi-storied concrete billets. A small area behind the stage was put in place for us to keep our bags— there were bottles of water and soda—some covered trays of vegetables. As the sun began to set and the courtyard seats filled up, I couldn't believe what I was seeing. Each and every audience member was carrying a gleaming black weapon—most of them were loaded machine guns.

After we were politely introduced, "Welcome Manito, all the way from Spokane, Washington!" and a strangely murmured cheer wafted over the stage, our charismatic and always optimistic frontman, Dave, offered our thanks for the invitation and our sincere appreciation for their service, shared how excited we were to perform for them, and then added, "We'd like to start by taking a request. Because you're all armed, we'll play whatever you want." That got a laugh. The first laugh we'd heard since we crossed over their fence.

So we started in.

Never before have I felt like I did that night. Never has music communicated so strongly or eloquently. These songs suddenly meant more than they did before. Each melody was a shared memory. Each chorus was a piece of home. Soldiers were on their feet dancing with their weapons, pumping fists, singing along— simply wonderful and surreal. We were doing our job, and doing what we came to do, take them home for a short while—escape the danger for a few hours—remember joy.

Our final song was the Eagles' Hotel California. Landing on the final note I stood up from behind my kit and waved to the smiles and the guns waving at me—the weirdest damn thing—I crossed the back of the stage and descended back to our greenroom spot. I was winded, sweating, and feeling the adrenaline rush from the show and the enthusiastic audience. Looking to my right, I was startled by a large figure I hadn't noticed, a few feet away. Towering there was a young African American man, roughly seven feet tall, ammunition bandoliers crisscrossed his chest, an M60 machine gun cradled in his arms, and, oddly, shining tears running down his cheeks. He stood staring at me.

"Hi," I breathed, still trying to catch my breath from the finale, "I didn't see you there."

He didn't respond right away, but after a moment he said, "Man, I fuckin' love that song Hotel California." His voice quavered slightly. His eyes became glassier. "Reminds me of home. I fuckin' wanna go home, man." He couldn't be much older than eighteen. He's just a kid.

"I love that song, too," I told him.

We chatted for a few minutes about Southern California and where he lived and where I had lived for a short year of my life in the early 90s. For a moment we shared memories of the beach, drives down the Pacific Coast Highway at dusk, relishing, curiously enough, the perfume of L.A. smog. Before we parted, he back to his duties and me back to mine, he pulled me into a bear hug of an embrace and said, "Thank you for coming to play, man. Means more to me and all the guys than you'll ever know. We'll never forget it."

I told him that I would never forget it either and I thanked him for his courage and his spirit. I told him, "You'll be back on the beach soon."

We've always known this was our mission, we musicians from home. We bring song and light, we bring home with us, and we bring memories both old and new—and tonight, surrounded by the dark dangers just beyond the fence line, we feel like we're truly doing our job.

I'm not able to define or describe the wonders I'm experiencing/seeing/living on this tour—on any tour for that matter. There is always more to the picture—I simply want to reflect these things with as much accuracy and emotion as I can. To capture the memory—so others might share through what I record—and, of course, so I won't forget. I wish I could see more clearly. A dream I have, perhaps—but I'll keep trying. I think my friend Cary would understand. He recently said to me: "Once a dreamer, always a dreamer."

The memory reminds me I am alive.

I slide the journal between its companions on the shelf and rotate my chair to the sunlit window. All of that was decades ago. It is marvelous that Cary's name appeared in that random entry. Makes me smile. I wonder if he had invented the word *gigmentia* by then?

I close my eyes. The spiral notebook containing my first writings on becoming a drummer enters my thoughts. I was fourteen. At the top of the page I had written, *Diary of a*

Drummer. I stand, cross the room, and rifle through a couple of boxes. *Voilà.*

December, 1983
Not much to write considering the band is at a basic stand still. And I do stress, The Band. *Us three guys haven't been able to come up with a name yet. My brother Bob is on bass, and Robert is on guitar. Anyway, as it turns out, we sound pretty good.*

I wish I had more time to play. I want to get good.

    I get a chill. I still wish I had more time to play. And write. I still want to get good.

    Oscar Wilde's quote: "Memory... is the diary that we all carry about with us," comes to mind suddenly. Glancing back up to the journals on the shelf, I try to work out just how this fascination with keeping memories scribbled onto paper became important to me. Was it some elementary school teacher, Mrs. Bohanek, Mrs. Dennis, or Mr. Squitcherino, that first suggested the practice? Was it my Uncle Stan whose lifelong love affair with the written word influenced me? Is it the love of poetry and lyrics—specifically well-crafted rock music lyrics? Or all of the liner notes and tour books and tales of traveling musicians? Is it because I love the idea that J.R.R. Tolkien wrote a story about Bilbo Baggins writing his adventures into a red leather-bound book, and later passing it to his nephew, Frodo Baggins, to finish (not to mention Frodo passing the pages to Samwise Gamgee in the end)?

    Or is it some fearful understanding that is buried deep within me that says, *Without memories there is only death—without memories there is nothing.* Mom's memory is fading. All of my grandparents suffered dementia. I should just accept it: I, too, will likely face it one day—or rather, it will face me. I wonder if I will recognize its face. *Without memories, there is only death.* I wrinkle my nose at the thought and chuckle lightly. *Take it easy there, fella,* my mind says, *that's a little heavy, don't you think? Lighten up.*

Maybe it is time for a scotch. I look at the clock. It is after three. Yes. Then I remember a loved joke:

If Alcohol can damage your short term memory,
Imagine the damage Alcohol can do.

Cheers, Mom.

CHAPTER 20

SHOWRUN #2

The RUB plays on. From backyards, to big rock lounges, to one of my favorite kinds of venues: the tiny shoebox room with a bar.

In the late 1980s, the small town of Sandpoint, Idaho had a vibrant music scene and was often called Coeur d'Alene's stoned, hippy sister (well, we used to say that). Blues groups, singer-song writers, jam bands, and the occasional hard rock act performed at a number of venues there on weekends year-round. Unfortunately these days, many of those great bars have shifted to DJs or have done away with live music altogether. Today, however, a small club on Sandpoint's main street, or First Avenue, has taken up the legacy. The 219 Lounge was once the ultimate nicotine stained, dollar bill wall-papered, ashtray flavored, hangover decorated, slurred-speech church-dive-bar of dreams. A place that scared most women. Up until the first decade of the twenty-first century, it was the late night coffin nail for barflies and the last stop for last call after all the other bars closed. Hazed with cigarette smoke, the room glowed with neon red light, the ceilings were low, and the booths and dark nooks aroused the Bukowski of every would-be drinker, whether they knew who Bukowski was or not. Our group of friends seldom called the bar by its given name, the 219. Instead we chose a title more apt to its effect and beastly appearance. We called it the 666.

Later, because of so many wonderful (and seedy) times spent there, we removed its devilish reputation and upgraded its name to 667: neighbor of the beast.

Now, in this century, new ownership came in and bathed the beast. And it cleaned up nicely. Ceilings were raised, exposing the early twentieth century tresses, brick work, and aged wood. Paint, new floors, new ventilation and air conditioning, a glistening wall of alcohol, and voilà, most women weren't afraid anymore. While I'll always miss the weirdness of the old dive bar, The 667, the new place still has some ghosts to remind us of its past—most of which is found in the room's vibration. Remember, I said Sandpoint is the hippy sister. That's right, the room has vibe—and to make it truly shake, just play music.

Upon The RUB's arrival that hot July afternoon, the bartender wears a wide-brimmed cowboy hat and thick glasses. He sets out three shots of tequila and welcomes us with big smiles and genuine excitement. We've played here a couple of times before, and like the bartender, we know how the vibration is going to rattle the beast tonight.

This is the gig that's standing room only and well over capacity. This is the show where the beer is mist in the air. This is the performance that takes place both on stage and amid the throng of howling, singing, gyrating music fanatics. This is the small town bar where you don't want to stop playing until the police show up and make you stop. This is a show where bass and drums are locked together and the machine crashes through the room—all the way out the front door to the line of people waiting for the chance to get in. These kinds of tiny venues and shows are truly, unequivocally what rock and roll is, and should always be: celebration, elevation, communion.

The next day, Sheree and I are driving across the gridded yellow fields of the Palouse on our way to the Coeur d'Alene Casino. A little hungover. A little fatigued. And to tell true, a bit of dread hangs in the center of my stomach for the show to come.

Casinos are, well, lame.

I know better than to preface a performance with such negativity, but I've not yet played a casino and felt satisfied with the outcome. Always, it seems, after leaving a casino, I feel as if I've lost something. This is likely the way most people feel, though I don't gamble. In fact, there's a monetary reward for bands that play casinos—the gigs pay well, and that's nice, to be sure. But there's a cost. It occurs to me suddenly that I might very well be gambling by performing amid the din of chiming bells, flashing slot machine lights, and focused poker faces—maybe I'm gambling with my soul.

Never mind all that. I turn to Sheree and say, "At least load in will be easy—tonight we're using the lounge's full backline."

Another fringe benefit for most casino gigs—this lounge has full PA, lights, guitar and bass amps, and a top of the line DW drum kit and cymbals—all ready for us to step on stage, quickly sound check, and perform without the tedium of hauling, lifting, tinkering, and assembling. A refreshing thing: to plug and play.

After we're ready to go, Cristopher, Sheree, and I sit at the bar and watch and listen to the shuffling, ringing, whooping commotion that is a casino floor. I can't help but think of Mom and one of her favorite pastimes: slot machines. She would often invite me to come down to this casino to gamble with her—I would decline saying, "Casinos are lame." She'd grin mischievously and reply, "Not with me, I win. I'm lucky." I notice a woman about Mom's age a few feet away feeding a machine coins. The thing gobbles from her hand happily.

The show is strange in comparison to the night before. This state of the art music venue was created and built for rock shows but alas, the room has no vibe (or maybe the wrong vibe). Surrounding us is the contrived excitement of beeping and hooting gambling machines and plumes of blue cigarette smoke. Most gamblers tend to give off a sad disposition—a yearning undefined—and they don't vibe well with live music. This is mainly due to the sole fact that they didn't come here for music. They'll wander in to get a drink, sit, and listen for a few minutes while they assess the damage they've just done to their bank account—wrestling with their belief in luck.

Nevertheless, we believe in brightening things up as best we can, and a casino should not be an exception. Though the audiences are not huge, we play with everything we have, as usual. Cristopher's father, David, arrives with a few other members of Cristopher's family. Our friend from Schweitzer Ski Resort, Andrea Bates, joins us on stage to sing The Who's, *Baba O'Riley*—which always gives me chills.

We play the next night as well. The audience has tripled, which is nice. But still, it's a casino.

Then comes another show at Borracho, our favorite downtown Spokane venue. My journal only says this:

Borracho—packed patio. Blurry, hot, loud, good.

The following night we perform another charity show for the Community Cancer Fund at the Coeur d'Alene Resort Golf Course on the lake. On the bill are a couple of other bands, one of which consists of good friends of ours, the band Royale.

Another bulleted journal entry.

Community Cancer Fund show—Golf carted in gear. Full backline—Josh Fry from Royale provided a wonderful vintage kit to play. Sky is clear blue. Hot. Why is the stage facing a golf green? Who are we playing for? Lots of very wealthy people here. Ended show with Pink Floyd's Comfortably Numb. *Seemed appropriate. Proved affective.*

From golf course to a mountain top wedding reception—I stare out from high over Lake Pend Oreille from Schweitzer ski resort as a black storm cell crosses the valley. Lighting flashes. Thunder rumbles. The heat of the day is uncanny.

We dress in what Cristopher calls our rock and roll formal attire—which for my band mates is their usual stage clothes with the addition of a suit jacket, or substituting the ripped jeans for not-so-ripped jeans. For me, I'm always somewhat formal. I straighten the tie around my neck, finish adjusting the drums, and step out onto the deck to feel the rain on my face. I see Cary napping on a ski lift chair beneath an awning. Below, on the emerald grass, the bride in white and the groom in black walk hand-in-hand under the slate grey sky. She raises one arm, as if feeling the drops on her palm. I imagine her saying to her soon-to-be husband, *Rain on your wedding day is good luck.* That makes me smile.

CHAPTER 22

A PLAN, OR, PLAN A

"You about split me in two," Mom tells me, strangely alert and focused today. "I thought your shoulders would tear me apart." I look at Sheree with an embarrassed smile. "Birthing your brother was one thing, but you, Michael, you about killed me." I shake my head. "Mom. . ." I whine as I squint, trying to shake the image out of my head.

For the last half hour, Sheree, Mom and I have been talking about our kids. Sheree spoke of her three children and her three grandchildren. Mom watched Sheree's mouth. I wondered if she was connecting the dots or if somewhere in Sheree's stories, she lost track and gave up. But after Sheree got into the stories of birthing her children and her gratitude for the relatively easy child labor she experienced with all three, Mom's attention perked up. Then she pointed her finger at me and blurted out, "You about split me in two!"

We all laughed.

She carried on, "You came out bald as a billiard ball. Big eyes." And she continued to share details of my coming into the world that only she could share. Only she could know. Of course she had shared these memories many times over the years, but these days it is a comfort beyond comforts to hear her speak about something that I feel certain dementia cannot drive from her—likely because such memories don't reside in her mind but rather in her heart. She tells of the difficulty with my eyes as a baby—that I had to be placed in an oxygen tent for a couple of weeks—falling off a chair, cutting my lip, and having to get stitches—when I broke my arm—then later, my other arm—that I was always scribbling in a notebook. . . A mom loving hard on her kid. As she spoke I noticed that she was speaking mainly to Sheree. And Sheree, like a mom will, followed along with deep empathy, feeling each memory as if it were her own.

"And you weren't supposed to be a boy," Mom says.

"I know," I agree.

"You were supposed to be Dawn Michelle. That was the plan," she says grinning.

"Didn't mean to wreck the plan," I mutter.

"Well," she says after a long blink and a glance at the abandoned middle school across the street. "There was a miscarriage between you and your brother, you know. Maybe that was my Dawn, maybe not." She sighs, "None of that was in the plan, either."

She pauses and asks about my Michael. I tell her that he is doing fine and that he is over at his Mom's. "His birthday is tomorrow," I add.

"Oh, how exciting." She looks at Sheree, "Now, his birth was scary. That plan didn't go as planned."

I nod and say, "No, not quite."

"But it all came out good in the end."

"Yes," I agree.

"Have you told Michael about all that?" Mom asks.

I shrug, "Kind of. It's a little above his pay grade at the moment, but I'm sure one day he'll appreciate the tale."

A shadow crosses Mom's face. "Share the memory, honey, so you don't forget. So he won't forget." Then she offers an uncomfortable smile, "When is his birthday?"

"Tomorrow, Mom. Tomorrow he'll be ten."

A decade ago, life was quite different.

The memory floods back.

2008, SUMMER

The little one's arrival is weeks away. His room is freshly painted. So are all the other rooms in the house. We thumb through kid accessory catalogues, we buy plastic bottles and fuzzy baby blankets—we make sure the insurance is in order. A pink sticky note of to-dos hangs on the refrigerator door—several of the tasks are checked off. At the bottom is the due date in big, bubbly, purple letters: *Four weeks and counting!!!!* Yes, with *four* exclamation marks—right and proper.

The birthing plan has been sketched out, inked, and rehearsed. A water birth is on Lisa's wish list, and we're both envisioning a claw foot tub, candle glow through steam, and a tray of strawberries and chocolate beside the door.

No doctors or sterile florescent hospital lights—rather, delivery in a home, with lace curtains, lavender rice pillows, and only myself, midwives and Lisa's mother, gently chanting the baby into this world. Instead of numbing the experience with drugs, Lisa will rely on the meditative states she has studied and practiced. Her doula's training over the last few months has inspired both of us to see childbirth as, well, natural. A *natural* childbirth. Something women have been doing since the beginning of time. Of course, if anything complicated transpires, we have a plan B. But we won't allow negative thoughts to pull us away from the vision. We want things to go according to our plan. Isn't that what everyone attempts? Lisa's only concern is not knowing the intensity of the forecasted pain, and if she can bear it. My only concern is Lisa and the coming wee one, and making sure that things go as close to the plan as possible. And it is a good plan. A very good plan. Plan A.

It is a late July Sunday afternoon. We sit in the shade of the house with our bare feet pressing down into the cooling grass. Lisa, myself and the band (and the band wives) are planning KITE's upcoming performances at *Montana's Rocking The Rivers Music Festival*, four days from now. Every summer the Jefferson River canyon sprouts a small city of camper trailers, big speakers, rock fans and rock musicians, and this year KITE is on the bill. And as we discuss the logistics, I can see the dust clouds already, and I can feel the sweltering weight of the sun on that wide open space. Under that wide open sky. The throngs of buzzed and staggering three day concert campers. The sharp wafting of porta potty stench. And I suddenly notice that I am sensing it all through Lisa. Eight months pregnant in the heat is challenging, but facing three days at a rock festival with limited facilities and the unsavory above notations is something to certainly prepare for. I smile considering our *birthing plan*. If only our *touring rock band plan* had candles, strawberries and steam. Maybe one day.

Each of us is feeling wary about her going on this trip, but no one speaks of it. The band, KITE: Monte, Scott, Mark, and myself, have discussed worst case scenarios and emergency plans, but we are convinced that the little bundle of joy will be arriving only when he is *supposed* to—not during our first, second or even third performance at the show. Mark, however, our consummate strategist, shares that he's researched the medical resources at the event as well as the distance and time to the nearest hospital. Just in case. . .

Accompanying us on this quick trip will be Lisa, Dani, and Scott's sister Tami and his mom, Barb. Barb and Tami have graciously offered the use of their space-ship motor home as a soft spot for Lisa to relax during the event. We sit in a circle on the soft grass, sipping cocktails. It is hot. Food lists: hamburgers, buns, pickles, cheese, condiments—eggs and pancakes for breakfast. Beer. Lisa requests watermelon. Lots of watermelon. Our friend Jeff will come too. He says he will supply the tequila —and tacos. We love tacos.

Lisa stands up and rubs along her navel.

Gear lists: drum kit, cables, mics, instruments, monitors, amps, pedal boards, rear screen projection gear. Et cetera.

We talk a bit about the new record and I share the difficulty that I've been having with a particular lyric. The band seems to like what I've already submitted but I'm not convinced that I've arrived at the right words. I tell them that I'm getting closer to a final version. Scott begins scribbling down songs for the set list and we all try to hear the starts and endings in our heads, and just how they fade into each other.

Lisa begins to wander out into Barb's and Tami's summer bloomed garden. She trails through geraniums, yellowwood, full moon maple, ginkgo, Russian sage, woolly thyme—lush flower beds and exotic trees heavy with drooping, late summer green. The lavender is swollen purple and fragrant. I watch her while listening to Barb tell of some of the spaceship's features. Onboard toilet, full kitchen, soft beds, entertainment center, and most importantly, air conditioning. *I should cut some of that lavender*, I think.

After a few more minutes and some debate as to the time we should leave, we finish the meeting. We put our glasses in the kitchen, we make a round of hugs and we walk to the car. Lisa is restless. She suggests that we rent a movie. On the way home we stop and wander around the video store. We rent two movies and return home. She is anxious.

When I wake up, she is standing beside the couch. She looks concerned. Her eyes are tired—afraid.

She says, "I don't want to freak you out, but I think I am having contractions." I sit up. Dazed. The movie isn't yet over. *When did I fall asleep? Is it the same day?*

"You're what?"

She tells me again. It registers, but I don't feel panic. I stand. "There must be some mistake. We're weeks away."

She nods. "I know that."

Of course she knows that.

We time the contractions. "Are they getting closer? Am I doing this right?" I wonder aloud.

"Maybe we should call," Lisa suggests.

I agree.

Braxton Hicks, false contractions, the burrito from lunch—any and all—the phone call to Lisa's midwife didn't have any conclusive, relaxing answers. We carry on monitoring, biting our nails—hoping that it is indeed a false alarm. I hear the ice-cream man jingling past our house. The pavement is cooling. The angle of the sunset is shimmering gold in the window. Lisa is lying on the bed. The air conditioner is heaving what cold air it can manage. I bring an ice cold towel and lay it across her brow. She smiles. She is worried. I call the midwife again.

I hang up and say: "Wine and a bath."

"What?" Lisa asks.

"Two of your favorite things," I say, smiling. "She says that if you drink some wine, it should slow or stop the contractions, that is, if it's a false alarm."

"What if it's not a false alarm?"

I consider this. "If it isn't meant to be—well—" I figured that she could fill in the blanks. Those blanks we never seem to fill in.

I draw the bath. I bring the wine. Lisa lowers her self down into the warm water. "Here," I hand her the wine. She takes a sip. A few minutes pass. Another contraction. Another sip. We don't talk. I hold her hand. "I think you really need to *drink* the wine." She takes a sip. "No, really take a drink." She eyes the wine cautiously. The red, medicinal juice—something she had not been able to enjoy for nearly nine months.

"Are you sure?" she asks.

"Yes." I say. I am in no way, *sure*.

Lisa takes a long pull from the earthen goblet. My uncle gave us those goblets, I think. At our wedding, I guess. Her swollen belly rises out of the water like a round stone. A dribble of wine drips down her chin into the water. She winces as another contraction comes on. I take the goblet and hold her hand.

A minute passes.

When she pulls her head away from the toilet bowl, she doesn't glare at me—she merely shrugs slightly and says, "I wasn't expecting that. I don't think I can drink the wine."

Apparently not. The toilet water is red. I flush it. She steps back into the tub and lies back.

The contractions seem to be lessening. They are sometimes five minutes apart, sometimes three. The light is failing. Night is climbing into the trees. I help her out of the bath and into bed. Still the AC is coughing, but at least it is somewhat cool. I pull a sheet over her and begin to consider our birthing plan. We have not yet packed the bag—but I've a good idea of what's needed: the tooth brushes, a couple of T-shirts, and the camera. The embroidered baby blanket that Lisa herself stitched together— miscellaneous toiletries—all into a bag. The cicadas are singing. One of our cats disappears into the kitchen like a fading shadow. I place the bag beside the door. I set the keys on top of the bag. I climb into bed beside her. I listen to her breathing. Another contraction and she stiffens. The AC puffs. I think I fall asleep, but it is imagined. Her hand reaches beneath the sheets and grips mine. Another contraction. Can this be happening? We've weeks until he's to arrive. What does this mean? But in spite of all the questions, I am strangely optimistic. *All will be well*, something inside me keeps saying.

So what. So the plan will be slightly different. I can still get the chocolate and the strawberries. And we *did* get a bath in. So the baby didn't arrive in the bath—but there was a bath—and bonus: a glass of wine. Alright, so it didn't go down perfectly— but no real harm done. A little vomit and all fixed. And certainly better now than in the middle of a thousand people during a rock performance—with only a wet wipe and a bottle of hand sanitizer for clean up.

I wonder briefly if I should call Scott and tell him that we should cancel. I push the thought away when Lisa sits up. I look at the clock. It is a little after four in the morning. "I think we should call again."

I flip the phone open. I dial. She is squinting from the bright bedside lamp, rubbing her eyes. We get the same advice: *wait and see*.

We struggle for sleep between contractions. We fail.

It is sometime around 9AM. I drive fast, but not too fast. I'm still bleary eyed, but alert. Lisa shifts uncomfortably in her seat. I turn to take a route behind a strip mall. It is a short cut that I thought clever when making the *driving plan*. After the first lurching speed bump, Lisa howls, "DON'T do that again!"

I curse myself. Why didn't I think of that before? *Speed bumps.* At the next bump I imagine the car to be Luke Skywalker's landspeeder and I gingerly edge it over the cement rib. She doesn't respond.

We halt at the longest red light in the history of red lights. When it labors itself to green, I mash the pedal to the floor and squeal the car around the corner and into the hospital parking lot. We arrive at the emergency room.

This wasn't in the plan.

The ER at the hospital was the last place we wanted to be.

The policy for the midwifery stated that a premature birth must take place in a hospital. *Good sense,* I think. But bad news for plan A. I try to keep Lisa in good spirits. We check in, we take the elevator up, and I start to make the calls to family and friends.

As we enter the room, I see it. "There's a bath tub in here!" I say.

And so there is. It is no time before I get the relaxing songs playing on our tiny CD player (Sting's John Dowland covers) and we get her into the tub. *There is still the chance of a water birth* —I can see her thinking. Lisa's mother Geri arrives, as do Scott and Dani. Dani sits tub side and glides her hand over Lisa's trembling tummy.

The wall-sized windows are photo-grey, but their shade cannot hide the depth of the July blue sky. I sit in the *tad-too-short-to-sleep-on* couch along the windowed wall and shake my head at it. Just another foot added on to the end could change the spirits of an exhausted father (note to architects: some people are six feet tall). The hospital's ventilation system hushes the room with an even breeze of synthetic cool. The weird, recycled air scent. Hanging tubes, stacked boxes of latex gloves, glass cylinders full of cotton swabs, locked drawers, metal trays with sharp stainless instruments—a big plastic bottle with white letters: ALCOHOL. My mind flashes to a glass of scotch. The hospital bed is soft and can adjust to bend like a sandwich maker or a hang glider. On rolling stands are a couple of monitors. They flash lines and numbers. Neither of which I understand. No color in the room save the baby blue of the sheets and the taupe hued walls.

I hear the water turn on in the tub again.

There's a little talk between her mother, Geri and me. Nothing longer than a few utterances about the excitement or what Lisa will be needing next. The change of plans isn't mentioned. I glare at the taupe walls, hoping that by some trick I can turn them to oak panels—and the curtains to a wispy green, and the locked cabinets to a roaring hearth. But all I see is taupe. Then I see the word *taupe* in my head. Then I suddenly find that I dislike both: the color and the way the word looks. I walk back to the bathroom door and look in on Lisa. She is lying in the bath with a towel draped over her. She looks up and smiles through the steam. It is a black and white photograph.

All day long she bears contraction after clenching contraction. Her determination for a *natural* birth is still holding. She refuses pain medication. Hours pass. By four in the afternoon we can see the little one's head (*not so little,* Lisa reminds us all). She is dilated. She has pushed. Pushed hard. Over and over again. No baby. There is some concern that he is stuck. Our doctor suggests an ultrasound to determine the issue.

When the caesarian section decision is made, Lisa begins to cry. After all the precautionary steps, the right foods, the right exercise, the focused and meditative visualization, the journaling, the encouragement from friends and family, it has come to this. I attempt to turn what seems like a failure into a mere *change of plans* by reminding her about the bath—and that I can still run out and get the chocolates and the strawberries. She nods along as I trippingly console. Another contraction claws through her. Then her tearing eyes begin to glisten into smiles. She laughs lightly.

"So much for the plan. Fine." She raises her hand, offering up a high-five: "Hit me with them sweet, sweet meds, baby. Bring, it, on."

Moments later, she is groovy. At least that is what she is saying. And she loves everyone. She even thinks the taupe walls are soothing. My anxiety lessens. The doctor comes in to tell us about the procedure. As he works through the description, I can't help but think about what a *real,* natural birth might have been like in a time before *real* doctors, anesthetic, hospitals, and clean water. Back when a baby's health was determined by how bones landed in a bowl—when the best pain reliever was a leather strap for the mother to bite down upon. But a C-section, back then? I shudder to think of it. The impossible choices.

I grip the bedside. Lisa puts her hand on my forearm and groovily tells me that it will be okay.

Her head is in my hands and she is looking up at me. A blue sheet wall crosses between us and the doctor's procedure. Lisa feels nothing, but her eyes are trained on me and begging for any kind of distraction. My fingertips trace the features of her face and I attempt to casually tell her about a lyric I'd been working on. That is all I know about creating: writing and performing. Songs mostly. Some short stories. A couple of failed attempts at novels. A third novel I really would love to pursue full time. Hours and hours of molding sentences, crafting lines into verses —hoping that they make a difference to someone, somewhere. But the creation that she is about to bring to life is beyond compare. Our son, Michael.

But I still say something like: "There's this one line I can't get quite right—and it is really bothering me." She nods and seems to understand that somehow such a thing is important.

I tell her how brave she is. A clear oxygen mask is over her mouth and nose. Her doula and midwife are near at hand, "Ready to be a mama, Lisa? We're almost there."

She's coherent, she's fading, she's coherent. She tells me that it seems warm in here. I look around, searching for the nearest AC ventilation grate. I can't find it. But when the table begins to shake beneath her, her eyes gape open, pulling my face to hers.

"It's okay," I say, "he's a little wedged in there from all of the pushing."

"I'm worried," she breathes out. Then she begins to chant and call to the baby. "Michael, come on out baby. It's time to come on out. Come to mama, baby." She repeats this over and over, half awake, half droning in a kind of prayer. I feel the heat of tears in my eyes. I cradle her head, trace her hair line with my fingers, gently—slowly. "It is starting to hurt," she says. "Almost there," her doula assures us. The table quakes from side to side again, and someone says:

"He's out."

I glance up and watch the doctor hand my little pale boy to a group of nurses gathered around the receiving table. "There he is," I say, and I look down at Lisa.

Her face is pleading. "Why isn't he crying?" she asks.

The room is strangely quiet. I can't see the faces of the nurses due to their masks, but their eyes look concerned. "They are sucking the fluid out of his lungs," our midwife says. Still no sounds.

Lisa: "It is starting to hurt." She says to me, "Go make him wake up. Go make him wake up."

Doctor: "We need to put you under, Lisa."

Someone, quietly: "No pulse."

Lisa: "Not until I hear him cry. Mike, wake him up!"

I obey. I stand and cross the short distance to the receiving table. Michael's body is a translucent pale blue and stained with wide, purplish bruises. I shoulder myself into the circle of nurses and lower my face to his. He is not alive. It occurs to me that I am looking at my dead son. Lisa's head is turned toward me. Her eyes are again wide and pleading. "Mike!"

"Michael," I say, or yell. "This is your father. It is time to wake up. Wake up. Wake up!"

And somehow I think of how this wasn't in the plan: my baby boy not moving, not breathing, his little face and body smashed. And somehow the line in that lyric that I'd been having trouble with suddenly seems easy to grasp. I finish the line in my head—because that is what you do—you keep going—you don't give up when nothing seems to make sense—when things don't go as planned. You roll with it. You take it as it comes. You stay on target. You don't let go. The show must go on. This, I guessed, was my first lesson of fatherhood, and my first words to my son.

"Wake up! It is time to wake up. We've so many things to do and see. . ."

There is a sputter. His right arm moves slightly.

Then, from across some distant boundary, from some inexplicable dream state, from the long sleep, Michael Scott Koep coughs out a pained and quiet cry. With that cry his pale body surges with crimson heat—oxygen floods his system. His limbs and face welt with a rush of blood and his little legs kick. I snap my gaze back to Lisa and her expression is quiet and relieved. "Stay with him," she commands, then she calls to the doctor: "Hit me."

Again, I obey. The nurses roll Michael's table out of the surgery room toward the Neonatal Infant Care Unit (NICU). I hold his pink little hand as I stoop-walk over him down the taupe hallway. My knees are unstable and I suddenly feel nearly two days of no sleep. I am teary and confused. But he is here. He is alive. I am thankful that we are in the hospital despite our home-birth vision. And I am thankful that Michael is surrounded by a group of experienced doctors and nurses. He looks beat up, but everyone assures me that he will be just fine. As we enter NICU, I stand back as the group of nurses connect him to the machine of the hospital: tubes and wires, IV and heart monitor, plastic oxygen hood and feeding tube, gauze and ice. They swab his nostrils, clean his ears, prick and poke—and all the while his little voice whispers out hoarse cries and breathy, rhythmic wails.

I am torn. I must stay with Mike but I want to learn about what is happening with Lisa and if she is okay. Just as he awoke, she went to sleep. I am suddenly afraid. What if there are further complications with her surgery? Why was the table shaking so violently beneath her? Michael was stuck? What does that mean, stuck? What happened to the *natural* part of this birth?

Luckily, the wall behind me feels solid and I lean into it. I watch the nurses dance around my little bruised boy. What if it's just he and I that make it out of here? The thought occurs to me that we didn't plan for this. The unwrapped plastic bottles in the basement, the neatly folded baby clothes in the closet, the catalogues of toys, the diapers—the half drunk goblet of wine beside the tub in our bathroom. None of those things seem to matter anymore. I realize how little I understand about where I am and where I am going. What if there is some hidden condition, a tumor? What if she lost too much blood while the table was shaking? There is still so much to do and to see.

Fear.

I try to focus on the numbers, blinking dots and moving lines on the screen above Michael's bed. Red, green and gold information trundles across its face. Earlier I felt that it was a completely different language, but now I find that I understand it, and I feel a little foolish. It says, simply: my heart is beating this fast, my blood has this much oxygen in it, and this is how warm I am. There is nothing more. Nothing else to understand at this level. It can't provide a read for how you feel about the sunshine or the rain, or which you prefer. No contentment readout. There's not a ratio to blink out goals accomplished, aspirations achieved or if your emotional needs are fulfilled. Nor does it list your failures, your sacrifices or your mistakes. No answer to that difficult line in the poem that one searches for. The screen tells only what is most important, if you're alive or if you're having difficulty staying that way.

Above the sink beside Michael's table is a mirror. I meet my own eyes—and there is the monitor that lists what the hospital machine cannot. I begin to read the conditions. I see memories and I see the best laid plans. I see concert tours. I see shows in the evening and museums with my little family during the day. I see the three of us in the bow of an ebony boat exploring venetian canals. There's the long road back to the past. The fights over the route we should take, the disputes about the pursuit of art, the anger that neither of us are getting what we want or need. There's that weird regret that you can't quite put a finger on—but is brushed aside, year after year for the sake of the bigger picture—the commitment. The marriage. The staying true to what you said you'd do. Even when it is hard, bruised and not going quite according to plan.

But what the mirror tells me, most importantly, is that I need sleep. My eyes are blood-shot from exhaustion and tears, and the shape of my face seems strangely deflated. Maybe it is the sterile air in this hospital. Is the AC on? Maybe it is the taupe walls and the shaded windows that block out the sunlight.

Or maybe I just need sleep.

The doula and midwife appear in the mirror and seem to take pity on me. "Come with us for a second, will you?"

They lead me down a hall toward a small kitchenette area: stainless steel coffee dispenser, small fridge stocked with apple juices, yogurt, crackers and cheddar, muffins. There's a microwave oven. Inside something had exploded—yellowish stains and brown crumbs. The doula fills a paper cup with ice and sets it on the counter. Out of her purse she produces a plastic bottle—a single shot of Crown Royal. She twists the seal and pours it. The ice crackles. "Your friend Scott sent this to you. He thought you might need it. I meant to get it to you sooner, but I forgot." Dear, dear, Scott. I sip it gratefully. But as I do, I see that she had been crying.

"Are you okay?" I ask.

"Yes," she tells me while she looks at the midwife. "It's just—this is all pretty traumatic."

The midwife lays a motherly hand on my shoulder. "We're so happy that everything worked out for the best."

"The show must go on," I say. The whiskey is stinging in my mouth. "But you two must have been through this kind of thing before, right?" I wonder briefly if Scott has more of this elixir.

The women don't answer. The doula begins to cry again. The midwife says: "You don't seem to understand how close we were to losing both baby and mom, do you?"

I hold the booze in my mouth. The fume of it rises up through my head and I can feel the early buzz—that first easing of muscle, of tension, of fear. "I thought—" I swallow and cough. "I thought that we did okay—in spite of our plans being destroyed." They both nod at me. They look as if they want to change the subject. "You mean we were in *real* danger?"

They nod again—now realizing that they shouldn't have said anything—at least not yet. I feel a sudden jolt of panic. "Well, what about now?" I put the cup down on the counter and start to move out toward the hall. They stop me.

"Now, we're relieved. Everything is fine, now."

"That is what you said before."

"No really," the midwife says. "In all of my years, I've not had this difficult a delivery—with these kinds of complications—but the two of you are amazing. You were both so brave, and strong. Unwilling to see anything but the little guy being born."

The doula broke in, "When you—" she sobbed, "when you told him to wake up—that there was stuff to do, things to see—I lost it. As soon as he woke, I had to leave the room."

I pick the cup back up and pour what's left into my head. "The show must go on," I say. "And thank both of you for all you're doing and have done. And thanks for the nice words—but I don't think we ever thought we were in that much danger—so you guys managed to fool us," I lie.

The midwife smiles. "You two made it happen."

I let the idea sit for a moment. *What choice, when the plan fails?* You don't stop—you do what you've said you're going to do, even if it seems impossible. I feel a wave of vertigo. The walls seem to curve. Lines seem to swirl. I suddenly realize that I'm a father. I am a dad. I'm Michael's dad.

"Well, he's here," I say, "and that was the plan."

CHAPTER 23

NICE

The three advantages of dementia:

1. You can laugh about the same jokes again and again.
2. You meet new people every day.
3. You can laugh about the same jokes again and again.

Or you can play the same songs and venues again and again. Wait, that's *gigmentia*.

Before walking to the car, I decide to sit on the porch for a few minutes and listen to Walter's leaves whisper in the morning breeze. It is another gorgeous blue sky. Sprinklers hiss and mist rainbows. I place my gig bag at my feet and take a deep breath.

It's a nice feeling.

Over the last couple of weeks, I've made the final edits for the third book of my *Newirth Mythology* trilogy, *The Shape of Rain,* and I've completed the art for the cover. With my designer friend, Pat Fanning, we've made the necessary tweaks to get the entire project print-ready. The thrill of that delivery to my publishing company was a wonderful feeling of completion mixed with a sad longing I'd not expected. As mentioned before, these characters have been making noise in my head, telling me tales, and keeping me company for a little over two decades, and I am becoming all too aware of how much I will miss their voices here at the end. Andreas and I are now starting to put our energies toward a book launch event on the release date of 10 October, 2018 (10/10). In the spirit of our previous launch parties, I've been working out how to create the climactic scene from the third book for people to step into—like a theme-park. It could be tricky, given that the setting is a gothic Venetian hall during a masquerade ball—music by none other than Jimmy Page of the mighty Led Zeppelin, and Ann Wilson of Heart.

This will take some planning.

I sigh. Walter sighs. The coming few days promise to be challenging. Not only because of the daunting task of playing the Iron Horse again with our own light rigs, stages, and PA as in previous shows, but there is also a street fair called *Art On the Green* happening in downtown Coeur d'Alene. This massive event attracts thousands, who wander from the top of our little town's main street, Sherman Avenue, all the way down to the main campus of North Idaho College. The fair's midway is crowded with hundreds of vendor tents, food stops, live music, and art collections. This year, Andreas has decided that we should have our own booth in the fair to celebrate the book series and herald the coming of the final installment, slated for release this fall. When he had first mentioned the idea, I thought it was a good one. When I realized it was on a weekend that The RUB was to play the Iron Horse, I felt a slight tremor of fear. *Do I have the energy to pull double duty? Will I survive?*

And if all of this isn't tough enough, on Sunday The RUB will perform at the band shell in the city park for the Taste of Coeur d'Alene music festival.

Thankfully, we've decided to call in our long time friend and sound engineer Ryan Fencl to join us for the coming chaos. For me, Ryan always brings with him positivity, a relentless work ethic, and a personality that meshes well with our trio's sometimes tricky idiosyncrasies. Knowing that he'll be nearby gives me some relief.

So, a two nighter at the Iron Horse, a book show event for three days with two book signings, and a festival show on Sunday.

This is going to take some planning.

Yesterday, Thursday, I began setting up the Iron Horse backdrop, my drum stage, and I loaded my kit, monitors, and light rig into the venue. I then filled Samwise with all of the necessary items for the street fair, including the pop up 10x10 tent, ample amounts of burlap so that I could cover the structure to give it that medieval look, two wood tables, all of the branded signage, a dozen white roses, a couple of swords, along with a

few other props, and finally several boxes of books. With the help
of my niece, Gerry (we call her, *Bean*), the booth went up without
a hitch—and, if I may say so, if there was a contest for the most
artistic and inviting structure, we would have at least made it into
the top three. I then returned to the Iron Horse to finish setting up
the drums, running the mic cables, and getting the light rig in
place. Unfortunately, the club was filled with a loud and
boisterous host of Karaoke singers, and accessing the stage area
became nearly impossible. In the end, I was forced to abandon
my efforts without finishing.

Now I sip my coffee and listen to Walter. He whispers, "Get
going, you're running out of time." Michael steps out onto the
porch and sets his backpack on the stair. He hands me a wooden
sword, then draws his own. "Prepare to die," he says.

"I am your father," I reply, standing and preparing to die.

He pauses, "Star Wars or Princess Bride?"

"Both," I say, as I attack.

Dropping Michael at his mom's, I drive to the Iron Horse and
finish setting up by noon. The streets outside are packed with
fair-goers. There's an air of fun and excitement. Heat is already
too much to bear.

I walk down a block to the tent displaying my work and see
Bean talking with a group of people. All of them are holding my
first book. She introduces me and I get the opportunity to chat for
a few minutes with these new potential readers. They ask if I
might sign their books. I tell them yes, only I'm scheduled to do a
signing later in the day at three; I ask if they could come back.
"Besides," I tell them looking down at my set-up-work-clothes,
"I'll look a little more presentable then." They tell me they'd be
happy to come back.

That's nice.

I rush home, shower, pack my gig bag, and return to the booth.
As I approach, I'm delighted to see a line of people waiting,
books in hand. Bean has set up my signing table, complete with

quill and ink. I set my bag down and say to the first person in line, "Thanks so much for waiting in the heat," and scribble my name across the title page.

The fellow replies, "Thanks for signing."

That's a nice feeling.

I sign books for close to an hour. Several friends and acquaintances stop for a signature and say hello. There are new potential readers, many from out of town. More than a few say they're from California, though they try to skirt around mentioning it, fearing, I assume, they'll be immediately branded as a part of the mass migration North Idaho has been witness to over the last couple of decades. Most folks born and raised here aren't terribly happy about the influx. I'm okay with it. As long as anyone moving here leads with kindness, I've no issue at all who calls this place home. Besides, even if they aren't kind, they soon will be. After all, Canada is only a couple of hours north, and it has a way of sending its wonted friendly vibe southward. Canada is a good influence.

Then suddenly I am surprised by Jim Bruce and his wife Jill. We greet with hugs and the genuinely warm questions of old friends, like, "How are you? How long has it been?" Jim and I have known each other since high school. An accomplished drummer, Jim took up a percussion position in the Pacific Northwest's cult band Black Happy in 1990. The eight piece outfit consisting of two guitars, two drummers, bass, and a hard hitting horn section, slammed funk, metal, and pop genres together (with a dose of quirky humor) earning them their own unyielding and unique voice as the new wave of grunge came crashing across Washington State from Seattle. In those days, it was truly a thrill to watch friends from our little Idaho town create a name and a sound so creative and hip—world-class hip. Their James Brown tightness, Metallica weight, and punk-like energy earned them a loyal following that endures to this day. I was a fan. I'm still a fan.

Signing their books, I suddenly remember that Jim's group Black Happy is mentioned during a medieval battle in the final book, *The Shape of Rain* (medieval battle and modern rock band —weird, I know, but it's true—in the tradition of Zeppelin and vikings for example—anyway, see page 249 of book three). Handing him the books, I share that fun anecdote, ending lamely with, "If you can believe that!" Jim appears to be genuinely pleased with the mention, even if a little confused. I tell him I'll take a picture of the page and send it along. He says he would love to see it.

That's a nice feeling.

After signing the last few books I grab my bag, give Bean a kiss on the cheek thanking her for all of her help, and run home to pick up Sheree. We pick up Michael and drive out to my brother's home for dinner. Bob graciously attempts to fulfill my request for pasta (drummer fuel) and delivers to me a delicious, but a-bit-too-creamy chicken rigatoni dish. Knowing the cream factor could be debilitating and cause serious cramps when I'm playing later this evening, I receive the plate gratefully with a scared glance to Sheree, but I only eat a few bites. Moments later she dials a local Italian restaurant and orders a plate spaghetti and a chunk of bread for us to pick up on our way back to the Burrow.

In a blink, I'm behind the drums at The Horse, finishing up the third set. It is difficult to breathe—the heat is hammer-like. The crowd is loud, demonstrative, and overflowing with live music spirit.

Cristopher calls one of our long medleys and we launch in to the opening bars. While I hold down a solid four on the floor kick snare pattern, I subconsciously plot out the next events for the lights and fog that I control with my left foot. I black the stage out and quickly move my foot down to the fog machine button and begin filling the stage with atmosphere, so that when we kick in to the chorus and the lights come up, the fog will illuminate like lighting behind a cloud. And that looks pretty neat.

And so, the chorus comes. My foot smashes down on the light switch, and the crowd's energy bumps up a notch with the effect. However, there's something not quite right. Trying to keep my concentration on the song and drum parts, I glance down to my foot switches and note that the fog machine is still activated. I tap my left foot onto the control. No change. I feel a stretching grin and a jolt of adrenaline as I attempt to stop the machine from pushing out smoke. No change. When I glance right to Cristopher, he is buried in a pillow of fog. To my left, Cary cannot be seen, hidden in a cloud of mist.

"Holy shit!" I yell, laughing.

In moments, the lights dim, the throng of people, not four feet away, disappear. The fog becomes so thick that even my drums and cymbals blur out. Suddenly Cristopher's head pokes through the cloud. His eyes are wet with tears—but I see they are tears of laughter.

"Holy shit!" he yells over the pounding music we're hammering through. "What—what's going on?"

Snot is dribbling from my nose. Laughing uncontrollably now, "Can't shut the fog machine off!" I shout.

Then Cary's disembodied head appears hovering over my hi hat. He, too, is grinning. He offers wide, questioning eyes. In answer, I shrug and play on.

Crashing to the song's end, I stand, turn, and kneel down at the back of my drum stage and attempt to follow the fog machine power cord to its electrical source. Vision is smudged. The light is dim. Ryan's face appears through the veil and he says, "You got this?"

"I think so," I tell him. Laying hold of what I believe to be the correct cable, I thread it back to a power strip and pull the plug. I crawl to the right of my drum stage and peer down to see that the machine has indeed stopped.

"It's off," Ryan says laughing. "Let's have a look at those tomorrow."

The crowd is still applauding and hooting, but there are a few voices sounding concerned. Cristopher shares over the mic that we've had a slight fog machine malfunction. There's a few, "No shit. . ." responses from those close, but we can't yet see them. Iron Horse bartenders and friends Bryce and Benny materialize from out of the mist. Bryce asks, "Is everything okay?"

I'm still in the throes of laughter, "Yes," I tell him. "Just a malfunction. Sorry for the scare."

"We'll open the doors," Benny says in good humor.

"That's a good idea," I agree.

"You guys smoked out the entire house all the way through the restaurant," Benny smiles.

"Oh, man," I say shaking my head. "I don't know what happened."

"Dude," he offers, "that was absolutely hilarious. Just hilarious."

A breeze gently enters the stuffy bar, and smoke pours through the doors into the night. We decide to take a break and retreat down to the basement. Sipping our drinks and laughing, I'm struck with how much fun we have together. Cristopher claims that the smoke machine debacle is perhaps the funniest moment he's ever had on stage—maybe in his life. Cary and I nod and agree. We each tell our respective stories of how we experienced it—when the fog caught our attention—how the world faded away—how we couldn't communicate over the din of the music —how, for a few minutes, we were each isolated and alone and yet we were all crowded into a room with hundreds of people— but still connected and pounding out the song. What could one do but begin to laugh, almost maniacally?

Another version of gigmentia, maybe.

"Can we do that again?" Cristopher chuckles.

We all wish we could.

And that's nice.

CHAPTER 24

TRIFECTA OF AWFUL

My stomach aches. Deep within my abdomen is a kind of nervous, fearful worry. I grip the arm of my chair to keep my toast down and stare up into Walter's leaves for comfort. A few minutes ago, I made the awful mistake of clicking on a social media link that posted a review of my first book. I make it a point to stay far away from reviews for a number of what I think are very good reasons. The most important one is to maintain my focus on writing the stories I love and adore above the opinion of others. After all, I'm trying to write what I like to read. Another is to make sure I steer clear of the feeling I'm currently feeling: sad inadequacy.

The review I had the *pleasure* of accidentally reading while I sipped my coffee this morning went like this:

"I wish [The Invasion of Heaven] was a short story because I don't think I can slog through the excessive "mundane" detail to get the juicy bits. And it's a trilogy!? Ugh. Pulp. This is drivel. Terrible idea, bad writing, and weird narration. It's a trifecta of awful!"

Excessive "mundane" detail? Why is *mundane* in quotes?
Slog. Mundane. Pulp. Trifecta of awful.

Ouch. Isn't that a little mean? Why would someone be so mean?

It is certainly not the first time I've encountered a bad review, but for some reason, today, it stings a little more than other days. I'm unsure why. Perhaps it is because of the coming release of book three in October—how difficult it was to produce and finish —the decades of thinking about it, crafting it, creating the world —trying hard to get better with each paragraph.

Slog. Mundane. Pulp.

Maybe I'm just overly fatigued from yesterday's double shift of book event and signing, and RUB rock show at the Horse. When I reach to my phone to check the time, it rings.

It's Dad. I lift the phone to my ear and take a deep breath trying to ignore the nausea.

When the call ends, I set the phone down on the table and stare up at Walter again. My stomach ache has intensified. Hot tears are in my eyes. I lean my head back.

"Fuck," I whisper.

Then, to my astonishment, I chuckle lightly at the image Dad has just described: my gentle mother, handcuffs secured around her wrists, and a burley policeman looming over her at the ER is so incredibly bizarre, I can't help but see humor in it. But the truth is far from funny.

Dad called to tell me that over the last couple of days Mom has been telling stories of a basement bar she's been frequenting at Guardian Angel Retirement Community—call it her imaginary speakeasy. According to her story, she'd been meeting Dad down there and dancing to a band, having cocktails, and socializing with a wide range of finely dressed characters. There was one night that Dad was accosted by a group of men who wanted to beat him up—which of course made Mom fearful—but the band played on and the dancing continued, and Dad and Mom waltzed the night away. There were a number of other hallucinations Dad shared with me—things we have heard before. Since the latest diagnosis, we've been expecting to hear stories like this more frequently.

However, yesterday morning, Mom couldn't locate her telephone. She had told Dad a couple of times that she believed one of the nurses was hiding it from her, or had stolen it. Being agreeable, Dad said he would check into it. Mom suddenly told him not to worry and that she would handle the thief herself. Apparently, Mom confronted the nurse and laid hold of her wrist, demanding that her phone be returned to her. Mom's fingernails dug into the young woman's skin hard enough to draw blood.

Incensed, Mom held on, frantic, frightened, and determined she was in the right. The panicked nurse called for help. The police were called. Mom was handcuffed, put into the back of a squad car, and taken to the Kootenai Medical Center Behavioral Health ward.

When Dad arrived, Mom was seated calmly on a treatment bed with her cuffed hands in her lap. The kind policeman assured Dad that she would not be placed under arrest and the cuffs were simply a precaution to keep her from hurting herself. Strangely at ease, Mom didn't appear to understand what had just happened.

Because of Mom's violent behavior, Guardian Angel would no longer be a care option. Dad can not care for her at home. The decision had to be made to admit Mom to the psych ward until the family could organize and come up with a plan.

While she was being admitted, Mom's blood-curdling screams tore through the walls. A doctor managed to give her a sedative, but it didn't assuage her fury. Dad could only stand by and support as best he could. After an hour, it was suggested that he should leave and allow the staff to get her settled. Reluctantly, Dad stepped out, his hands shaking, his heart broken.

This morning she's calmed down a bit, but she's unable to reason or remember why she's there. Her hallucinations have increased. In response, the doctor has increased her medication.

"Dad, why didn't you call us?" I had asked, shocked at the news.

"It would have made things worse," he replied. "If things could be worse."

"What now?"

Dad paused, sighed, and said, "I don't know."

Sheree joins me on the porch and I share what I've learned. She holds my hand. She tells me that she's here. We sit for a while longer in silence, until I rise and say, "Well, I should get going. I've got a signing in an hour." Sheree stands and pulls me into a long hug. It helps.

Bean has been working the booth for most of the morning. As I approach, I can see by her expression that she has heard the story, too. We don't say much about it. We fall into an embrace.

She says, "This sucks."

"Yes, this sucks," I agree. "How about a joke?"

Her head still on my shoulder, she says, "I could use that."

"I really hate dementia. You know why?"

"Why?"

"I can't remember."

"Shut up," she says.

Another line forms for books to be signed. I try to stay light, but I'm finding it difficult as if the fog debacle from the last night's performance has not yet cleared out of my skull. However, the good nature of the average street-fair reader is fine medicine. I talk with people about their favorite books. I scribble down a couple to add to my *to read* list. One nice older woman with huge pink hoops for glasses asks if I am related to Ray Koep. "He is my grandfather's brother." Her eyes sparkle and she tells me a quick story about meeting him when he was running for mayor nearly forty years ago. I sign her book and she thanks me.

"Your book's story takes place here in town?" she asks.

"Yes," I reply. "Here, Sandpoint, Priest Lake, and Italy."

"Oh my," she gushes turning the book over in her hands. "I know I'll love it."

"That's what I was shooting for," I say.

Slog. Mundane. Pulp.

"I hope you have a lovely day, young man." She lowers the book into her bag as the next person steps up. He is tall, lanky, and wears equally large black framed glasses.

"So there's three books. A trilogy, right?"

A trifecta of awful, I think. My stomach hurts again. I want to tell him that he'll only like it if he is in for slogging through excessive "mundane" detail to get to the juicy bits. I shake the thought off. "Yes, the third book comes out this October."

"Sweet," he says.

Later, at the Burrow, I tell Sheree I'm going to take a nap. She tells me that this is probably a great idea.

When I wake to get ready for the second show at the Horse, she has prepared the perfect drummer-fuel meal: linguine pasta, marinara sauce with mushrooms, crunchy bread with garlic and butter, a tall ice water, and hot coffee. *Oh, sweetheart.*

The audience is again spirited, energetic, and appreciative. I notice that blood has misted all over my kit from a split knuckle. *Not again*, I think. Downstairs, between sets, Ryan tells me that the band is sounding good. "You and Cristopher are a fucking machine, man!" That makes me smile, but I'm distracted. "And Cary is killing it. Just killing it. So enjoying the band tonight!" I smile more. Sweat stings my eyes. My knuckle is crusted with dried blood.

From out of my gig bag I pull my journal and scribble a few notes.

August 4, 2018
Evening: Sticks—thrown and caught seven for seven. Quite funny. We'll see by night's end. Completely scared with Mom's situation. Focus is lost. Cut myself on a fill—hi hat caught my left hand—bled all over kit. Hurts, but sort of feels good. I'm hitting hard tonight. Strangely accurate and strong. Probably a healthy purge of anger and confusion over Mom's plight. Hard day. A very hard day.

Ryan hands me a shot of tequila. He nods at the journal. "What are you scribbling?"

I look down at the page. "Oh, just journal stuff. Keeping track of as many details as I can."

Excessive "mundane" details.

"Like your hand?" he points. "I saw you wiping the blood away between songs. I love it! I mean, sorry you cut yourself, but that's good rock and roll. People don't usually see those kinds of details."

I laugh lightly, "You mean *mundane* details?"

He thinks a second. "No, people these days don't seem to give a shit about details. They want stuff easy and fast. But nothing good is easy, right? The good shit is in the details."

My hand throbs. Ryan throws back his shot and says to us, "You guys are killing it." Turning to the door, he says, "See you up there." He leaves. Cristopher and Cary chat quietly. I look down at my journal and write—

Today:
Mean review
Lost and can't focus
Mom in handcuffs
Trifecta of awful.

I think I'll go play drums now.
The good shit is in the details.

CHAPTER 25

LOS ANGELES

Not long after my first book was published, Andreas and I started exploring what it would take to bring the Newirth Mythology to the big (or small) screen. Both of us being huge fans of movies and *Invasion* possessing a focused cinematic quality in its delivery, it seemed inevitable that we would need to start our *Hollywood 101* education sooner than later. One of the first things I thought important was to reach out to friends in the business.

Anthony Nelson and I went to high school together. Way back then he was already a talented illustrator and story teller. He was also a gifted actor for the local playhouses as well as a uniquely funny stand-up comedian. Anthony even created the cover and in-sleeve art for an EP called *A Change of Tune* I had recorded just after high school with my friend Andy Day for our group, Us. Shortly after that project's release, we parted for our respective adventures until Facebook brought us back together in 2014. Seeing his profile, I noted that he had started his own production and signatory company, and had penned a number of compelling scripts, produced TV shows, and was creating incredibly imaginative and original content. Reaching out was a delight— not only to catch up, but also to be taught by such a gracious and thoughtful teacher.

At that time he was living in West Seattle. While I was working on the second book, I drove over to visit Anthony one weekend to begin envisioning my trilogy as a movie or streaming series. His enthusiasm for adaptation and cinema was intoxicating—and he started my wheels turning.

But there were two more books to finish before I could completely dedicate myself to the endeavor. So, in between crafting *The Newirth Mythology*, my movie education continued as I read every book on film I could get my hands on. I spoke with writers, professors, actors, producers—anyone that would take the time to share a little of what they knew. I became an armchair casting director and started lists of actors I saw playing my characters. My dream cast: George Blagden as Loche Newirth, Emma Watson as Helen Newirth, Emily Hampshire as Astrid Finnley, Ben Whitshaw as William Greenhame—and Viggo Mortensen as Dr. Marcus Rearden (I even met Mr. Mortensen and got the chance to tell him my wish, if you can believe that—a story for another time). Bookshelves beside my desk began to fill with screenwriting manuals and filmmaker biographies. Years passed and, as book three received its publication release date, I felt it was time to meet with Anthony again—to see what could be seen.

We spoke on the phone a little over a month before and he informed me that he had finally, with some reluctance, moved to Los Angeles. I filled him in on the final book's coming release, the preparations for the launch, the craziness of the summer festival season for The RUB, and that I'd love to fly down and meet with him to further my education. As I expected, he opened his arms and said, "Get down here!"

Now, having gotten down here, I sit in a restaurant and read the journal entry I just made.

August 7, 2018
Freaky LA.
Barney's Beanery: just down the hill from the Andaz Hyatt House—sort of kitchy, old-school diner-esque w/ newspaper menus, vintage motor-bikes as sculpture, not a single open space on the walls—plastered with rockstars, actors, license plates. . .A rock history palace filled with a trillion starlit memories.
Still foggy from last weekend (no pun). Taste of Cd'A show went well on Sunday. Cristopher hosted the entire event and did well with organization, hospitality, and all else. There was good camaraderie between bands. Sound was quiet but clear. Ryan's handling of the front of house lessened my anxiety.

Twisted up over Mom. I feel like I should have canceled this trip. Dad insisted that I carry on carrying on.

Meeting with Anthony's partner, screenwriter Todd Samovitz, this evening. Another meeting tomorrow with Anthony and Todd. Lots to learn. Strange being in LA again. Strange to think I lived here in the early 90s trying to build a career as a rock musician. Now, I'm back with yet another far reaching ambition. A TV show? What?

Well. . . yes. Any questions?

Goodness.

This is a fact finding journey. A trip to learn what it will take to bring this concept to the table. What are the pieces? Who are the people? What forms do I have to fill out? Where are the hoops? Freaky LA.

As I walk back up the hill to my hotel after the meeting, my head buzzes with countless questions. Speaking with Todd was a delight and yet another enlightening encounter. He is thoughtful, smart, artistic, and driven. Good qualities, to be sure. He cut his teeth as an illustrator, then as a drummer (definitely good people), then as a lawyer, then as a screenwriter. He told me that my books have everything they need to succeed as a series— especially, he said, "Because the source material is so well imagined and written." *Blush.*

A good meeting. And a good amount of vocabulary reinforcement. Words like *pitch, pitch bible, pitch deck, treatment, tagline, log-line*—all words I've heard before and read about regarding the sale of a script. It's exciting to hear them used in a real context concerning the *property* (there's another one) that will eventually be called NEWIRTH.

The next morning, walking from my hotel to Mel's Drive-In on Sunset, I find a roll of two hundred dollars lying on the pavement. I stop, stare at the bills, wonder, and then look up the street. A car stops at the light beside me—a window rolls down and a man with a weird smile says, "Hey, your lucky day!" He has obviously seen the money, too.

I say, "And a bummer day for someone." About a block up is a person walking. "Could be his," I say as I stoop to gather the money.

"Maybe," the guy in the car says. "But if not—it's your lucky day. I'd keep it, bro."

"Aww, that's not cool," I reply.

I start to jog up the sidewalk. The person ahead wears a grey sweatsuit, hood is up, and carries a bag with a long strap.

"Excuse me," I call as I get closer. Turning, I see an African American man with striking features—big brown eyes, full lips, and a carved jaw.

"Did you happen to drop some money?" I ask.

His hands quickly drop to his side pockets. As his eyes widen, he says, "I did."

I hold the bills out for him. I nod to the intersection behind us, "Back on the corner." I smile.

"God bless you, man," he says taking the bills. "How stupid of me."

"Have a great day," I offer as I pat his shoulder and continue on.

A couple of blocks later, I arrive at Mel's Diner and get a table on the patio. As I sit, the man appears beside me and stops. He says, *Information Dominance Corps, US Navy*—retired." He adds, "Thank you, again. Very kind of you."

"Glad I caught up to you."

He shakes my hand and walks on down Sunset.

Information Dominance Corps, US Navy? What the hell is that? Google tells me:

Monitoring chatter. Analyzing data. Protecting networks. Breaking codes. In the Navy, the offensive and defensive use of information is the ongoing, critical responsibility of the Information Dominance Corps (IDC) – a dedicated team of problem solvers who help secure America's freedom by giving our Sailors the edge they need to make every mission a success.

Cool.

Later, over a classic scramble with ham, potatoes, toast, and a cup of hot coffee, I go over my notes from last night. I groan at the learning curve ahead.

After breakfast, I attempt to scribble out a book blurb for Michael Herzog's soon-to-be released book, *This Passing World: The Journal of Geoffrey Chaucer.* Honored to have been asked to contribute my experience of reading this long-in-the-making book, I scribble a few thoughts into my journal. I scratch most of those thoughts out. What remains reads like this:

Michael B. Herzog provides for us a glimpse of an achingly human Geoffrey Chaucer grappling with wordcraft, love, and the murderous dangers of the 14th Century English Court. Here is an aging poet's rumination—charmingly pensive, funny, frightened, and decidedly focused as he watches his life and the world around him passing away. Here is breathtaking prose, heartbreak, hope, and ensnaring intrigue. Here is a beautiful book.

I close my journal and stare into my coffee.

I think of a cigarette. It has been over ten years since I've smoked. How the two are meant for each other—coffee and smokes. Though I could never return to the habit, my memories of sitting at a table in a diner drinking coffee and smoking while talking with a friend are many and missed. Raising my eyes, the patio area is lit with sunlight—and I'm reminded of my friend Greg White.

Years ago, Greg was a last minute fill-in for our usual bass player who couldn't make one Eastern European tour. Greg and I had yet to actually play together, having met just a few days before we flew. It was on a morning like this, in Hungary, (could it really be—a little over two decades ago?), he and I got acquainted, and became fast friends. Over smokes, coffee, and breakfast, we talked into the afternoon about music, books, art, and his time in the military when he served in the Middle East during Desert Storm. Across the street was a gothic Catholic church casting long shadows over the neighborhood. Down the block was a nightclub with a green neon sign.

That morning in Europe, I shared with Greg the working premise I had for the first book of my not-yet-published trilogy. I was nearly through a first draft at the time. He was genuinely interested told me he wanted to read it as soon as I was done.

Though there is much more to this story, in many ways, Greg's belief and encouragement ultimately brought me and my work to this point—a completed psychological thriller trilogy and now, a step toward development for TV.

If it wasn't for that morning with Greg in Hungary—coffee and smokes—our bass and drums rhythm section connection (Greg, I must add, is a monster musician)—I might not be sitting here on the Sunset Strip scribbling.

I lift my phone with a smile to send him a note concerning coffee and smokes when I see that Dad has called.

A surge of adrenaline hits.

Calling him back, he tells me that Mom won't, or can't, eat. It's been three days with no food. Her hallucinations have become worse. Her hysteria has lessened slightly but only due to increased medication prescribed by her doctor.

Dad uses the word *Hospice*.

"I wish I could tell you that there was something you could do. . ."

"Me, too," I say.

"Well," he brightens, "There is. Get your work done down there, it's important. Mom would want that. Then get home."

"I will, Dad," I tell him. A tear wells up.

We hang up.

Glancing up the Sunset Strip, I take a deep breath. I steady a wave of vertigo. We knew this was coming for a long while, though, we are all shocked by her rapid shift. I sit down and try to process. But I am strangely calm. Almost unfeeling. Almost numb.

I finish my coffee.

To distract myself during the Lyft ride, I Google the location of my next meeting, The Beverly Hilton, chosen by Anthony. I remember asking him, "Isn't that the location of an awards show?"

"Yes," he had said, "The Golden Globes. I thought it fitting given our subject."

"Well, I like the way you think!"

Like many Los Angeles hotels, it has its share of stories: JFK and Marilyn Monroe supposedly did a deed or two on the premises—this is the spot where Madam Heidi Fleiss set up shop creating the biggest Hollywood prostitution scandal to date—and sadly, this is where icon Whitney Houston drowned in her suite's bathtub, due to an overdose.

I loved Whitney. Damn it.

I tuck my phone into my bag and sit back. I shake my head.

Entering the main lobby, I cannot help but sense glamour and decadence. Its iconic glass doors, its marble floors and columns, its gold and hardwood accents, and how it sparkles like ice in a glass of scotch—makes me wish I would have worn a suit and tie. The room is packed. Finely-dressed men and women cluster in small groups, sipping cocktails, and visit. Some entertainment gala is underway, and as I cross over the massive star-engraved tiles, I imagine that I've stepped into a 1960s picture—expecting Frank Sinatra to appear beside me and say something like, "Cock your hat, kid. Angles are attitudes. Now, let's get a drink."

I feel a tap on my shoulder. I turn to see an attractive woman wearing a long, ice blue dress, and a wide brimmed hat swooping down over one eye. "Hello," she says. She is holding a long lensed camera. She raises it slightly.

"Hi," I say.

"I wonder if you would do me a favor?"

"Yes, of course," I tell her.

She hands me the camera. She then points to the courtyard through the doors at the far end of the lobby. "I wonder if you might shoot my picture out there? It is a lovely garden area, high green hedges. It'll match what I'm wearing."

I note tiny baby blue forget-me-nots in the pattern of her dress.

She leads me through the lobby and out onto green grass surrounded by leafy hedges and flowers. She crosses the lawn and poses. I snap a few photos. She changes positions. I shoot a few more. When I hand her the camera, we turn to walk back inside. She thanks me and disappears into the gala.

Coming back into the lobby bar, I see Anthony. We embrace and he then leads me through the chatting crowd to a table beside the pool where Todd is waiting.

It is wonderful to listen to the two discuss the concept of NEWIRTH becoming a streaming series. Again, for me, it is an exercise in new terminology and craft. *Contacts, connections, pitch package, treatment, option, development, production, et cetera.* Anthony is concise and makes sure that I'm understanding the complexities of his industry as he attempts to draw a straight line from the book to the screen. The line is not straight. I'm not even sure there's a line.

Then there's a reality check. They share a litany of Hollywood pitfalls, ego trips, tragedies, loser "no talent" executives and agents, thievery, back stabbing, greed. Harvey Pepper's voice whispers, *Fucking lizards out there, Michael. Beware of those reptilian vampires!*

"Surely, there must be great folks, too," I say, with hope. There's a faint tone of pleading in my voice. "Champions for a great story, great art—to make something timeless, right?"

After a pause, they glance at each other, then back to me. They both nod. "Sure," Anthony says, rather unconvincingly, "sure, there's a few of those out there."

I suddenly feel very young. Quite naive.

I scribble notes into my journal as they switch-hit lecture. I ask a thousand questions and they do their best to answer. Before we know it, it's late. My brain is full.

On the ride back to my hotel I think of Mom. I think of her favorite TV shows.

CHAPTER 26

THE RIOT HOUSE

My hotel, once known as the Hyatt House, or famously—the *Riot House*, is one of many iconic landmarks in Los Angeles. I take my book, laptop, and journal up to the top floor and find a small cabana beside the pool. The mid-day air is humid and warm. I breathe in and catch a faint whiff of pot. *Perfect*, I think.

This is my second visit to this rock-and-roll hotel. The first time was when I flew down to attend the aforementioned book conference a few years ago. During that time I was working on a particularly delicate, dangerous, and seedy scene in the second book, *Leaves of Fire*. Essentially, I placed Helen Newirth into a well-documented moment in Led Zeppelin history in which my young character visits guitarist Jimmy Page in his Riot House suite—with all of the dustings of 70s groupies, seductive starlight lifestyles, the sparkle of glitter eye shadow, and the hypnotic pulse of Zep's *Kashmir.*

That was the intention, at least. I gave it my best shot. Hell, I was only five years old when all of that was going down.

Which is why it was important for me to stay at the hotel if I was going to write about it. *Research.* I stayed two nights and wandered the halls (which have all been remodeled and updated to a rather forgettable early twenty-first century aesthetic), the main lobby (which has been transformed into a kind of tombstone for a bygone era, complete with guitar sculpture, larger-than-life pictures of rockstars, and the restaurant, named *The Riot House Bar and Restaurant,* but seems strangely unabashed as to its namesake), and I met with the hotel manager to ask a few questions and see if there was a formal tour (there was not a tour, but the manager was gracious, shared some wonderful stories, and showed me around to various wall plaques and famous rock photos framed and placed around the main lobby and mezzanine).

My beloved guitar player, Cary, joined me for drinks on that first visit to the hotel (I've failed to mention that Cary and his wife live in Idaho and also keep a home in Santa Monica—this made our meeting rather convenient). Avid fans of rock history, Cary and I reveled as we sipped our martinis and wandered around looking for ghosts. On the roof, we stared out over the Hollywood Hills and the Sunset Strip snaking its way west to the ocean. If only we had a TV to hurl over the edge.

That brought a smile.

What horrors, wonders, freakish parties, seedy moments this rooftop pool has seen? How many of these innocent rooms have been trashed and ripped to shreds by a drug addled rockstar for reasons quite beyond rational explanation? I shake my head at the chaos and the childish, narcissistic stupidity of such recklessness.

Then, as the bartender delivers my cocktail, and I sit back in the cabana, I remember. . . *I'm in a rock band.* Why is it that some part of me *gets it?* Can such behavior be romanticized?

Another smile.

Just four floors below, from room 1015, Keith Richards must not have liked the program he was watching that day—his TV plunged to the street and exploded on the pavement. You ask, would I like to try it? Well, maybe. Maybe, part of me.

No, I've never thrown a TV from a hotel balcony. But I have, in a drunken haze during an after-show party in Ketchikan, Alaska, kicked a door down, as the owner, bandmates, and a group of last-call partiers egged me on to do it, because, in truth, our guitar player was passed out inside and he had the only key. As I stood before the door, staggering and swaying, my eyes blurred at my target and with a bit of a run, I gave the door a mighty kick. An instant later I found myself on the floor, slumped against the opposite wall. The flimsy door deflected my foot and I bounced off it like a rubber ball—or better, a drunken idiot. Chortles filled the corridor. A bottle was passed. I was lifted to my feet, steadied by my hammered and enthusiastic band mates, and I charged again. With a crash it splintered open. Fun. Strangely satisfying. But it's no riotous flying TV.

I've never witnessed anything as utterly insane as, say, Ozzy Osborne beside a hotel pool wearing a sundress and snorting a line of fire ants up his nose to impress the members of hard rock's, Mötley Crüe. But I have witnessed a hotel room full of drunk and drugged folks play a drinking game around a table, chanting in unison: "Spin the fuckin' eye! Spin the fuckin' eye! Spin the fuckin' eye!" Threading my way to the inner circle that night, I discovered a coffee table surrounded by a group of people kneeling, glasses of booze at the ready, and their attention glued to what looked like a small, white sphere, spinning in the center of the table. As it slowed and stopped, it looked very much like an eye ball. Its gaze halted on one of the booze-holding participants. Laughs burst out and everyone pointed at the woman. She tilted her glass and gulped the alcohol down. As the chant began again, "Spin the fuckin' eye!" a man's hand reached down, lifted the eye ball, and raised it up. He then popped it back into the empty socket in his head, let it nest there for a couple of chants—its iris misaligned with his other eye—he then tapped the side of his head and it dropped onto the table in a slow spin. Fun. Strangely satisfying. But its no riotous nose-hit rail of genus Solenopsis (that's the scientific name for red ants—I had to look it up).

I've never throttled a Harley Davidson motorcycle through a hotel lobby like the tales tell of Zeppelin's John Bonham. But I have ridden a bell cart down the hall—pushed by my bass player. Fun. Strangely satisfying. But it's no riotous hog revving an unmuffled long block across a mezzanine.

I've never taken a chainsaw to a hotel room desk set, bed, TV and dresser, grinding them all to splinters and fluff as the Eagles' mythology of Joe Walsh mythologizes. But this one time at an after party, I accidentally spilled a beer on my guitarist's bed. I traded beds with him—and later swiped some fresh sheets from a maid's cart before we crashed. Fun. Strangely memorable. But it's no Husqvarna hotel room murder.

Clearly, there is no comparison between my experiences and those recorded in the debauchery tome of rock history. While I may be holding back a good number of stories that my Mom would certainly not approve of, the truth is, as a traveling rock musician, I kind of get it: the madness. I think it's safe to say that nearly every traveling musician gets it to some degree, too. The road, the friendships, the searching, the homesickness, the hunger and need to get to the next show without a hint that you'll find success, even if you knew what success looked like. There's a heartbreak and yearning only assuaged by allowing yourself and your respective traveling circus to unleash a bit of *craziness* from time to time.

For most of my touring career we dreamed of being able to *afford* a hotel room rather than imagining the trashing of one. On those special nights, five of us would crowd inside with gratitude, for there were soft pillows, blankets, and still silence. While the giant acts roaming the touring circuits may have had parties taking up a whole floor with rooms reserved for drugs, others for orgies, and a few for both and more, we might have had a beer in our Super 8 room and watched Letterman before one of us was snoring. Sure, craziness ensued from time to time, as did, as fate would have it, the painful consequences. No comfy limos or jets for us—no, back then we had a seat on the van beside the rack of effects and the bass drum as we bounced down the freeway to the next show. The circus lifestyle and the uncertain future becomes a part of you after a while. You learn to flow—or you break. And sometimes throwing a TV out the window seems like the only thing that makes sense, perfectly acceptable, and necessary. In the end, only a smile remains.

I'm reminded of a line from *Leaves of Fire,* when a young Helen Newirth (Helen Storm in her early years) visits the Riot House to try and seduce Zeppelin's Jimmy Page. "And Miss Storm learned quickly—the code that came with the lifestyle— most of its elaborate constitution communicated with a simple *smile.*"

I nod to the bartender and smile. Another cocktail appears before me a minute later.

NO THROUGH TRAFFIC

Brown skies.

Flying into Spokane, I feel dread. A murky haze of forest fire smoke hangs like a pall over the entire region. It is that time again.

The Pacific Northwest has come to expect a pattern of browned-out summers since the mid nineties. We call it *Fire Season.* Stifling heat, gunky air, apocalyptic sunsets, and an overwhelming sense of doom has recently been predicted for a staggering thirty days a year. For me, the season is horrid, abysmal, and, a word I don't like ever to use, hated.

A digital bank clock shows the temperature at 104 degrees. The freeway ahead smolders and blurs in the heat.

There is only one thing to do today when I get home. Go to the beach.

After dropping off my bags at the Burrow, changing into swim trunks, and filling a cooler, I drive over to pick up Michael. Seeing him fills me with joy. On the way to pick up his best friend Finnley for our trip to the beach, I share the news about my Mom, his Nana. He doesn't say much at first. He looks up at me and asks, "Are you okay?"

"Well," I tell him, "I'm sad."

"I am, too," he says. "She's been sick for a long time. Almost my whole life."

My eyes widen slightly. "True," I say. *For much longer,* I think.

"She's not going home, then?" he asks.

"Not this time."

He looks out the window. I reach over and thread my fingers through his hair. No words come.

The three of us arrive at the beach and spread our towels out onto the sand. We run into the cool water of Lake Coeur d'Alene, swim out a few yards, and look at the sky. It's the color of dust. The air tastes like ash.

While the boys swim and splash, I return to my towel and take a deep breath. A cough immediately follows.

I check my phone and tick through the gig details for the coming weekend. Two shows: one at Gozzer Ranch, a 700 acre private golf community overlooking Lake Coeur d'Alene—the other one is a fund raiser called *Ales for the Trail* at McEuen Park for the upkeep and maintenance of our local network of biking trails. Both promise to be challenging, given that they are outdoors beneath this ashen sky. The good news is that they're both plug and play.

Next, I dial Dad to learn how Mom is doing. He tells me that tomorrow morning we'll be moving her to Hospice.

I hear myself ask, "So, that's it, then?"

Dad pauses. "I'm afraid so."

Michael calls from the water, "Dad! Come on!"

"I'm going to jump in the lake," I tell Dad.

Dad says, "You should. See you tomorrow."

Morning heat. There's a slight humidity from the sprinklers that shut down a few minutes ago—the smell of wet, warming grass beside the hospital sidewalk. I stop at the door. Printed on the glass: *Circle of Life—No Through Traffic*. I read it over and over again trying to get my head around the paradox. I point the sign out to Bob and Dad. They shake their heads at it. Mom has been here for the last few days, and it appears the sign is right. No through traffic.

Inside, she is asleep—sedated. She has not eaten for days. Her skin is grey. Her lungs rattle like stones in a box.

Not long after transport, we get her settled into a room at Hospice, a few miles north of the hospital. The floors are fake wood. The walls are the color of clay. A shadow from the tree outside darkens the window. The air is cool. We sit on chairs beside her. The four of us are together. Mom and Dad, and their two sons.

The nurse has just left, informing us of what we can expect. The word *dyspnea* enters into my working vocabulary. It means *air hunger*. We're told she could go long periods without breathing. The congestion we're hearing is due to her inability to clear fluids from her throat and lungs. Morphine dispels the pain. Her skin will be cool to the touch. Her mouth and lips will appear dry. She could pass in hours. Or days. The nurse believes that Mom can hear us and that our words will be of great comfort to her as she transitions.

I wonder.

Her pink, stuffed bear with a white nose is snuggled in next to her cheek. It matches the pink, violet, and baby blue flowers on the blanket. A clear tube juts out from the covers and disappears underneath the bed.

I try to remember the last time I told her that I loved her.

I can't remember. . .

CHAPTER 27

THE SHOW MUST GO ON

At 3:30PM the following day, I am driving the tight lake shore curves around the lake. Finn's AC struggles against the outdoor temperature of 105 degrees. The skies are a dismal brown haze.

Tonight's stage is perched on a swath of green grass looking west across the lake. Directly across, the other side is lost in smoke. Behind the stage is a field of dry brown weeds. As I pull in, Cary stops me and has me park over a part of the drive away from the dead grass. "A single spark from your car or muffler will start this hill on fire," he tells me.

Our good friend and master engineer Jeff Angel and his crew are running the sound and lights for this show, and handling the majority of the heavy lifting. However, even the task of setting up just our personal gear in the heat is vexing. After soundcheck, I go to Finn to grab my gig bag, but I've left it at home. I say a few bad words and tell Cristopher and Cary that I'll be running to get it.

Despite the mistake, I'm happy to feel the air conditioning for the forty-minute round trip. Driving along the shore, I consider stopping for a quick swim—but I decide there isn't time. *Maybe after the show*, I think.

When I get back, I learn that Cary and Cristopher were somehow refused a second drink at the cocktail bar by a rather unpleasant bartender who was instructed to limit the band's sipping allowance. Astonished, and not a little pissed off, I go in search of the manager to get to the bottom of the sacrilegious, villainous, and insane edict. Who in their right mind would refuse a member of The RUB a second cocktail when we are invited here to play? How could any bartender with any inkling of sense follow such a ruling? Has the heat and smoke caused brain damage to some of the weaker of our race? Verily, it must be so!

With all I have been dealing with, no one tells Cristopher that he cannot have a beer. No one! And on a show day?

Luckily for the manager (and for the Gozzer-RUB relationship), I am intercepted by a couple of Gozzer club members who are RUB fanatics and friends. Before I can reach violent rage with any authority, these angels-on-high place the band and crew on their personal tabs with the instructions: "Give them whatever they want. They're The RUB for godsake!"

Our friend singer songwriter Robby French is performing at the halfway point on the hill between our stage and the clubhouse above. He sings Prince's *Purple Rain*—and it is a delight to my ears. I give him an appreciative smile as I pass, as well as a gesture of prayer—how we all long for a deluge of rain right now. *Make it happen, Robby. Prince, send rain.*

I find Cristopher and Cary in a chilled, stone wine-cellar at the bottom of a stair below the main bar. I deliver the beers. They've been busy arranging to have our dinner served here. We toast. We eat a rich sea bass, rice, and asparagus, and we manage to calm our nerves in the wake of the daft bartender.

Mid-dinner, I share with them the sudden shift with Mom. They listen and try to console me. There is little they can say or do. Listening, today, is enough for me.

The show is loud. The lights criss cross the stage and reach far up into the smoky night, like massive neon columns. The crowd of maybe two hundred people sings, writhes a bit, and lets loose their concert-going spirits even while wearing golf shirts and ball caps. We are encored twice. A third is coaxed out of us as I try to leave the stage. Stepping down backstage and removing my sweat-soaked shirt, I turn to see a rain of hundred dollar bills fluttering all over the drum kit. A few moments later we launch into one more and end strong. I'm not wearing a shirt. I wonder suddenly why I don't make this a usual manner of dress, like many other rock drummers.

Tear down is relatively easy—I only have my drums to deal with. The sky is pitch black and feels thick with smoke. On the way around the lake, I find a small turn out. I park, pull off my shoes, rush down an embankment, and dive into the dark water. It is heaven. I float on my back and stare up into nothing.

The next morning at Hospice, Dad, Bob, Bobbi, Sheree, and I surround Mom. Dad holds her hand and tells her softly, "I love you." Sheree's hands rest on either side of Mom's face. I know Sheree is administering Reiki.

I stand and walk over to the television hanging on the wall. I click it on.

"Mom should have some music in here, don't you think?" I say with some incredulity. "I mean, if she can truly hear. . ."

I tap the remote control. A blue menu appears on the screen and I'm delighted to see a long list of satellite music channels. When I see *Elvis 24/7*, I select it.

"Nice," Bob says, "Elvis has entered the building."

The King sings, *We're caught in a trap / I can't walk out / Because I love you too much, baby.*

I thumb the volume to a moderate level and turn back to Mom. I want to believe The King's voice can reach her.

By noon, the sun has scorched the sky to a blinding white sheet. High smoke has shrouded any vestige of blue. McEuen Park's grass seems to brown by the second.

I walk with the sound engineer back to the front of house, describing how I would like my kick drum to sound. He nods and says he'll do the best he can, but he complains that he's been getting a lot of grief from the city. They've been micromanaging the volume and have sent a guy down with a noise meter to make sure we're not violating the sound ordinance. "They'll shut us down." He then begins complaining about the heat—then about how he is under-compensated for his services—then about. . .

His voice turns into a kind of hypnotic drone—negative and useless. I hold up my hand and say, with a tone I'm not used to hearing from my mouth: *pissed-off*, "Turn it up or go home. This is a rock show! Remember? Remember?"

At that moment, our friend, host, and promoter for the show, Tyler Davis, appears and places his hand on my shoulder. "Don't worry. It'll rock. Now come back stage and let's have a shot." I let out a heavy sigh.

I shoot the tech a glare—then a good natured wink, just because. "Let 'em arrest us," I say.

Tyler will make sure it sounds good, I resolve.

"I heard about your mom," he says entering into the backstage area. "Really sorry to hear it."

"Thanks, Tyler."

Singer songwriter Lucas Brookbank Brown is opening the show tonight with his unique funk-folk vibe. Folks begin to arrive and find places in the grass to sit. Sheree and I eat slices of pizza beneath the blue pop-top tent backstage.

By the time we take the stage, it is obvious that the heat is keeping people away—or is it the sound? All through our first set, I watch the sound tech talk to his friend behind the front of house desk, rarely looking up at us as we are performing. Though

I cannot hear the main PA out front—if it is anything like the monitors—weak, too quiet, and squeaking with feedback—I can't imagine the audience of some three hundred people is enjoying the show. I surely am not. We continue to work through the issues. The tech continues to have a conversation with his friend.

The break does not come soon enough. I march off stage, around to the front of house, and interrupt the sound tech's conversation.

I say, cooly, trying to avoid bad words, "Excuse me, I'm so sorry to interrupt, but I wonder if you'd like to know about some needs we have onstage for the show you're running sound for? I know you two are talking about something frightfully important, but I thought you should know the monitors are feeding back and. . ." My anger is rising. The tech gets the hint and starts to apologize.

Heat, exhaustion, sadness—I turn and walk away before I do serious damage.

The second set is better. The tech's eyes are glued to the band. The audience even begins to pull itself out of its sluggish, heatstroke trance to dance.

Sheree drifts into view on the left side of the stage as we start into the Tom Petty song, *Here Comes My Girl*—a song we have never played the same way twice because I've never learned the lyrics. Of course I love Tom Petty's lyrics, but for me, making the lyrics up every time makes the song slightly more interesting— and more fun. Whether or not anyone agrees with me doesn't matter—especially today.

Today's verses are about how Sheree held Mom's head in her hands.

I sing how she called the power of the Universe to thread its light into Mom's eyes.

How she looked at me and told me it was going to be okay.

How Mom is going to fly.

Then Mr. Petty's perfect words rattle out:

But then she looks me in the eye and says
  "We're gonna last forever"
And man, you know I can't begin to doubt it
No, 'cause it just feels so good, so free and so right
I know we ain't never goin' to change our minds about it,
      hey
Here comes my girl[22]

Sheree's arms are above her head. Her blonde hair swings like ropes of sun. She flashes her grin at me and spins and twirls to the music, and for a song or two, I forget about forgetting.

---

[22] From *Here Comes My Girl*. Lyrics: Tom Petty ©1979. From Tom Petty and The Heart Breaker's album *Damn The Torpedoes*. Geffen Records.

CHAPTER 28

MOM

"Mom?"

I watch her. The pink and purple flowers move slightly as her chest rises and falls. The bubbling in her throat halts. The room is silent save Elvis' singing, *Don't be cruel, to a heart that's true.* A few long seconds later, with a sudden inhalation, the sound of drowning again fills the room.

It is late afternoon. Dad has gone home. It's just the two of us.

"Mom?"

I think of the copious journal notes I've been keeping this summer and how many pages I've tapped out trying to make sense of this season's shows and the life that surrounds them. I'm trying hard to capture the color of the days, the spinning leaves in Walter's branches, the tiny details that can suddenly vanish from memory if I'm not paying attention—Michael's brown eyes narrowing as we battle with swords, Sheree's warm hand in mine as we sleep, the soreness of my arms from bashing the drums, and Mom asking the same questions over and over.

She struggles for each breath, her lungs roiling and churning.

"Mom, I'm sorry I can't help you, but I'm here."

I'm frustrated. I wring my hands. I search for words. So many words to reach for.

"Mom, I haven't been able to cry. I don't know what's wrong with me, but I. . ."

Love Me Tender begins from the small TV speaker.

"Mom, there's so much to say, and I don't know if you can hear me, but I want to tell you that it's okay to go. We'll be alright." I shake my head trying to believe she can hear my words —that she can understand them. "Can you hear me?" I squeeze her hand.

How many words have we shared? How many stories have I told her about my life—the life she gave me? How many memories? *Those damn wide shoulders of yours*, I hear her say. *Thought they'd split me in half.*

What is the last thing I want to say to my mom?

And after all the words I've spoken, written, sung, I wonder about the very first word that sparked from some neurological synapse in my infant mind, translated into meaning and formed in my mouth. The first word I likely said to her. A word I've probably used more than any other. I feel a slight smile. What other word could it be?

Mom.

I say, "I love you," my eyes blur as a wave of tears rise, "Mom."

Diana Denise Koep, 1946 - 2018

CHAPTER 29

THE DAYS THAT FOLLOW

Dad calls the following morning to tell me that Mom passed at 11:22AM. We talk briefly about the next steps. Before we hang up, he asks, "Are you alright?"

I look across the counter at Michael eating a grilled cheese sandwich.

"I don't know, but I think so," I say.

"You tell me if I can help you, okay?"

"Okay."

I share the news with Michael. He circles into the kitchen and gives me a hug.

I call Sheree. I call Andreas. I call Mark. I call Cary. I call Cristopher. I call Scott. I let them all know.

I spend an hour or so calling others.

In the late afternoon, Sheree, Michael, and I drive to Dad's house. Bob, Bobbi, Bean, and Nic are there. We sit on the porch and sip scotch. The sunset is pink.

Pink at night, sailor's delight. Pink in the morning, sailors take warning.

It feels like Mom is simply taking a nap in her bedroom. The thought is comforting.

Loading my smaller red Yamaha drum kit from out of Finn and across the sidewalk, I tell myself, "Don't cry. You're here to play a gig. Don't cry." If there is a show where I could possibly lose it, this would be it.

The 315 Martinis and Tapas, Greenbriar Inn is a Nationally Registered Historic property located in downtown Coeur d'Alene. Built in 1908 by master brick layer, Harvey Davey, it has been a family home, a boarding house, a bordello, an apartment building, a health and welfare headquarters, and a convent. With as many lives as the building has had, we like to think it is now having the best of them due toour dear friends Bob and Kris McIlvenna turning the place into an old-world bed and breakfast specializing in delicious tapas, handcrafted cocktails and martinis. Oh, and for a couple months out of the year, The RUB plays a quiet dinner set in its small dining room every Tuesday, from 6 PM to 9 PM.

And when I say dinner set, I mean just that. There is usually a person eating dinner within the reach of my hand, as I play my drums. One might think that a drum kit and drummer in such close proximity to a plate of seared Ahi and a shimmering Vesper martini is an ill pairing indeed. In most cases I would agree wholeheartedly. However, in the case of the 315, the tables closest to the band are always the first reserved. And it's these folks that sing along with us for the entire show.

It should be noted that we perform at a freakishly low volume in a dining room—a level we call, *featherlight.* We still use a small PA speaker to amplify our voices, but we spend much of the night singing off of the mic. In other words, most of the time, our instrument volume is low enough for our natural singing voices to ride over the top. In the end, the show turns into a restaurant sing-along. Most of the time it feels less like a show and more as if we're playing in our living room, surrounded by our friends. Intimate. Warm. A true delight. And the martinis are exquisite.

Though tonight has all of the elements of our usual 315 evening of laughs, wine, and song, I'm ungrounded. It occurs to me that there are only a few shows left until the season finale at Live After 5. An encouraging thought, but it is fleeting. Before I throw the door open, I check my emotional state and take a deep breath. *Don't cry,* I think.

Cristopher and Cary meet me with a group hug. They do well not to engage me too deeply. Instead, Cristopher orders us martinis (a gin martini for Cary, a Vesper for me, and for Cristopher, a filthy dirty gin martini garnished with three jalapeño peppers and an olive—he calls it a *Crüxtini*™). We ring our glasses together. "To Mom," we say.

Slowly the room fills with familiar faces. The RUBBISH arrive and offer their kind condolences and warm hugs. *Don't cry.* The owners, Bob and Kris McIlvenna, pull me close and tell me they're there if I need them. *Don't cry.* Aunt Mel gives me a wink from a table away. *Don't cry.* At the bar, my friend and bartender Michael Irby slides a fresh Vesper to me. His eyes are kind. *Don't cry.*

Behind the kit, I listen to Cary vamping a progression I don't immediately recognize—then I am singing The Beatles', *Dear Prudence.* It's lulling feel is the perfect vehicle for my delicate condition. As the song ends, Cary begins *Hide Your Love Away*— a song we've never played but somehow I'm hitting all the words (due to my brother's healthy prescription of Beatles from my youth). Following hard upon is *Hello Goodbye*—another we are not sure on, but we pull it into existence without too many misses. *I Am the Walrus. Michelle. Come Together.*

We're laughing as we fumble. The audience throws out their favorite Beatle songs. We try every one of them. A couple fall flat —horrible misses—but hilarious in their attempt. Others take flight as if we've played them for years. We play over an hour of Beatle songs finally arriving at *Hey Jude.* The entire room sings the *na nas* with just the right abandon, just the right buzz, just the right McCartney intention. It is magic. The Beatles are magic.

At the end, the room explodes with applause. Cary and Cristopher are grinning at the strange wormhole we've just come through. I can feel a grin, too, but damn it, I'm crying.

The following night, the three of us ride together for a multi-band show at our favorite tequilaria in Spokane, Borracho. With a full backline provided, we are asked to perform a 90 minute set— which is fine with us, given the intense August heat, combined with the browned-out smoky skies. Despite some difficulty with the sound tech's inability to follow Cristopher's instructions, and Cristopher and Cary having to set up on opposite sides of the drum kit (Cary has always been stage left, Cristopher, stage right) due to the provided backline, the audience is, as my journal blurbs: *appreciative and engaged.* So that's good.

Immediately after the show, we pile into Cristopher's truck. With trailer in tow, we drive west on I-90 to get some distance in for a Wedding we're booked to play in Ridgefield, WA, the following evening.

Weddings. . .   Set up in a barn. No greenroom but found a shaded glade to relax and snooze before show. Glad I don't have to change into my stage clothes in the parking lot. I've done that a few too many times. . .
Gardens are plush—manicured—deep green—no smoke in the air—
What a relief.
Talked with Cary about Mom—ghosts.
Weddings are tedious things...

The return drive is relaxing. Over the truck's excellent stereo system, Cristopher cranks up couple of new songs he has been crafting. The drive along the Colombia River gorge is a perfect accompaniment to the soundtrack. As the miles tick away, he disc jockeys old performance recordings of The RUB, snippets of some of his current playlist, and prime cuts of a band the three of us played in during the 1990s, Head of Beef Band.

I watch the blue strip of river pass. Kite surfers scratch across the water with the high winds.

Later, at the Burrow, Dad calls to inform me that Mom's funeral has been scheduled for the following Thursday. He has already put together the service and the reception, both to take place at St. Thomas Catholic Church in downtown Coeur d'Alene. I offer a number of ideas we could consider to celebrate her life, but by his tone, I sense he's not in a good place to brainstorm. Instead, I pivot to putting together some kind of visual presentation for friends and family. He tells me that would be fine.

He then shares Mom's obituary:

Diana Denise "Dee Dee" Koep passed on August 14, 2018 at the Schneidmiller Hospice House. Born in Coeur d'Alene, March 8, 1946 to Orville M. and Leona B. (Owens) Weiser, Dee Dee joined her sister Jackie and brother Bob. She attended schools in Coeur d'Alene, Central School, Coeur d'Alene Junior High and CHS, where she was a member of the famous Vikettes drill team. She graduated in 1964. In 1963 while selling hydroplane tickets she met Ken Koep of Coeur d'Alene. They married in September in 1964 and had two boys Bob and Michael. While the kids were young she sold Fashion Two-Twenty Cosmetics and many times was top in sales for the region. Dee Dee later worked at Harvey's Clothing store on Sherman Avenue. Her claim to fame was as one of the concierge at the new Coeur d'Alene Resort. She played Mrs. Claus for many Christmas celebrations at The Resort as well. Later, when Dee Dee was out and about town she was often sighted by children—they would point and say, "There's Mrs. Claus." It warmed her heart.

Dee Dee enjoyed the years being with friends at pot-luck dinners and parties, and with her family, there was never a time that an anniversary, birthday, graduation, or holiday went by without a dinner and a hug at home. She said, "I'll make my Red Devil's food cake." (The green bean casserole recipe is still a secret.) Dee Dee and Ken enjoyed boating and spending summers at Priest Lake's Low's Resort where they found a new family of friends.

I'm not sure who wrote it, but I love that there's a mention of the green bean casserole secret. A secret I cannot reveal, even here.

CHAPTER 29

THE PICTURE TABLE

On the basement floor of the St. Thomas Parish Center, there's an event room that feels like a middle school cafeteria—quite unlike the rich roman opulence of the nave, transept, and altar across the street. White linoleum floors, pink walls accented with brown metal frames around the doors and windows, and crucifixes, crosses, and fish make up the overall decor. Random crosses hang below the stair railings, beside the elevator door, and on the bulletin boards.

Just inside the door, Sheree, Michael, and I have pulled together three card tables and set them end-to-end to make one long table. We've covered it with an ironed piece of burlap. Atop that we've set a number of large stones down the middle, with a dozen white roses, interspersed. Finally, we have arrayed about a hundred photos from Mom's life—some in frames, some leaning against the rocks, some overlapping on the surface as if they might be sitting beside one's morning coffee at one's own kitchen counter. That was the idea, anyway. A physical photograph to encounter as if it were your own—to hold a picture.

Dad and I discussed my creating a video presentation or a slide show, but I couldn't bear it. Crossfading pictures of Mom's life to the sounds of some Elvis song for five to ten minutes seemed appropriate for a seventieth birthday celebration, but for a funeral—well, for this artsy fellow—no can do. Had someone else made such a feature, I don't think I would have been able to watch it. To me, the whole idea seems to cage a person's life inside a box. One gets to experience her history in less time than it would take to eat a sandwich—from baby picture to first grade, from graduation to marriage, from children to retirement, from retirement to— well. . . and the song ends. Certainly, the opposite can be argued. But again, for this artsy fellow—no can do.

Instead, I figured that, while Mom's closest gathered at the reception following the intensely frigid Catholic farewell (which consisted of a disconnected priest murmuring out a monotone litany of Mom's life from a yellow sheet of paper, in a church Mom didn't even like, with a vibe that would never allow an Elvis song), I could provide a different kind of experience—a visceral one, if you like, where folks could surround the table of photos, pick up one of our family photos, and reminisce. To the person beside they'd say, "Look at this one." Or they'd say, "Oh, I remember this. . ." All the while, a collected memory of Mom is in their hand.

I stand a few feet away and watch people pick through the pictures. Heads lean together as one is held up to share. A couple arm-in-arm point to a framed portrait of Mom as Mrs. Claus. A little girl on her tip-toes in a purple dress rests her chin on the table and stares into Mom's eyes.

There's laughter from time to time, too, as I had hoped. Included upon the table of pictures is a selection of photos that depict Mom with major celebrities like Elvis, Frank Sinatra, The Beatles, et cetera. All Photoshopped, of course. As a graphic designer, I've become quite proficient in Photoshop, and over the years, I've had enormous fun creating a fun-fictitious past for Mom as a kind of family joke for her birthdays. One year I placed Mom into a photo with Elvis Presley and captioned the photo with something like: *U.S. Press Corps. 1964 / Diana Koep and Elvis Presley / Promotional Photo.* As holidays and birthdays passed, her career and legacy as a Press Correspondent grew.

Eventually, one of the many photos found its way onto Facebook. You can guess the attention it got. Suddenly, Mom was asked about this mysterious past she's never mentioned. Friends of mine in the entertainment industry were suddenly chatty over my newfound celebrity-royal status. Comments over the photo often ended with, "I had no idea. . ."

Here are a few, just for fun.

U.S.Press Corp Conference
London, England
November 6, 1968

Ringo Starr, Paul McCartney, George Harrison
Diana Koep, John Lennon
At Abbey Road Studios

I let the prank run a bit before I shared the truth. Many thought it to be hilarious. Others cooly chuckled, either surprised that they were fooled so easily, or maybe upset because they liked the idea so well and hated to see it be fake. Either way, *don't believe everything you see on the internet.*

At the table even now, a couple is holding up a picture of Elvis and Mom. Their expressions are asking, "What's this? What's this? Why, I never. . ."

I smile. It is nice to think that the couple will take with them another memory of Mom. One last story.

CHAPTER 30

AUTUMN IS COMING

Andreas is excitedly checking down a list of to-dos over the phone. I love the sound of his voice when he's creating—it vibrates somewhere between laughter and focused madness. I glance at my notes as he lays out points, tasks, and scheduling. It looks like this:

—Shape of Rain Book launch confirmed: Oct. 10, 2018
—Davenport Hotel, Spokane
—Masquerade ball theme
—Make masks
—Design invite
—Food and wine (TBA)
—Music—Cary and Andrea (Jimmy/Ann)
—Scott and Eric to break out into a sword fight at event? Oh yes!

He covers a few more details concerning the book's printing, shares some news from our distributor, and ends strong with, "What do you say we plan a publisher/author meeting tomorrow night over a scotch?"

"You're a genius," I tell him.

"I know," he says.

I ask, "Are you coming to the RUB show tonight? Last of the festival season."

"Absolutely! Can't wait!" He pauses a moment, then asks, "How many shows have you played this season? Seems like a lot."

"Honestly, I'm not entirely sure—I have gigmentia."

Hanging up, I leave my desk and step out into the early September afternoon. Above is a light brown film over blue. Two squirrels speed across a high power line and disappear into a treetop. A smear of black clouds looms over the grey hills to the south. It's hot. I notice how the sunlight has begun its seasonal slant. Even through the smoke, shadows seem a little darker and stretch farther. I've been fascinated with this change in the quality of light since I was very young. It has always heralded the coming of fall, my favorite time of year.

I attempted to capture the feeling in a lyric, long ago. KITE's Monte Thompson wrote the music back in 2005 for the album *Sleeping In Thunder.* At the time, we felt we got close to saying what we wanted to say.

The Slant of the Sun

There's something about
A wing-snapped bird
Alone in the dust—
A black cat on the grass.
> *There's something about*
> *A grey eyed girl*
> *Alone in the back—*
> *Not a friend in the class.*
There's something about
The brown of booze
Before a broken man—
His brief case right beside.
> *There's something about*
> *A spider's web*
> *Across an open gate—*
> *Mom calls the kids inside.*
>> *It's the slant of the sun, I know.*
>> *The shifting of the Earth*
>> *In her wide, soft bed.*
>> *Come every September*
>> *She nods her head,*
>> *And the stars shake loose*
>> *And the shadows stretch out*
>> *And I notice that*

        There's something about
Empty wheel chairs
Outside the sliding glass doors—
The laughter in the park.
        There's something about
        A child's eyes
        The closet door ajar—
        And it is getting dark.
There's something about
The moon, the sea,
And the civilizations
Uncovered by the tide.
        There's something about
        A will to carry on,
        When a wing is cracked
        And the cat is on the lawn.[23]

That's as close as I can get to doing justice to the essence of the sunlight across the sky today.

Bounding around the corner of the house comes Michael with sword raised. I forget the dirty sky, the possible thunderstorm, the planet's tilt on its axis, and I pivot into a run for the front porch where I will find my sword. With him close behind, I lay hold of the hilt, turn, and parry just in time. Click, click, click—the sound of the wooden blades as they clatter and dance in the air. He presses, I retreat. I press, he retreats. Both swords begin to blur until they strike their targets simultaneously—his upper shoulder —my forward knee. We fall into the shaded grass of Walter's leafy canopy, laughing. Way up high, I think I see a single yellow leaf fluttering in all that green. I point to it and tell Michael, "Autumn is coming."

"Autumn is coming," he repeats.

---

[23] *The Slant of the Sun.* Lyric: Michael Koep ©2006. From KITE's album, *Sleeping In Thunder.* TreeARC Records.

The summer festival season has wound down. Over the last couple of weeks, The RUB has performed at the Kendall Yards Street Fair, another full scale show at Borracho, a private party at the Hayden Lake Country Club, and finished out August with three shows at Hills Resort on Priest Lake. My journal tracks the respective stick catches and throws from each show: 4/5, 6/9, 4/6 (and the three Hills performances), 3/7 (yikes!), 7/8, 9/9. Yes, nine throws and nine catches for a Happy Labor Day. Unbelievable, really.

One should have lofty goals.

And, thankfully, tonight is the season finale called Live After 5 in our hometown.

I tuck a bottle of ice cold water down into the side pocket of the gig bag. My folded shirt and tie are placed into the center hole. While my hand is buried within, I do a quick inventory. Warm up sticks, *check*. Practice pad, *check*. Banana, *check*. First aid kit, *check*. Sun hat, *check*. Journal, *check*.

Pulling into the backstage area, I see a massive spaceship of an RV parked behind the stage at McEuen Park. Tyler Davis, Live After 5's master of ceremonies, has managed to rent the house on wheels, squeeze it through the fence-line, across the sidewalks and between trees so we could have a proper greenroom.

"What do you think, Jones?" He says as I'm stepping out of Finn, his arms spread open.

"That's—that's for us?" I'm overwhelmed and delighted by his thoughtfulness.

"The RUB is playing tonight. Damn right it's for you."

I shake my head. "Dat must mean we gots to play good, don't it, Jones?"

"Yeah, Jones. Damn right you do," he says.

(We call each other Jones. To this day, I'm not sure why.)

Ryan Fencl appears. He gives Michael and me warm hugs. He offers his condolences. I ask how his son is. Moments later he and Michael start lugging my kit to the stage. From there, Michael and I pull drums from cases and set up the chrome hardware stands and mount the shimmery cymbals and suspend the drums and affix the kick pedal and place the snare and arrange the pieces together, as I've done all summer long—nearly all my life. I place a water bottle and the banana on the floor beside my drumstick caddy. Behind me, I click my beloved fan *on* and let a light breeze cross through center stage. My office for the evening. Just like the office from the last show. Stepping back, Ryan, Michael and I admire the beauty that is a drum set. Hovering cylinders with gleaming silver hoops, white round drum heads (albeit, a bit blood bespeckled) overlapped with round brass cymbals—the green circle of my cushioned leather throne at its heart. "Pretty," Ryan says as he starts affixing a microphone to the first tom. To Michael, he says, "You're getting pretty good at being a drum tech."

Michael nods, "It's pretty easy, really."

In the RV greenroom, Tyler is slumped in a leather seat, thumbing his phone. There's a table with a fruit and veggie tray, a multi-colored cheese board, a basket of warm breads, and a large bottle of Patron tequila towering like an ice sculpture on a shelf above. A cooler full of water bottles. A bucket of ice filled with Coronas for Cristopher. A bowl of green limes. There's even a hot water dispenser, tea basket and tea cups—Cary loves tea.

Try for a moment to feel what I'm feeling: appreciated—cared for—loved. A room, food, drink, privacy—a show to play—and time to get my senses focused to do just that. And if all of this hospitality isn't enough, there's air conditioning.

"Imagine that," I say looking around wide-eyed, "I don't have to change in the parking lot."

Tyler laughs. "Hell, no. Not on my watch, Jones!"

Once soundcheck is complete with our new favorite sound crew, headed up by our friend Elby—Cary, Cristopher, and I step down back stage, cross a narrow strip of grass and climb again into the cool RV. We pour our drinks of choice and take our ease listening to the air conditioner hum. Through a slit in the curtained windows, I can see long lines forming at the gate. At first glance, I recognize a few familiar faces. There's master harmonica player, Jess Kunz. There's Michael Irby. There's my brother, Bob, and his wife Bobbi. Aunt Mel. There's that girl and that guy from that one show, at that bar, that one time. . . A small family crowds together, holding their folding chairs, waiting for the line to move. I can see Amidy over at stage right selling a RUB T-shirt to a woman holding a beer. Two ball-capped guys, eyes red, share a vaping pen. I see Sara, Rodd, Dennis and Doug, The RUBBISH, setting up their seating just off to stage left.

Michael visits briefly. I give him a bottle of water and some fruit to munch on. After a few minutes, he tells me that he's going to go find his friend, Finn. Cary lifts his guitar and lets his nimble fingers tap the fretboard. It prompts me to pull my sticks out of my gig bag and begin warming my hands up. Cristopher shares with us his excitement that his kids will be at the show tonight. He then pulls from his own gig bag an orange zip-up turtleneck sweater, tight by the look of it, a pair of white trousers, and his white boots.

"Hey," I say, seeing his wardrobe choice. From out of my gig bag, I produce a white button up, short sleeved shirt, white shorts, and an orange tie. "Matchies," I lisp, with as much femininity as I can muster.

Cary says, "Hey," too. He raises up white bell bottom pants, a purply white blouse with orange piping and tosses it atop his orange sunburst Univox guitar. "People will think we've called each other."

We all laugh.

I look at these two men and feel an overwhelming sense of gratitude and peace. In the end, we're a family. We're dear friends. Despite our personal trials, our occasional brotherly bullshit, we make music together. Beautiful music. And memories. I am honored to be in their lives.

Outside, the opening act has started. Low end bass rattles the screen door. Slices of sun through the overhanging leaves wriggle and glitter on the windows, reflect blurry dapples of light on the floor. I am grateful that our little band has made it to the end of yet another festival season. I think of the asshat fight that broke out at Borracho and their getaway car smashing through heat-hazed afternoon traffic. I smell the generator fumes on the parade route from the firetruck deck. I hear our mean words from the fight in the basement of the Iron Horse—I taste the sea-bass at Gozzer—the smoke machine debacle blinding the entire Iron Horse. These are the moments. These are the adventures. There's no grammy award win. There's not a hit single. No fan club (though, there is a RUBBISH). But I do remember Cristopher lurching through my drum kit, cymbals and drums toppling over, in a fit of encore rock fury. I recall watching Sheree dance, spiraling like a wheel of gold as we start into any given show's third set. There's the way Walter's leafy head shaded the front lawn in the morning, my bare feet in the grass, my hot coffee in hand. Michael's voice asking, "When are you going to be done with your book, Dad?" His ferocious surprise attacks with sword. His sleeping face. There's the grey-haired custodian leaning on his broom at the back of that echo chamber of a hall watching us play after he had said, *"You're doin' a whole lot a good hitting those drums. . ."* There's Mom's cool hand in mine, as she listens to me tell her about drums, why pizza is better in New York, Sheree's hugs, margaritas, and how Michael is getting taller by the second—how quickly a second goes by—how quickly a day, a season, a lifetime. Reminding her of all I can think of. Even now, I'm collecting more, wishing that somehow I could share with her all of these *excessive mundane details.*

What has this festival season taught me? It has taught me how much I've failed to capture—and that the condition of gigmentia has a dual meaning. In one way it excuses me from the impossibility of possessing the wherewithal to remember, savor, relive every fleeting moment. Given the overwhelming amount of sensory experience—each lightning rod to pupil, pupil to firing neuron, to understanding, to the rush of oxygen, to a chill of gooseflesh, there's no way we can possibly take it all in. We couldn't survive it.

Thus, we have gigmentia.

Yet, in another way, gigmentia seems to prompt the opposite. It asks me to engage. Engage my mind. It tells me to pay attention—to collect. It begs me to try to complete what is inevitably impossible—or at least, to try as best I can—to keep the time.

Thus, I have gigmentia.

The memory reminds me I am alive.

Setting my empty glass on the table, I tell Cristopher and Cary that I've been thinking of writing a book about this summer's festival season—to try and capture what it's like to play some fifty shows, most of them completely different from the one before. To see if I can tell a story about us, and not at all about us.

They listen. Nod. I seem to detect in their expressions something like boredom. As if they're saying, "We're so ordinary. Who would want to read about us? About this?"

I would.

But they tell me they think that would be very nice, metaphorically pat me on my overthinking head, and start to prep for the stage.

I move to the back of the RV and change into my stage clothes. I tie the orange tie in the bathroom mirror. Cristopher is singing a single note. A continuous "Ahhhhhhh." A warm up, sure, but he sounds like an ogre, and he knows it, and it makes me laugh.

Cary asks, "What's the first song?"

Cristopher shrugs. "I don't know. Let's get on stage and take a look. We'll know. We'll know then."

Tyler's voice booms over the PA now. He gives shouts out to his sponsors, and thanks the city of Coeur d'Alene, and tells how delighted he is for another successful season. After a crashing cheer, Cristopher says, "Let's go."

We step down onto the grass. It is sunset. Narrow fingers of light break across the lake, onto the huge field, and silhouette more than three thousand people with their arms in the air. As we cross to the stage and climb the stairs, Tyler yells, "Won't you please welcome *The RUB!*"

A massive wave crushes my senses as we walk on. My feet stumble slightly as if bracing against a gale-force wind. I see my office, my drumsticks lying across the snare drum, the yellow banana on the carpet beside my floor tom. For a moment, I stand behind the kit and stare out at the thousands of faces staring up at us. Behind them is a gold sky pitching toward indigo, sailor's delight pastel pink above the water, and a streak of white slashing the lake in two. A sky, a lake, and smiles. I wave to everyone. I sit. I pull the sticks into my hands, glance at Cary on my left, then turn to Cristopher. A lightning chill rides up my arms and I hope that I will be able to remember what comes next.

ACKNOWLEDGEMENTS

My brother wanted to play the drums before I had any conception of music as magic—as a pursuit—as a career. I recall him saying, "Man, drums are cool. I want to play drums." Being the younger brother that copies everything older brother does (except for the mistakes, of course), I began my life as a hitter of things with sticks by trying to build my own drum set out of coffee cans. He helped me to build it. And he still helps me to this day. He is also the first bass player I ever jammed with. Thank you, Bob, for the many firsts.

To Morgan Hruska, my first real band mate, and the fellows in my early bands: Sean (Jackson) Tetpon, Scott Faulkner, Brian and Greg Nilges, Mike Mitchell, Robert Mitcham, thanks for sharing music with me.

A deep thanks to Jason Williamson for our many of hours spinning records together, creating art and music, and your relentless encouragement.

Thanks to more musicians and friends: Lane Sumner, Andy Day, Forrest Wolfe, Matt Hill, Tony Mariotti, Scott Haynes, Gary Ross, Tom Taylor, and Darin Schaffer.

Touring all those years, there's another cast of teachers, friends, and cohorts to thank for countless adventures and memories: Dave Dupree, Bob Burdett, Doug Smith, Heather Black Dupree, Monte Thompson, Mark Rakes, Scott Clarkson, Darren Eldridge, and Craig Shoquist.

Thanks to these fine technicians, business people, and fellow musicians: Tyler Davis, Ryan Fencl, Elby Farwood, Jeff Angel, Dan Humann, Gary Schultz, Aaron Robb, Andrea Bates, Dan Spaulding, Blake Braley, Tristin Hart Peirce, Jess Kuntz, Justyn Priest, Joe Welk, Josh Fry, Kevin Dodson, Brian Mahoney, Randy Palmer, Zach and Josh Cooper, Indian Goat, and the many others we've worked with and have come to know.

To The RUBBISH, Rodd, Sara, Doug, Dennis, Perry, Maggie, Renee, and the incredible audiences we've had the pleasure to play for, thank you for continuing to make memories with us.

To my partners and bandmates Cary and Cristopher, a heartfelt thanks for fifteen years as The RUB. Here's to many more.

This manuscript was originally much, much longer (those darned excessive details). Thanks to Michael Herzog who helped me to make the writing stronger, and considerably shorter, and Gerry Buchan and Jean Herzog for their wonderful copy-edit eyes.

Thank you to Pat Fanning and Adam Graves at Range for their design expertise.

A very special thanks to Anthony Nelson, Todd Samovitz, Chris Shafer, George Strayton, JD DeWitt, Kristin Kilmer, Tom Taylor, and Lisa Demaine for their part in bringing *NEWIRTH* into development for TV during the writing of this book.

A profound thank you to Andreas John, Mark Lax, Greg White, and all at Will Dreamly Arts for their tireless encouragement and loving support.

I am grateful to my dad, Ken, for his stories, recollections, and loving support to Mom and our family. Thank you Dad for all you do. Thanks also to Laura, Bobbi, Bean, Nic, Croz, Mel, Joe, Stan and Jolynn, Melissa, LaRae and Chris, Presley, Reese, Lyla, Kyler and Michelle John, Dave and Lisa VanHerset, Bob and Kris McIlvenna, Michael and Jai Irby, for being there, for the smiles, and for the shared moments while pages stacked up.

Thanks also to Lisa Perkins Koep and Geri Perkins.

Thanks to the fine people at Coeur d'Alene's Guardian Angel Homes and Schneidmiller Hospice House for their care and important missions.

In loving memory of Diana Denise Koep, Harvey Pepper, Lewis Hunter Stowers III (Chicken Delicious), Steve Gibbs, and Walter Perkins.

A hug and thanks to Allison McCready and Amidy Fuson.

Thank you to my lady Sheree Jerome who helped me navigate from show to show, page to page, who fills my heart and our home with light, and who kept my focus on the moon and stars when Mom was failing and the night was darkest. And to my son Michael, thank you for your surprise sword attacks, your brilliant imagination, and for suggesting that I include more drawings in this book.

Lastly, for fun, a list of all of the bands I've played in—so far.

Thanks to all who played in them, too.

The Flyers, The Bitchen Mitcham Band, Trio, Anthem, W.F., Vantage, Common Ground, Key Bo Rey, Us, Storm Season, Pride In Peril, August Rain, F.W., Fainting In Coils, Ralph, Manito, Band From Atlantis, Seed, KITE, Head of Beef Band, The RUB, Chum, Bubble, The Keef Green Trio, Robot Love, The Bobio Blouse Band, The Conquest of Bread, Skunk Fight, Leaf Tinted Monacle, Tea.

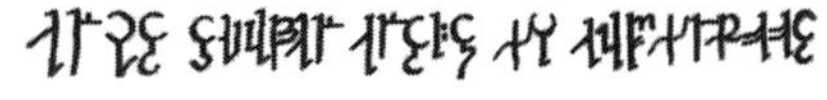

thia thave alyoth ni tunefore
~gallina~

Also from Michael B. Koep
THE NEWIRTH MYTHOLOGY TRILOGY

Stories change us. Loche Newirth's story changed the history of the world, and only now are we learning how. . .

IN PART ONE, *The Invasion of Heaven,* psychologist Loche Newirth is hunted after he sees a painting that opens a window onto the afterlife. A secret order seeking to control the art pursue him across the world, into madness and beyond. Loche's journal is left behind for his mentor Doctor Marcus Rearden to interpret. It tells of William, a diagnosed manic depressive, swashbuckling swordsman who believes he is over six hundred years old; Basil, a stoned and prolific painter and his perilous work that he must keep secret; Julia, a beautiful business woman who abandons everything for a love she never expected.

IN PART TWO, *Leaves of Fire*, Loche Newirth must face how his writing has shaped the lives of William, Julia and countless others. As a war breaks out between the immortals on earth and the inscrutable Albion Ravistelle, Loche seeks a path through death to find a way to end the conflict.

IN PART THREE, *The Shape of Rain*, discredited mythology professor Astrid Finnley is summoned to a secret archaeological dig site to translate an ancient script where she uncovers an unthinkable nightmare—a woman buried alive for over a thousand years. Meanwhile, Loche Newirth's assassination is ordered. But his former mentor Dr. Marcus Rearden wants him alive to torture, to command, to control. When Loche discovers his son is also a target, he flees and is vaulted back to the prehistory of his writings—to a time when a venomous army of gods lay siege to the City of Immortals, and his little boy stands in the balance.

Infused with intrigue and mystery, steeped in rich atmospheres and celestial horrors, saturated with twists and delightful intricacies, Koep's offering is a final mythology for a rapidly evolving New Earth.

WHERE BOOKS ARE SOLD
THE NEWIRTH MYTHOLOGY TRILOGY
By Michael B. Koep
ISBN # 987-0-9976234-7-5
Will Dreamly Arts Publishing